GLASGOW

GLASGOW

BY

David Daiches

ANDRE DEUTSCH

First published 1977 by
André Deutsch Limited
105 Great Russell Street London WC1

Copyright © 1977 by David Daiches

Printed in Great Britain by
Ebenezer Baylis and Son Ltd.
The Trinity Press, Worcester, and London

ISBN 0 233 96913 6

Contents

List of plates		*page* vii
List of illustrations		ix
List of maps		x
Acknowledgements		xi
Introduction		xiii
1	From Legend into History	1
2	Merchants and Craftsmen	10
3	Turbulent Times	22
4	Before the Union	36
5	'A road west awa' yonder'	46
6	Work and Play	61
7	Education and the Arts	77
8	Coal, Cotton and Iron	95
9	Into the Nineteenth Century	109
10	Reform	120
11	The Price of Progress	128
12	'The most aggressively efficient city in Great Britain'	147
13	The Face of Victorian Glasgow	158
14	Victorian Pomp and Circumstance	169
15	Entertainment High and Low	180
16	'The high, tragic pageant of the Clyde'	192
17	Before the Lights Went Out	204
18	Today and Tomorrow	216
	Select Bibliography	230
	Index	233

Plates

Charter of regality, 1450 (GDC)   *facing page* 50
Seal of the City, R. Lane, *Ancient Scottish Seals* (UA)   50
Seal of Bishop Bondington, c. 1250, R. Lane, *Ancient Scottish
    Seals* (UA)   50
The College in the High Street, c. 1660, J. Slezer, *Theatrum
    Scotiae*, 1693 (UA)   51
Glasgow from the NE, c. 1680, J. Slezer, *Theatrum Scotiae*,
    1693 (UA)   51
The Merchants' House, 1659, R. Stuart, *Views and Notices of
    Glasgow in Former Times*, 1847 (ML)   66
Glasgow from the SW, 1764, Foulis Academy Print (UA)   66
The Trongate, c. 1770, Foulis Academy Print (UA)   67
The Broomielaw, J. Swan, *Select Views of Glasgow and
    Environs*, 1829 (ML)   82
Snuff-box lid, 1820 (PP)   82
Salmon fishing at Govan (Graham Collection, ML)   83
St Vincent Street, J. Swan, *Select Views* (ML)   83
St Enoch's Church, c. 1885 (PP)   98
Theatre Royal, Dunlop Street, c. 1860 (PP)   98
Queen's Park Terrace, c. 1850 (RCAMS)   98
Glasgow University, 1974 (WR)   99
Botanic Gardens Gate, 1905 (TA)   99
Cruikshank frontispiece, 1858 (ML)   114
Stock Exchange, 1875 (JH)   114
View of the Clyde, Stratten & Stratten, pubs., *Glasgow and
    its Environs*, 1891 (ML)   115
The Barony Church, c. 1895 (PP)   115
Calton back court, 1890 (PP)   130
Temperance demonstration, c. 1910 (PP)   130
Scott's Electric Theatre, 1910 (PP)   131
Corporation tram, 1894 (PP)   131

PLATES

The 'Room de luxe', Willow Tea Rooms, 1904 (MC)   162
The 'Oak Room', Willow Tea Rooms, 1904 (MC)   162
The *Queen Empress*, 1929 (TA)   163
John Brown's shipyard, *c.* 1930 (KRS)   163
Scramble in Gemmal Street, 1955 (PP)   178
The Red Road Flats, 1973 (WR)   178
George Square, 1976 (WR)   179
Charing Cross, 1974 (WR)   179

Illustrations

The city crest, 'Senex,' *Glasgow Past and Present,*
   1884 (ML)   *title page*
Advertisements, *Glasgow Mercury,* 1784 (ML)   49
Characters of Old Glasgow, *c.* 1800 (PP)   72
Anderson's Institution, *Northern Looking Glass, c.* 1820 (ML)   89
Title page, *Glasgow Courant,* 1715 (ML)   92
'Awfu' weather', *Northern Looking Glass, c.* 1820 (ML)   118
Irish nationalists, *Quiz,* 1895 (ML)   137
Corporation Trams, *Quiz,* 1895 (ML)   149
South façade of St Vincent Street Church (ML)   164
Advertisement for Crouch's Wonderland, *Glasgow Amusements*
   and Pastimes, c. 1890 (ML)   187
Programme for Hengler's Circus, 1891 (PP)   191
James Maxton *et al., Bailie,* 1922 (DD)   197
Wee MacGreegor, J. J. Bell, *Wee MacGreegor,* 1900 (ML)   210
Glasgow Fair, *Northern Looking Glass, c.* 1820 (ML)   *back endpaper*

Maps of Glasgow

1847, from J. Pagan, *Sketches of the History of
Glasgow* (DD)   *front endpaper*
1560, *History of Glasgow*, R. Renwick and Sir J. Lindsay (ML)   16
1654, Blaeu's *Atlas* (ML)   34
1783, published by John Mennons (DD)   80–81

Acknowledgements

THE publisher is most grateful to the following people and organizations for permission to reproduce material from their collections: Glasgow District Council (GDC); John Hume (JH); The Keeper of the Records of Scotland (KRS); The Mackintosh Collection, Glasgow University (MC); The Glasgow Room, Mitchell Library (ML); The People's Palace (PP); T. & R. Annan & Sons (TA); The University Archives, Glasgow University (UA); The Royal Commission on the Ancient and Historical Monuments of Scotland (RCAMS); and to W. Ralston Ltd (WR) who photographed the UA collection; and to Bryan & Shear Ltd who photographed the ML collection.

The publisher also wishes to thank the following people for their generous help and advice: J. Fisher and the staff of the Glasgow Room, the Mitchell Library; Elspeth King, Assistant Keeper, and Michael Donnelly, The People's Palace; D. G. Mold of W. Ralston Ltd; Michael Moss, Glasgow University Archivist, and Anne Ross, Deputy Archivist; John Hume, Lecturer in History, University of Strathclyde; Public Relations Department, Glasgow District Council.

Introduction

A<small>N</small> attempt to write, in reasonable compass, an account of the development of a city with a history as long, rich and varied as that of Glasgow inevitably presents problems of scale. Some of these problems I have tried to solve in a somewhat subjective way, emphasizing different aspects in different periods to the degree to which they struck me as significant of the city's character at that time. Thus I discuss political issues in some periods – notably the seventeenth century, the early nineteenth century and the second and third decades of the twentieth century – more specifically than at others; I describe the industries of the late eighteenth and of the nineteenth centuries in more detail than those of the twentieth; I discuss education and schools in some periods and not in others; I have not always carried through to the present day accounts of movements whose origins or significant early mutations it seemed important to discuss; I have paused to be anecdotal at some periods and I have swept along without such pauses at others. While all this may make my history of Glasgow in some degree impressionistic, the alternative would have been to make it very long and probably very dull.

There have been many accounts of Glasgow, most of them written from the inside. This account, by an Edinburgh man, cannot claim to represent an insider's view. But it is the view of one who, in walking Glasgow's streets, talking to its citizens, reading and pondering the multifarious and often fascinating written sources of its history – from old Town Council minutes to nostalgic auto-biographies, from reports of trade and shipping to the outbursts of preachers and the jottings of diarists – and steadily acquiring the 'feel' of the city century by century and even decade by decade, has developed a deeply affectionate understanding of its character as it defined itself throughout the ages. Although this account does not have the frankly emotional involvement that some modern Glasgow writers have shown in writing of their city, for I have striven to make my picture objective as well as lively, it is very much the account of a friend and I hope it reads as such.

David Daiches
May 1976

CHAPTER I

From Legend into History

T HOSE who know Glasgow today might be surprised to learn that its history begins in sanctity. The first clear historical fact about the city is the appointment and consecration of Bishop John Achaius to the see of Glasgow in 1114-18. Bishop John began the construction of Glasgow Cathedral about 1124 and the building, of stone and wood, was consecrated on 7 July 1136 in the presence of King David I, that 'sair sanct for the Crown' who helped to impoverish later Scottish kings by his lavish grants to the Church. The Cathedral was built by the Molendinar burn, which rose in Hogganfield Loch and flowed south-west into the Clyde, before the Victorians made it into an underground sewer: the site was considered especially holy for there St Mungo was supposed to have built his original wooden church. St Mungo (Celtic 'my dear one') was the affectionate name given to St Kentigern: he is Glasgow's patron saint and he and the legends associated with him figure prominently on the city's coat of arms. The story of his life that has come down to us, narrated by the late-twelfth-century Jocelin, a monk of Furness, is almost pure legend, but the earlier chronicle known as the *Annales Cambriae* records the death of 'Conthigirnus' as having occurred in the year 612, and this we may accept.

Clearly, it could not have been simply the memory of the seventh-century St Mungo that prompted the building of a cathedral on this site. There must have been enough people dwelling in the neighbourhood to justify the presence of a bishop and service the ecclesiastical establishment. A charter granted between 1175 and 1178 by William the Lion to Bishop John's successor Jocelin (not to be confused with Jocelin of Furness) allowed the bishops of Glasgow the right to have a burgh at Glasgow (*ut burgum habeant apud Glasgu*) with a weekly Thursday market, which suggests that Glasgow had for some time already been a market town. Glasgow emerges into history, then, like so many famous towns on the Continent, as a bishop's burgh and a market town. It may have owed its position as a market town partly to its being in early times the lowest point on the Clyde where a bridge could be built, yet it must be remembered that the original Glasgow was set back from the Clyde and from the salmon-fishing village on its right bank by about one thousand yards.

Can we learn more about the significance of the site by looking at the geography and earlier history of the region? If you fly into Glasgow from the south or south-east on a clear day, you can see that the city lies in a vast hollow more or less encircled by barren hills and plateaux. The River Clyde flows north-west through this hollow, and though it widens into an estuary before turning south there is no steady widening and flattening of the landscape as the river moves towards the firth. To reach the hollow otherwise than by sea from the west or across the low watershed that divides it from the Forth valley on the east (a route apparently not favoured in prehistoric times) the earliest settlers in the region would have had to seek out the passes, of which the most obvious was the Biggar gap, a natural route from the North Sea coast between the Tweed and Clyde valleys. A more arduous route lay from the Solway Firth through Annandale and over Beattock summit. Routes westward to the Ayrshire basin – to be taken in a later age, like the Beattock route, by both road and rail – lay through the Lochwinnoch gap or, more circuitously, across plateau and moorland by Muirkirk. From the Clyde estuary there was access to the Highland north by passes and lochs.

As the first inhabitants of Scotland, stone-age hunters and fishers, pushed up from the south in the wake of the retreating ice age, something over six thousand years ago, they must have found the region thickly wooded. It was not until the arrival of a second group, stone-using agriculturists growing cereal crops and with domestic animals, that a start would have been made in clearing the forests and that parts of what we might call the Glasgow hollow were settled, however sparsely. The third element in Scotland's pre-historic population, the so-called Beaker folk, have left little trace in this region, but the fourth, whose origin and date of arrival remain quite uncertain, but who were certainly in southern Scotland before the Romans arrived in Britain, spoke a Gallo-Britannic language (a Celtic language of the branch known as P-Celtic) and were accomplished metal-workers and charioteers. These Britons, as history calls them, were organized in tribes. The early second century A.D. Greek geographer Ptolemy identified the tribe who inhabited the Clyde valley as the Damnonii. There is no evidence that the Damnonii had an *oppidum* – tribal gathering place and market – on the site of modern Glasgow. But they were in the Clyde valley when the Roman general Agricola pushed north into Scotland in A.D. 80 in search of a stable frontier for the Roman province of Britannia, which he governed.

Agricola built some forts in the Lowlands, and a whole line of them between the Firths of Forth and of Clyde, but was not satisfied to regard this as the northern frontier of the Roman Empire: he pushed further north with the intention of conquering all Caledonia, the name his son-in-law the historian Tacitus gave to the Highlands of the north, inhabited by tribes whom the Romans called collectively 'Caledonii', Caledonians, from the name of one of the tribes. (The Romans also called the inhabitants of North Britain 'Picti', Picts; this term was later confined to those who lived north of the Forth–Clyde line who are now known to have been a partly Celtic people, speaking a P-Celtic language akin to but not identical with British Celtic, but some speaking a non-Celtic language that may have been the language of the indigenous tribes.) Agricola was recalled from Britain in A.D. 84–5 and almost immediately afterwards the Romans abandoned the area north of the Forth–Clyde line, in spite of Agricola's military success there, because severe Roman defeats on the Danube forced them to turn their attention in that direction. But in dominating the Lowlands, Agricola had made some impression on the Damnonii of the Clyde valley, who appear to have acquired Roman pottery and glassware by trading with the Roman fort at Castledykes, in the Clyde valley near the present Lanark.

Agricola's forts in the Lowlands, except for an important one at Newstead on the Tweed, which was held until about A.D. 100, were given up after his departure. About A.D. 120 the Emperor Hadrian came to Britain, concerned not so much to push forward the frontiers of the empire as to establish an impregnable boundary. Between A.D. 122 and 128 he constructed a great stone wall that ran from the Tyne to the Solway, but the pressure on it from the tribes of what is now south-west Scotland forced the governor Lollius Urbicus, about A.D. 142 in the reign of the Emperor Antoninus Pius, to push the frontier forward and construct on the old Agricolan Forth–Clyde line a rampart of turf (on a stone foundation), surmounted by a palisade and with forts every two miles. By this means the Romans managed to contain the area between the Tyne–Solway line and the Forth–Clyde isthmus. It was now that lower Clydesdale was brought into the Roman communications system. What is known as the Antonine Wall stretched from Bridgeness on the Forth to Old Kirkpatrick on the Clyde, with a military road running beside it to the south. Further south, a road came up from Newstead on the Tweed through Castledykes and across the Clyde to Loudoun Hill and thence probably across to the coast at Irvine Bay. A further road must have linked the fort at Castledykes with a new fort built at Bothwellhaugh on the other side of the Clyde from modern Hamilton, and may well have gone on by the route later taken by the Drygate, Glasgow's first eastern entry, to the western end of the Antonine Wall.

After about half a century, during which the Antonine Wall served as a basis for defensive military operations against the northern tribes as well as a means of keeping under control the tribes immediately south of it, the Romans moved back their frontier to Hadrian's Wall. In A.D. 209–11 the Emperor Severus crossed to Britain and conducted a new campaign against the northern tribes, described by the third-century writer Dio Cassius as the Caledonians and the Maeatae (the name is perhaps preserved in Dumyat, the hill overlooking Stirling). But in spite of temporary success he was unable to dominate the country and after Severus' death at York in A.D. 211 his son Caracalla ended the campaign and returned to Rome. Henceforth Hadrian's Wall remained the frontier of Roman Britain; the Romans made sporadic forays to the north and perhaps some successful treaties with tribes there including the Damnonii, until the gradual draining away of the legions in the fourth and fifth centuries as a result of the attacks on the Empire by Germanic tribes. In the fifth and sixth centuries Angles, Saxons and Jutes, from North Germany and Denmark, occupied most of modern England pushing the now undefended Romanized Britons into Cornwall, Wales and the Lake District, which remained British. The Angles settled in the north and pushed into modern East Lothian and parts of south-west Scotland. The Damnonii now disappear into the larger unit of the Britons of Strathclyde, a kingdom which at its largest stretched from the head of Loch Lomond in the north almost as far as Stirling in the east, with its capital at Dumbarton. The Britons of Strathclyde kept up contact with the Britons of Wales and their chief enemies were the Angles of Northumbria: they alone of the British tribes in what is now southern Scotland were able to maintain resistance against the kings of Northumbria and keep their kingdom intact. They also fought the Picts on their north and the Scots (many of whom had come from Ireland with Fergus Mór about A. D. 500) on their north-west. It was to the embattled kingdom of Strathclyde that St Kentigern or Mungo came about the middle of the sixth century.

Legend has it that Kentigern was the son of Thennach or Thenew (a name which eventually mutated into Enoch, hence St Enoch's Square in modern Glasgow, which is near the site of St Thenew's chapel to which St Thenew's Gate – *gait*, way or street – once led). Thenew was said to have been the daughter of Loth, a Celtic prince associated with Traprain Law in East Lothian which was an *oppidum* of the British tribe Votadini. (Loth gave his name to the Lothians.) A certain Prince Ewen or Eugenius took advantage of Thenew's saintly innocence by getting into her bed disguised as a girl and so seducing her. The result was Kentigern, who was expelled with his mother by the irate Loth but found refuge in Culross, Fife, after drifting some time in an open boat in the Firth of Forth. There – the legend continues – Kentigern was tutored by St Serf or Servanus (who in fact lived about two centuries later), who in his affection for his pupil gave him the name Mungo. Under St Serf's influence Mungo became a missionary. He was miraculously led by two wild bulls yoked to a cart to what Jocelin (in 1185) said was in Mungo's time called 'Cleschu', in the kingdom of Strathclyde. There he was proclaimed bishop and consecrated by a bishop specially summoned from Ireland. He established a monastery on the banks of the Molendinar burn.

Many miracles are recorded of St Mungo. One was restoring St Serf's pet robin to life after it had been killed by some malicious boys. Another was associated with a frozen bough which he miraculously blew into flame. A third involves King Rhydderch of Strathclyde who is remembered as St Mungo's patron. Rhydderch's Queen had presented a ring given her by her husband to a soldier with whom she was having an affair. When the King discovered the ring on the hand of the soldier as he slept by the banks of the Clyde, he removed it and threw it into the river. Then he asked the Queen where was the ring he had given her. The distraught and repentant Queen confessed all to St Mungo, who arranged to have the ring found inside a salmon caught by a fisherman. This is why a robin, a tree, a salmon and a ring (as well as the saint himself) appear on Glasgow's coat of arms. The coat of arms also includes a bell, which represents the consecrated bell St Mungo brought back from Rome after a visit there. On his return he had addressed the people on a miraculously raised mound, which is the mound out of which the tree grows in the coat of arms. The motto, 'Let Glasgow flourish by the preaching of the Word', also refers to this occasion; it was later abbreviated to the more simply materialist 'Let Glasgow flourish'. There is an old rhyme referring to the items on Glasgow's city arms:

> Here's the Tree that never grew,
> Here's the Bird that never flew;
> Here's the Bell that never rang,
> Here's the Fish that never swam.

5

What is the origin of the name 'Glasgow', the little town by the Molendinar where St Mungo settled? Jocelin tells us that the saint established his episcopal seat 'in a country place [*villa*] called Cleschu, which means "Dear Family" and is now called Glasgu'. This would derive the name from the British Celtic *clas*, 'enclosed place or area, sanctuary, cloister, family', and *cu*, 'dear', and it is indeed possible that the name originally meant 'dear cloister' (but not 'dear family'). Or it could be *glas cu*, 'dear stream' (the Molendinar). But *glas* also means grey or green, both in British Celtic and in the Q-Celtic of the Scots, so the origin might be *glas cau*, 'green hollows'. *Cu* is Gaelic for 'dog', so the origin may be the Q-Celtic *glas cu* (British Celtic *glas chu*) 'greyhound', which some sources say was a nickname applied to St Mungo. Or it might be British Celtic *glas cu*, with *glas* meaning 'green' to mean 'dear green [place]'. Whichever explanation we accept – and perhaps the last seems most plausible – it is difficult to stand in Argyle Street today and think any of them appropriate.

Christianity was already practised in Strathclyde when St Mungo arrived there. The first Scottish saint, Ninian, had been active at Whithorn in Wigtownshire in the latter part of the fourth century. This area had come under Roman influence and seems to have embraced Christianity in the fourth century and asked (perhaps from Carlisle) for a bishop, receiving Ninian, whom Bede tells us had received instruction at Rome. Whithorn was thus the centre of the first Scottish episcopal see, called the see of St Martin after Martin of Tours, and although we do not know its extent and cannot be sure that Ninian himself extended missionary activity northward, there can be little doubt that the tradition of St Ninian was known in Strathclyde in the mid sixth century and that St Mungo founded his see in the light of that tradition. St Columba, a contemporary of Mungo's, came to Iona from Ireland in 563 and spread Christianity among both Scots and northern Picts. The influence of the powerful Northumbrian church was also felt in almost all parts of Scotland except Strathclyde, where the Britons seem to have resisted assimilation of their Christian practices to the general Roman pattern (as established in England by the Synod of Whitby in 664) for several centuries.

The Britons of Strathclyde came temporarily under the military control of the Northumbrians in the 670s, but the victory of Bridei, King of the Picts, over the Northumbrians at Nechtansmere (Dunnichen) in 685 put an end to this and restored the independence of Strathclyde. The Strathclyde Britons continued to play an important part in political and military activities in northern England and

6

southern Scotland (we use the name Scotland for convenience, but of course it did not yet exist). King Bridei was a son of Bile, a former king of Strathclyde, and this indicates a dynastic relationship between Britons and Picts, although they did war with each other and in 750 King Teudebur of Strathclyde defeated the Pictish King Oengus. Increasingly Scots from their kingdom of Dalriada, to the north and west of Strathclyde, settled among the Strathclyde Britons. About 843 Kenneth MacAlpin, King of Scots, joined the kingdom of the Picts to his own kingdom of Scots; the new unified kingdom became known as *Alba* in Scots Gaelic and *Scotia* in Latin. Gaelic, the Q-Celtic language of the Scots, ousted the Pictish form of P-Celtic and overt Pictish cultural and political influence disappeared. But the union of the Scottish and Pictish kingdoms under the auspices of a Scots king, with the result that we now talk of Scotland and not of Pictland, did not mean the total subjection of the larger Pictish element by the smaller Scottish. There was a merging, but precisely how it took effect and why the overt signs of Pictish culture disappeared we do not know.

The MacAlpin kings, having absorbed at least southern Pictland (there is some doubt about the degree of authority they exercised in the far north), turned their thoughts to southward expansion, and inevitably threatened Strathclyde. When in 1018 the Scots under King Malcolm II defeated the army of Bernicia, the Anglian kingdom in north-east England and south-east Scotland, at the battle of Carham to establish the River Tweed as their frontier, the south-eastern boundary of Scotland was defined. In 1015 on the death of King Owen the Bald of Strathclyde (who was related to the House of MacAlpin) no further king of Strathclyde emerged and the area, after various transitional arrangements, became part of the Scottish kingdom. So at last we find Glasgow in Scotland.

Although Glasgow flourished in its small way throughout the Middle Ages, it was not among the really important towns of Scotland. The great bulk of Scottish seaborne trade was carried on from East Coast ports with the Low Countries and the staple ports, while politically and militarily Glasgow remained relatively isolated from the centres of intrigue and the main routes of invaders. It was Edinburgh, so much nearer the Border, that invading English armies made for, and it was that city together with Stirling, Perth and Falkirk that were centres of the perennial struggles between the Scottish kings and their nobles. The great battles of pre-Reformation Scotland – Bannockburn (1314), near Stirling, and Flodden (1513), across the Tweed from Coldstream – were fought well to the south or east of Glasgow.

Glasgow does figure in the wars of independence the Scots waged against the English King Edward I in his attempts to impose his rule on Scotland at the end of the thirteenth and beginning of the fourteenth centuries. Bishop Wishart of Glasgow organized a short-lived revolt against Edward in 1297. William Wallace, the first great leader of the fight for Scottish independence, was born on the other side of the Clyde in Renfrewshire and was involved in some skirmishing in Glasgow. The late-fifteenth-century verse account of his exploits attributed to the legendary Blind Harry, which is at least as much romance as history, tells of various escapades in and around Glasgow. Once, after personally killing a group of five enemy soldiers east of Cathcart on the south side of the Clyde, Wallace collected his men and withdrew across the wooden Clyde bridge to Glasgow, though he could not stay there long as the Bishop's Castle was held for King Edward by the martial Bishop Beck of Durham.

> Our [over] Clid that tyme thar was a bryg of tre;
> Thiddir thai past in all thair gudlye mycht:
> The day was gayne, and cummyn was the nycht.
> Thai durst nocht wylle ner Glaskow still abide;
> In the Lennox he tuk purposs to ryde.

On another occasion Wallace attacked the Bishop's Castle and when Bishop Beck and his garrison came out to repel the attack and forced Wallace and his band down 'the playne streyt' (presumably the High Street) his uncle Auchinleck with another force of 140 men, who were concealed 'on the baksid of the toune', emerged from the Drygate and put the English to flight. It was at Robroyston near Glasgow in 1305 that Wallace was betrayed to the English. But Robert the Bruce carried on the struggle, and within a few years all the English garrisons in Scotland (including one in Glasgow's neighbouring and rival burgh of Rutherglen) were ousted.

Glasgow was nearer the front line when the Norsemen attacked and settled in northern and western Scotland, establishing a sea empire based on Orkney which lasted from the tenth to the thirteenth century. But they never appear to have penetrated up the Clyde as far as Glasgow, presumably because it was too shallow. The defeat of King Haakon's expedition at the battle of Largs (on the Ayrshire coast) in 1263 ended the Norse threat.

If the dear green place gave no sign in the eleventh century of ever growing into the teeming city of later generations, it had its strong religious traditions, which led to the re-founding of the see of Glasgow early in the following century, and it must have had sufficient inhaditants to provide the necessary services. As we have seen, by the late twelfth century it was both a cathedral city and a market town: a papal bull of 1172 refers to it as a *civitas*, city. In 1190 the annual July Glasgow Fair was established, which still flourishes today. By the thirteenth century we have a reasonably clear picture not only of ecclesiastical activities and of municipal organization, craft activities and community life in general but also of Glasgow's physical shape.

CHAPTER 2

Merchants and Craftsmen

THE map of medieval Glasgow is not difficult to construct. There was the Cathedral on high ground on the west bank of the Molendinar burn, with the bishop's castle and the bishop's palace (mentioned as two separate buildings in 1258) nearby. The original cathedral was destroyed by fire in 1172 and Bishop Jocelin (1175-99) was responsible for its re-building and for the erection of a tomb for St Mungo. Only a few fragments of Jocelin's cathedral remain. The building we know today was begun by Bishop William de Bondington (1233–58) and the Choir and Lower Church were completed in his lifetime. The Nave, though begun earlier, was not finished until the very end of the century. Further important additions were made by Bishop Cameron (1426–46) and Archbishop Blacader (1483–1508) who built the fine Aisle on the south side. South from the cathedral towards the Clyde ran the High Street, which was crossed roughly at right angles, just below the cathedral, by Rotten Row coming in from the west and Drygate from the east. This cross formed the first centre of Glasgow. The second centre, which proved more important and more permanent, was where the north–south line of the High Street, and its continuation Saltmarket was crossed by the Trongate and Gallowgate. This was (and is) Glasgow Cross; here the Mercat Cross and the Tolbooth were erected in the first half of the fifteenth century, and here was the centre of Glasgow in the seventeenth and eighteenth centuries. The Mercat Cross was taken down in 1679. The first Tolbooth was taken down somewhat earlier and a new one, with steeple, erected in 1626.

The word 'gate' (originally 'gait') in the names of these streets means 'way' or 'way to', though it is doubtful if Gallowgate meant 'way to the gallows'. Rotten Row is believed by some to derive from the Gaelic *rathad an rìgh*, 'way of the king', but this seems unlikely, as the earliest form of the name that has come down to us is 'Raton-raw' (1283). It is more likely that the element 'Rotten' in the street name derives from that sense of the word 'rotten' (with the dialect form 'ratten') given in the Complete Oxford English Dictionary as 'of ground, soil, etc: Extremely soft, yielding, or friable by reason of decay'. Trongate is the way to the tron, or public weighbridge. The meaning of 'Dry' in 'Drygate' remains uncertain.

There are documents from the thirteenth century mentioning burgesses of Glasgow who were bakers, skinners, dyers and fullers. In the record of the sale of a 'burgage' (tenure of property) in 1285 we find the first reference to Glasgow Bridge, a wooden structure on the site of the modern Victoria Bridge. It is not easy to see why the bridge was built downstream of the High Street–Saltmarket line, unless it was to avoid the point where the Molendinar flowed into the Clyde, which was at the southern end of this line. There was a ford just west of this junction, and it may be that the bridge-builders wished to preserve this ford as an alternative means of crossing the river. The fast-flowing Molendinar burn was used to turn the town mills, thus proving more useful than the shallow Clyde which at low tide was in places no deeper than fifteen inches. It was many centuries before the Clyde at Glasgow was made properly navigable: until this happened cargo for Glasgow carried by sea-going ships had to be off-loaded on to 'gabarts' (lighters) in the Firth of Clyde or brought by pack-horse from Irvine on the Ayrshire coast. The Clyde was most important to medieval Glasgow as a source of water and of fish, notably salmon. The broad, shallow, sandy-bottomed river was subject to periodical flooding, and there are many records of disastrous floods.

The medieval picture is one of ecclesiastical overlords and active merchants and craftsmen. The Bishop of Glasgow owned the customs of Glasgow, and it was to the Bishop that the right to have a weighbridge was granted. It was the Bishop, too, who appointed the provost, bailies and serjeants of the town. When in 1450 James II granted the city what is known as a grant of regality, the object was not to make Glasgow a 'burgh of regality' with a new and higher status: it was to the Bishop and his successors that the grant of regality was made, to have the city of Glasgow *in liberam puram et meram regalitatem*, 'in free and perfect regality'. 'Regality' meant the rights of the Crown in matters of administration and justice. In two charters of 1476 and 1491, granted by James III and James IV respectively, Glasgow is called *civitas seu burgus episcopatus*, 'city or episcopal burgh'. But although the Bishop was in ultimate legal control, the burgesses operated their own courts dealing with transfers of property and tenancies and with disputes concerning these and other matters. We learn from a precept under the privy seal of Robert III in 1397 that the weekly market day was changed from Saturday to Monday, but there is no record of when it was changed from the original Thursday.

There were Scottish burghs whose powers derived from a feudal superior, and these were known as burghs of barony, and others whose powers were granted directly by the crown – the royal burghs. (The relatively late term 'burgh of regality' raises questions about which historians differ.) Medieval Glasgow could be described as a burgh of barony whose feudal superior was the Bishop. Rutherglen, three miles up the Clyde on the other side of the river, had been a royal burgh since David I created it one in 1126. The difference between the two kinds of burgh was not significant in the Middle Ages, but there was nevertheless a rivalry between Rutherglen and Glasgow, with the former anxious to exert its trading monopoly over Glasgow. A clause in Rutherglen's charter forbade the sale of anything that had not already been offered for sale in its burghal market and Glasgow had to fight Rutherglen in order to exercise the right granted to it to have its own market. In 1226 King Alexander III forbade the bailies and serjeants of Rutherglen to take toll or custom in Glasgow. Another rival to Glasgow was Renfrew, six miles down the Clyde on the left or south bank of the river: this too was one of the burghs created by David I, although about 1160 it was granted to Walter Fitzalan, first high steward of Scotland, and his heirs, who were in fact the royal house of Stewart, so that the castle built by Walter Fitzalan on a hill by the Clyde (still called Castle Hill) was the original seat of the Stewarts. In 1404 Robert II created his son (later James I of Scotland) Baron of Renfrew, a title still borne by the Prince of Wales. Further still downstream, about fourteen miles from Glasgow on the north or right bank of the Clyde, was Dumbarton, Gaelic *dun Breatuin*, 'fort of the Britons', originally called Alcluith (*ail Clud*, 'rock on the Clyde'), the ancient capital of Strathclyde, which already had a long and eventful history when Alexander II created it a royal burgh in 1222. Dumbarton too was a rival of Glasgow and in 1243 its bailies had to be ordered not to interfere with the Glasgow burgesses, who were to be as free to trade in Argyll, Lennox and elsewhere as they had been before Alexander had granted Dumbarton its burgh charter. Quarrels over trading rights between Glasgow and its neighbouring burghs flared up intermittently for centuries, with Renfrew and Rutherglen taking the offensive against Glasgow. In 1450 James II had to order the men of Renfrew and Rutherglen to cease preventing the passage of goods to and from Glasgow market and the taking of tolls in the barony of Glasgow. The burgesses of Dumbarton were reproved in 1469 for preventing those of Glasgow from buying wine from a

French ship in the Clyde and told not to behave in that way again. In 1542 a royal decree ordered Renfrew and Rutherglen to allow merchandise to pass peacefully to Glasgow. But there were also instances of co-operation between the burghs, as when Glasgow and Dumbarton agreed in 1499 to respect each other's rights on the Clyde and in 1456 Glasgow, Rutherglen and Renfrew co-operated in an unsuccessful but prophetic attempt to deepen the Clyde at Dumbuck, east of Dumbarton.

We shall have a lot to say about the commerce and industry of Glasgow, but it is important to remember that until late in the medieval period Scotland, like England, was essentially an agricultural country. As I. F. Grant has put it: 'The country folk themselves mainly lived by local agriculture, and, in addition, furnished the main exports of the country, wool, hides, herrings and salmon. The folk of the burghs merely exported these and imported commodities and manufactured goods. Their own little industries – cloth and leather goods were made – probably merely supplied local needs. In any case, neither industry nor commerce sufficed to maintain even the embryonic Scots burghs, for they were largely, perhaps mainly, agricultural communities.' All the Scots burghs received considerable grants of land in their charters, and these the burgesses cultivated. It has been pointed out that 'the very pattern of the old burghal rigs [series of strips of arable land] can be traced right through the ground plan of Glasgow'. At one time the burgh of Glasgow owned 1,768 acres of arable land, in addition to large commons and isolated crofts. Fishing in the sea lochs that opened off the Firth of Clyde was also important for Glasgow, which developed a considerable export trade in salted and barrelled herring.

Throughout the fifteenth century Glasgow developed apace. About 1410 the old wooden bridge across the Clyde was replaced by a stone bridge of eight arches. Some forty years later William Turnbull, Bishop of Glasgow (1447–54), a learned and ambitious man of considerable influence both within and outside the Church, persuaded King James II to solicit from Pope Nicholas V a Bull founding the University of Glasgow. After the granting of the Bull in 1450 King James granted, in 1453, a letter under his own Great Seal according the university a number of significant privileges. The desire to emulate St Andrews, which had had its university since 1413, may have been one of Bishop Turnbull's motives, but he must also have considered his city a natural site for a university, since the preamble to the Bull founding it, presumably using arguments furnished by the Bishop, pointed out that in Glasgow 'the

13

air is mild, victuals are plentiful, and great store of other things pertaining to the use of man is found.' The original university building was in the High Street near the Cathedral, a proximity which symbolized the importance of the Church not only in establishing Scotland's second university in Glasgow but also, through the zeal of Bishop Turnbull, in formulating its original constitution defining its academic structure and presiding over its early development. The constitution provided that the Bishop of Glasgow should be Chancellor of the University *ex officio*, but the practical head of the University was the Rector, chosen annually by the four 'nations' which roughly corresponded to the four western sees in Scotland, Glasgow, Galloway, Argyll and the Isles. The teaching was done by Regents, who were not specialists but took students of a given year in all the subjects they were required to take throughout the whole of their course. The 'Grammar Scule' or High School was founded before the University – the first reference to it is in 1461. It was run by the burgh, and was first sited on the west side of the High Street.

Emulation of St Andrews was even more evident in the steps that led to Glasgow's becoming an archbishopric in 1492. St Andrews had been raised to an archbishopric in 1472 and Glasgow's Bishop Blacader was anxious that Glasgow should not remain inferior to that city. He persuaded James IV to support him in this, and in 1489 the Scots Parliament announced its emphatic approval. On 9 January 1492 Pope Innocent VIII promoted Glasgow to archiepiscopal rank, with the dioceses of Dunkeld, Dunblane, Galloway and Argyll as suffragans. (Dunkeld and Dunblane were later transferred to St Andrews and the Isles to Glasgow.) Blacader himself became the first archbishop. Rivalry between Glasgow and St Andrews, like that between Canterbury and York in England, continued to produce unseemly bickering. 'While it is obvious', George Pride has remarked, 'that, if Scotland had to have two archbishoprics, the choice of Glasgow was right and indeed inevitable, while, too, the move furthered the good repute and attraction of the western city, the sad truth is that the arrangement exaggerated the already top-heavy form of the ecclesiastical establishment of Scotland and increased the tendency to starve the parochial clergy in order to make a brave show at the higher levels.'

In Glasgow, as elsewhere in Scottish burghs, the distinction between merchants and craftsmen was at first jealously guarded by the former, although Glasgow was unlike other Scottish burghs in its relatively late development of merchant guilds and in its late development of the organization of merchants known as the Guild

Merchant or Merchant Guild. It was not until 1605 that the Convention of Royal Burghs (which, despite its title, had Glasgow among its members from its foundation in 1552), after criticizing Glasgow's failure to adopt 'the comely order of other free burghs', induced the city to form one. The result of this reform, embodied in the Letter of Guildry, was a conspicuous improvement in the relationship between merchants and craftsmen, who from now on operated in unusual harmony, with a Dean of Guild presiding over the affairs of the merchants and a Deacon Convenor presiding over those of the craftsmen, each with a seat on the Town Council. Glasgow then developed two unique institutions, the Merchants' House, which looked after the poor, the widowed and the orphaned of merchants' families and the Trades House, which did the same for craftsmen. The former was built in the Bridgegate about 1659 (only the steeple now survives) and the latter (at first known as the Alms House) was also built in the seventeenth century, in Old Kirk Street at Cathedral Square. A new Trades Hall was built at the end of the eighteenth century.

Craftsmen had been given the right to organize in crafts in Scottish burghs by Mary of Guise in 1556, when she was acting as Regent of the country. Skinners were incorporated as a craft in Glasgow in 1516; Tailors in 1527; Weavers in 1528 and 'Hammermen' (who included blacksmiths, goldsmiths, saddlers and others) in 1536. By the beginning of the seventeenth century Masons, Bakers, Cordiners (Shoemakers), Coopers, Fleshers (Butchers), Bonnet-makers, Barbers and Surgeons (a single craft), Wrights, Maltsters and Gardeners were all incorporated. In 1604 the numbers of Craftsmen in Glasgow were recorded as follows:

65 tailors	21 skinners
55 maltsters	21 wrights
50 cordiners	17 fleshers
30 weavers	11 masons
27 hammermen	7 bonnet-makers
27 bakers	5 dyers
23 coopers	2 surgeons

In the same year there was a total of 361 craftsmen to 213 merchants. The first Glasgow merchant known to us by name is William Elphinstone, who exported salmon and herring to France and imported brandy and salt at the beginning of the second decade of the fifteenth century.

Throughout the latter part of the fifteenth century the burgesses of Glasgow seem to have been strengthening their part in municipal

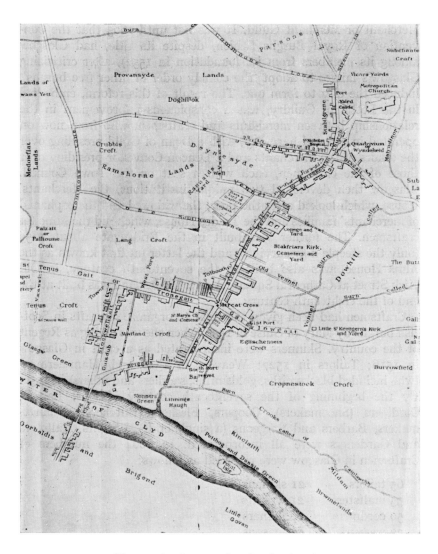

Glasgow in about 1560, clearly showing
the linear development of the city and the two crossroads

government. John Stewart of Minto is recorded as the first provost
of Glasgow in 1472 (and we find Stewarts of Minto among the provosts
of Glasgow for over a century afterwards, until resident burgesses
took the place of neighbourhood lairds as provosts). In 1492 a letter
of King James IV confirming Glasgow's privileges was addressed to
the burgh and not to the bishop. In the decades before the Refor-

mation came to Scotland there was some conflict between the burgh court, operated by the bailies, and the Church authorities on judicial matters. But it was not until 1560, when the Scottish Parliament formally embraced the Reformation, that the provost and bailies temporarily ceased to be appointed by the archbishop. Glasgow's power to elect its own magistrates was not yet, however, established. The charter of 1611, which declared Glasgow a royal burgh, reserved the archbishop's power to nominate the magistrates, and when Charles I confirmed this charter on 16 October 1636 the rights of regality were reserved for the Duke of Lennox and various taxes were ordered to be paid annually to the archbishop and to the Crown. Under the Commonwealth the city received the right to elect its own magistrates, although the position changed again at the Restoration of 1660 and it was not until 1690 that a new royal charter and an Act of Parliament finally secured for Glasgow Town Council the right, long enjoyed by other cities, to choose its own magistrates. These bailies, as they were called in Scotland, were at first two in number but the number rose to three by the end of the sixteenth century. The councillors varied in number between twenty and over thirty; at the beginning of the seventeenth century there were twenty-three, twelve merchants and eleven craftsmen, and shortly afterwards the number settled down at twenty-five, thirteen merchants and twelve craftsmen. The councillors chose the treasurer, the master of work, and the water-bailie, whose job was to watch over the river, collect dues and prevent the improper dumping of ballast. Of the council's paid officials, the foremost was the town clerk, but there were others too, including the procurator (legal officer) and the city's ministers and schoolmasters, as well as certain officers appointed, as the council minutes show, for particular purposes as the need arose or when a persuasive candidate presented himself.

We have records of the Town Council proceedings from 1573. Five years later John Leslie, Bishop of Ross, published from his exile in Rome his Latin history of Scotland (*De Origine, Moribus, et Rebus Scotorum*) which was translated into Scots nearly twenty years later by James Dalrymple. Here, in Dalrymple's translation, is what Leslie had to say about Glasgow:

> Two myles abone the toune of Renfrou is a gret and ane large village vpon the watir of clyde named Goeuan [Govan]; because it brewis gude ale commended through the hail land. Frome this beyond the watir of Clyd distant vthiris two myles is a noble toune to wit of Glasgwe quhair is ane archbishopes sait. Surlie Glasgow is the

maist renoumed market in all the west, honorable and celebrate: Afor the haeresie [i.e. the Reformation: Leslie was a staunch Roman Catholic and principal adviser of Mary Queen of Scots on religious matters] thair was ane Academie nocht obscure nathir infrequent [poorly attended] or of ane smal numbir, in respecte baith of Philosophie and Grammer and politick studie. It is sae frequent [i.e. attracting great numbers of people], and of sik renoume, that it sendes to the Easte cuntreyes verie fatt kye, herring lykwyse and salmonte, oxne-hydes, wole and skinis, buttir lykwyse that nane bettir, and cheise. Bot, contrare, to the west (quhair is a peple verie numerable in respecte of the commoditie of the sey cost), by vthir merchandise, all kynd of corne to thame sendes.

Leslie, exiled abroad, went to Rome in 1575 to try to further the interests of Queen Mary, who was by this time imprisoned in England. The burgesses of Glasgow had accepted the Reformation eagerly, and were involved with the Catholic Mary only in that the battle of Langside (then outside the bounds of Glasgow), where in 1568 her supporters and her opponents met and Mary was decisively defeated so that she fled to England and imprisonment, was fought on their doorstep. Mary's husband Darnley, however, had close connections with Glasgow. His great-uncle, the second Earl of Lennox, was Honorary Provost of Glasgow when James IV visited the city in 1510. His father, the fourth Earl of Lennox, owned a house in the Stable Green Port, to the north of the Cathedral. It was while visiting his father there (or perhaps in his new house at Limmerfield Lane, off the Drygate) in 1567 that he developed smallpox. Mary persuaded him to come to Edinburgh to convalesce, and there he was murdered at Kirk o' Field.

With the abolition of papal authority in Scotland by the Scottish Parliament in 1560, Scotland had become officially Protestant, with the Kirk as theoretically the sovereign authority. James Beaton (nephew of the better known cardinal) was then Archbishop of Glasgow and no supporter of the Reformation. He fled to Paris, with many of the Cathedral's treasures and its great collection of relics. The Cathedral itself was damaged in the anti-Romish rioting, but there is a tradition that the craftsmen of Glasgow banded together to prevent the destruction of the building of which they were so proud; in August 1574 the citizens voluntarily subscribed for the Cathedral's repair.

We get a lively picture of Glasgow life and Glasgow problems in the late sixteenth century from the minutes of the Town Council. Not only did the Council promulgate statutes and ordinances (with the formula 'it is statut and ordanit that . . .') regulating trade and other activities in the town; it also summoned people to appear and hear its judgement on the offences they had committed or disputes in which they had become involved.

On 23 January 1590 the bailies found to their horror that there had been squatters in the Tolbooth. It was 'filthillie usit be certane persones repairing thairin, nyght and day' as a result of the negligence of the officers in forgetting to lock the door. On 12 March John Mure, tailor, and John Touris, cordiner, were fined, the former for throwing a stone at Margaret Stewart, John Touris' wife, and throwing stones at her pigs, and the latter 'for streking of the said John Mure twyss on the left chulder with ane quhingar [hanger, or short sword] to the effusion of his bluid'. On 4 June the Council ordained that henceforth annually on 'Whitsuntwisday' the Provost, Bailies and Council should ride the marches [boundaries] of the burgh and city of Glasgow and then hold 'the Court of Perambulatioun of the Marchis of the Burgh and Citie of Glasgow'. At this Court they dealt with offenders whose offences against what we would call town planning had been revealed in the riding of the marches. 'They find falt with ane chop biggit [built] out vpoun the hie gait be David Ramsay, potter, in his land, lyand [lying] in Stokwall, contrair to all good ordour, and evill example of otheris.'

The accession of James VI of Scotland to the English throne in 1603 and his removal to England seems to have had no immediate effect on the tenor of life in Glasgow. In 1589 the citizens of Glasgow were taxed to the tune of 'twentie thousand punds' to be given 'to the Kings Majestie, for the furtherance of his Hienes marriage'. There was less enthusiasm for the tax imposed in 1608 to help finance the government's campaign to bring order into the Western Isles. The Council minutes of 8 April 1609 noted that 'the stent set down for outrecking of the men of weir [war] to the Ilis conforme to his hienes proclamatione' had not been completely paid to the appointed collectors, who were the Dean of Guild for the merchants and the Deacon Convener for the crafts. A week later the Council minutes record complaints that truant schoolboys and apprentices were playing destructive games in city fields, causing 'grit skaith and hurt' to the 'neytbouris yardis lyand nixt and ewest to the uther yards quhare the pastymes forsaid are hauntit, and usit in breking thair treis and destroying of thair herbis and seidis sawin in ye saidid yardis'. Owners of alleys and yards were forbidden to allow such pastimes in them, and the master of the grammar school was ordered to arrange for archery practice for his pupils as a more useful and less destructive pastime. An ordinance of 15 December 1610 ordained that the lepers of the Hospital (St Ninian's Hospital, erected as a lepers' hospital in the middle of the fourteenth century as a result of a plague of leprosy which visited Glasgow and wrought considerable havoc: it was on the Gorbals side of the river, between modern Crown Street and Main Street) 'sall gang onlie upon the calsie [causeway, or street] syde, near the gutter, and sal haif clapperis and ane claith upon thair mouth and face, and sall stand affar of qll [while] they resaif almous, or answer under the payne of baniching thame the toun and Hospitall'. On 25 January 1612 one Richard Herbertson, flesher, appeared before the Provost, Bailies and Council accused of 'the maist barbarus bangsterrie' against another flesher, James Watson, and his son John. And the next day he killed 'the said James Watsounis grit dog, maist necessar and profitable for him worth to him the sowme of £40'. He was sentenced to be imprisoned until the following Monday the 27th and on that day to be put in the stocks at the Cross, with the dead dog laid before him, after which he was to be 'put in sure ward' until he was able to find sureties that would guarantee compensation to John Watson. In July a Highland fiddler was accused of forcing a young damsel, 'but hard to be verifeit'. However, he was found to be 'ane idill vagabound' and was put in the stocks before being banished the city, on pain of hanging if he returned.

On 5 January 1628 it was 'found expedient that the calsey fra the croce [cross] down to the Salt Markett be put out and laid als neir as can be to the buiths on baith the sydes of the gaitt to make the Hie Street braid'. On 13 April 1638 William Anderson, dealer in salmon, was reproved for the exorbitant prices he charged for salmon tails, 'far exceding the pryces that was wont to be takin of old', and maximum prices were fixed 'auchtpennies for the taill of ane lytil salmond, and sixtein pennies for the taill of ane meikle salmond, and that under the pain of deprivatioun'. At the same time, 'for the regard they beir to the said Wulliam' they allowed him to charge, during the pleasure of the Council, a maximum of 'twelf pennies for the taill of ane lytil salmond, and two schillings for the taill of ane meikle salmond'. William Anderson does not seem to have reformed as a result of this consideration afforded him, for we find that in February 1644 he was again reproved for overcharging for salmon.

Meanwhile, Glasgow, like other cities in Scotland, was feeling the effect of religious and political controversy. Before turning to a discussion of Glasgow's position in these conflicts, we might pause to note that by the early seventeenth century Glasgow was a thriving small town with citizens renowned for their skill and enterprise. Its population, calculated from the bills of mortality, has been estimated at about 4,500 in 1560 (as compared with 9,000 for Edinburgh and, in 1572, about 2,900 for Aberdeen). By 1610 it was 7,644. In 1535 Glasgow was eleventh on the 'stent-roll' (amount of assessment or taxation) of the Convention of Royal Burghs; it was ninth in 1557, and fifth in 1591.

There were two significant movements among the Scottish burghs in the sixteenth century, according to the pioneer economic historian of Scotland I. F. Grant. 'One was the definite emergence of Edinburgh as the capital of Scotland . . . The other was the increasing size and wealth of Glasgow, which was to come to full fruition two hundred years later.'

CHAPTER 3

Turbulent Times

BEFORE the Reformation, preachers of the reformed religion were subject to trial and execution in Glasgow as elsewhere. John Knox tells us of a young Franciscan, Jerome Russell, 'a young man of meek nature, quick spirit and good letters', and 'one Kennedy, who passed not eighteen years of age', a talented young Scottish poet, being apprehended in the Diocese of Glasgow for their reformation principles in 1538. The Archbishop of Glasgow, Gavin Dunbar, was reluctant to sentence them to the customary death by burning, saying, 'I think it better to spare these men, than to put them to death', but those whom Knox called 'the Beasts that came from the Cardinal' [Cardinal Beaton, Archbishop of St Andrews] insisted on the extreme penalty and the two were duly burned at the stake. Cardinal Beaton was himself murdered in 1546, and fourteen years later, under the influence of forces both religious and political, the Scots Parliament passed three Acts which destroyed the Roman Church in Scotland by abolishing the authority of the Pope, annulling all Acts not in conformity with the Confession of Faith they had already passed, and making the celebration of Mass a criminal offence. The young Queen Mary was in France, and now a Catholic, married to the sickly young king of France; while Scotland was torn between pro-French and pro-English factions as well as by the traditional conflict between the Crown and the Baronage. This meant that the powers forfeited by the Roman Church did not pass to the Crown, as they did in the English Reformation, but soon devolved upon a religious body of both lay and clerical members, the General Assembly. It also meant that no Scottish monarch favoured the form of Reformation adopted by the Scots Parliament in 1560 and conflict between those accepting that form as representing the essence of the Church of Scotland and a royal authority preferring forms more congenial to monarchical power was to be a feature of Scottish history for over a century.

The conflict came violently to the surface when Charles I, through

William Laud, his Archbishop of Canterbury, issued, without reference to the General Assembly or the Scots Parliament, a Book of Canons which styled the King the Head of the Church and ordained that a new Service Book, popularly known as Laud's Liturgy and seen by many Protestant Scots as Popish in tendency, should be exclusively used in Scotland. The reading from this Service Book caused disturbances in both Edinburgh and Glasgow in the summer of 1637. In Glasgow Archbishop Patrick Lindsay (the post-Reformation episcopacy in Scotland had had a chequered history but in 1637 the Church of Scotland still had bishops, thanks to the adroit manoeuvring of James I) asked Robert Baillie, presbyterian divine, Regent of Philosophy and later Professor of Divinity at Glasgow University, to preach a sermon at the diocesan synod urging on the congregation the duty of conforming to the Book of Canons and the Service Book. Baillie asked to be excused, on the grounds that he had not yet been able to examine them. At first the Archbishop insisted, then he asked William Annand, minister at Ayr, to preach instead. Annand (later to become Dean of Edinburgh and a learned theologian with Anglican sympathies) duly preached in favour of Laud's Liturgy, much to the anger of what a nineteenth-century church historian has called 'the female Puritans of Glasgow': on the following evening several of them attacked him and he was lucky to escape with his life. The next day the magistrates of Glasgow, together with some of Baillie's friends, escorted him out of the city for his own safety. Nobody inquired too closely into the instigators of the attack, 'for', wrote Baillie, 'numbers of the best quality would have been found guilty.'

Objections to the Book of Canons and the Service Book were political as well as religious: petitions of protest poured in to the Secret Council (the Scottish Privy Council), including a notable one from Glasgow entitled 'Supplication of the Town of Glasgow' which stated that the people of Glasgow were 'appalled with fears' to see themselves summarily deprived of that liberty in serving God which both State and Church approved by public authority, and forced to embrace another, 'never so much as agitate in any General Assembly, or authorised by Parliament'. On 24 February 1638, the minutes of the Glasgow Town Council record, three bailies of the city were elected to ride to Edinburgh and confer with the other burghs of the kingdom about what could be done.

Charles I ignored all protests and steadily headed for confrontation with his Scottish Presbyterian subjects. One result of this was the production of the 'National Covenant' in February 1638, in which the signatories bound themselves to stand by each other in firm defence of the true reformed religion; although the Covenant also professed loyalty to the King, it was in uncompromising opposition to his religious policies for Scotland. 'So long as this Covenant is in force,' wrote Charles to the Marquis of Hamilton, 'I have no more power in Scotland than as a Duke in Venice; which I will rather die than suffer.' Conflict was now inevitable.

It was in these circumstances that on 21 November 1638 a historic General Assembly met in Glasgow Cathedral. The Lord High Commissioner was the Marquis of Hamilton and, knowing that the Assembly had been packed with Covenanters, he tried to terminate the meeting on the 29th, attacking the constitution of the Assembly and denying its validity because it professed to hold authority over bishops. Hamilton abruptly left the Assembly and issued a proclamation forbidding all further meetings and requiring all members to leave Glasgow for their own homes within twenty-four hours. But the members ignored Hamilton and continued the Assembly in his absence. They repealed or annulled various acts of preceding Assemblies from 1606 which they considered offensive, repudiated the new Service Book and Book of Canons, and formally charged the bishops with having acted against the laws of the Church of Scotland. Of the fourteen Scottish prelates, six were deposed and eight were both deposed and excommunicated, some on patently absurd charges. Episcopacy in Scotland was abolished. The Earl of Argyll, known as sympathetic to the Covenant though not yet a Covenanter, with his powerful private army, was welcomed as a supporter of the cause. The stage was set for war.

In February 1639 Glasgow Town Council made regulations concerning a 'Wapinschaw' (inspection of arms). On 10 April it provided for a hundred men to be sent out 'to the border, to the comoun defence, and to be maintenit upone the comoun charges of the toun'. On the 13th it elected George Porterfield captain of this company, who 'ar to martch in my Lord Montgomries regiment' as promised to Lord Montgomerie by the provost, bailies and Council. On 16 April it was ordered that all the inhabitants should carry 'musquattis' and have ready two pounds of powder per person. A further fifty men were sent to the Border. In May and June we hear of further plans for drilling companies and for the 'defence of the good comoun cause in hand'. The city's silver plate was sent to Edinburgh, 'conforme to the direction of the committee of supplie for the comoun cause'. All this was part of Glasgow's reaction to the brief confrontation between Charles's army and the Covenanting forces, known as the First Bishops' War, which brought the two armies face to face at Duns Law and produced a temporary peace (without any actual fighting) in the Pacification of Berwick, signed on 18 June 1639. But Glasgow knew that further conflict was inevitable. On 30 June the Town Council ordered that a wall should be built at the foot of Stockwell Street, with a gate in it, and another wall 'from the lit-hous to the custome-hus', also with a gate in it, and yet another between the bridge over the Clyde and the house of a certain John Holmes, 'in ane cumlie and decent forme, and with all convenient diligence'.

The General Assembly met again in Edinburgh in August 1639 and took an even more extreme line than that of the previous year in Glasgow, going so far as to recommend making subscription to the Covenant compulsory. The Scots Parliament, in the absence of bishops and other spokesmen for the King's view, approved all the Acts of the Assembly. Charles, incensed, prorogued Parliament against its will until the following June. A Scots Parliament met without royal recognition or a royal commissioner in June 1640, declared itself a valid Parliament, and proceeded to pass a number of revolutionary Acts, including making the Covenant compulsory. Glasgow supported the Covenanters. Patrick Bell, who had been Provost of Glasgow in 1638, was sent by the provost, bailies and Council to Edinburgh at the end of May 1640 'to attend the doun-sitting of the parliament, the second day of Julii [actually, June] nixt' and instructed that in the event of the King's not authorizing the continuing of the Parliament he should join with the other members in resolving and concluding 'sik things as they think most conducible for the publick good, and for the preservation of thair liberties, lyfis, and estaites' and consent to whatever they decided.

The result of all this was the so-called Second Bishops' War. A Scottish army under the veteran General Alexander Leslie (with the Marquis of Montrose, who was soon to become disillusioned with the extremism of the Covenanters' leaders and change sides to campaign for King Charles, leading a contingent of 3,000 horse and foot) crossed into England on 20 August 1640 and after a ridiculously short campaign thoroughly defeated a royalist army under Viscount Conway near Newcastle. The Scots then occupied Newcastle and soon afterwards all of Northumberland and Durham also. The victorious Covenanting army agreed at Ripon to advance no further on condition of receiving £850 per day subsistence from the territory occupied. After the English Long Parliament had ratified the terms the following year, the triumphant army returned to Scotland, their pockets bulging.

The Town Council of Glasgow was now concerned to get the endowments of the archbishopric made available for the support of 'ane minister . . . in place of the Bishop, and for ane competent allowance out of the said Bishoprick, for upholding the great kirk [cathedral], and for helping the poor of the Bishops Hospitals and gramer scoolle'. On 4 December 1641 Patrick Gillespie secured a letter of presentation as minister of the High Kirk in place of the archbishop but opposition by Robert Baillie and others delayed the official appointment until 1648. For twenty-three years – from the abolition of bishops in Scotland in 1638 until after the Restoration – there was no Archbishop of Glasgow.

Scotland was not at first involved when civil war between Charles and his opponents broke out in England in August 1642. The Scots were, however, involved with the Irish rebellion towards the end of 1641, and the Glasgow Town Council minutes of 8 December 1641 record a contribution to the cost of transporting men to Ireland. In 1643 the English Parliamentary forces sought help from Scotland against King Charles, and the result was the treaty called the Solemn League and Covenant, an agreement between the two parties cast (on Scottish insistence) in an uncompromisingly religious form. Both the English Parliamentarians and the Scots bound themselves to reform religion in England and Ireland 'according to the Word of God and the example of the best Reformed Churches', and the Scots undertook to send a large army into England to be paid for by the English Parliamentarians and used as they decided. Glasgow was enthusiastic about these measures. On 12 December 1643 – a month before Alexander Leslie, now Earl of Leven, crossed into England with an army of 18,000 foot and 2,000 cavalry – the Town Council sent a drum through the town with an announcement requiring 'all to inroll themselffs for the present comoune expeditioune'. Glasgow men played a part in Cromwell's victory over the royalist army under Prince Rupert at Marston Moor in July 1644.

Royalist hopes centred on Montrose, now on the royalist side. He had been in England with Prince Rupert, but eventually decided to break through the cordon of Covenanters in the Lowlands and return to Scotland to raise the royal standard on the Braes of Atholl above the River Tilt on 28 August 1644. This signalized the beginning of his royalist campaign in Scotland which, after brilliant successes, ended with his defeat at Philiphaugh in September 1645. Two days after Montrose raised the royal standard the Town Council issued a proclamation ordering 'all maner of persones between sextie and sextein to be in readiness with the best armes, and to this effect, to cum out presentlie with ther several capitanes, with matche, powder, and lead, and also to provyd themselfs with twentie days' provisioune, to marche according as they sall get ordours, vnder the paine of deathe'. On 26 October they sent to Holland for 'six score' sword blades. But as Montrose's army moved nearer Glasgow the city fathers began to wonder whether their conspicuous opposition to him and his cause was a good idea. After Montrose's decisive victory over the Covenanting forces at Kilsyth on 15 August 1645 – only a few hundred escaped out of 6,000 – the Glasgow magistrates sent an apology for their lack of loyalty and congratulated him on his victory. Montrose sent a message of assurance to the city, and on 18 August he entered it after a deputation from the Town Council had met him outside the walls and offered the equivalent of £500 sterling for his soldiers, with a plea that their city might be left unharmed. Montrose, though he agreed to this request, was unable to control looting by some Highlanders in his army who had never seen such material prosperity as they found in the Saltmarket and the Gallowgate: a Highland army always expected loot if victorious. But Montrose honoured his promise to the Town Council, and hanged some of the more conspicuous looters in an attempt to put an end to the practice. Finding the temptations of Glasgow too great for some of his army, however, he withdrew the army in a couple of days and moved six miles up the Clyde to Bothwell. Before he left he borrowed £50,000 Scots (£4,166 sterling) from the city, which he never found an opportunity to repay.

Montrose issued a proclamation to the chief towns of Scotland, summoning a Parliament to be held in Glasgow on 20 October. But his decisive defeat at Philiphaugh by General David Leslie, nephew of Alexander, on 13 September put this out of the question. Instead of housing a properly constituted Parliament acting with royal authority, Glasgow now found itself occupied by Leslie and his triumphant Covenanting forces while the Committee of Estates (a Scots parliament acting without royal authority or royal or episcopal representation) proceeded to take a bloody vengeance on Montrose's supporters. 'The Committee of Estates,' recorded the Glasgow bailie James Burns, 'sat down in Glasgow. They sat in the Tolbuith Hall when three prisoners were condemned for treason: Sir William Rollo suffered first, a large scaffold being erected above the cross, and was beheaded at four afternoon, the 21st October: and on the morrow the 22nd, Sir Philip Nisbet, and Ogilvie of Innerquarity, a lovely young youth, suffered. They were all three beheaded . . . Those who were most forward for Montrose ran great hazard of life and fortune; those who had taken protections, were fined in six years rents of their estates, and the third part of their moveables, live as they list.' Leslie borrowed £20,000 Scots (£1,166 13s. 4d. sterling) from the city, remarking that this would pay for the interest on the money

Montrose had got. On 22 May 1647 a Town Council minute makes clear that the money was not yet repaid.

The Earl of Lanark, 'be vertew of the commissioune grantit to his Lordshipe by the Lordes and others of the Committee of Estates of Parliament', discharged the Provost and other officers and asked the Town Council to elect the Provost and other officers from a new list. The bailies declined, resolving, the Town Council minutes record, 'to stand firm to the ordour they have been in vse to choise their Magistrats out of the present Counsall, and no otherways'. The Earl then discharged them from electing any member of their Council or any accessory, on which the Council formally protested in favour of the preservation of the liberties of the burgh in electing their magistrates and against the election not being 'perfyted this day'. But the Earl had his way. He 'suspendit, or dischargit of their offices' the 'Provost, Balleis, and wholl Towne Councell (except George Porterfield)' because they 'war accessorie to ther sending to and capitulating with James Grahame [Montrose]'. On 13 March 1647 the Town Council ordered that henceforth no one could become a burgess or 'Guildbrother' without first subscribing to the Covenant.

By the end of 1647 the English Parliamentarians had become disillusioned with their Scottish allies and the latter were equally disillusioned with the failure of the Solemn League and Covenant to establish Presbyterianism in England. Charles was now a prisoner at Carisbrooke Castle in the Isle of Wight, and there three Scottish commissioners (including the Earl of Lanark) met him and concluded a secret treaty known as the 'Engagement', which promised Scottish support for Charles if he would agree, if restored to power, to establish Presbyterianism in England for three years and to suppress Independents and other sectaries. Charles balked at making the Covenant compulsory, but he undertook to have it confirmed by Act of Parliament. So once again a Scottish army marched into England, but this time in support of the King. At the end of May 1648 Glasgow expressed its disapproval of the decision to go to war in support of the King. The Town Council petitioned 'the Ryt. Honourable Noblemen and vthers of the Committee of War of the Sheriffdome of Clydisdale', stating that the city was not satisfied of the lawfulness of the military action in favour of the King and asking the Committee 'to tak in guid pairt that the posture of war is not so spidilie advancit as the order issued by you did require'. With great respect and politeness, they asked that Parliament should be supplicated to clear the lawfulness and necessity of such proceedings. But the Committee of Estates, meeting in Edinburgh, supported the military action against the English Parliamentarians: Covenanting influence was waning among the Scottish nobility, and the deep suspicion of the King's intentions was not now shared by the majority of the Estates. On 8 July 1648 a Scottish army crossed the Border, to be destroyed by Cromwell on 17 to 19 August at Preston, Wigan and Warrington. The doubts of the Glaswegians were vindicated.

The Scots could not accept the execution of King Charles in January 1649, and six days afterwards the Scottish Estates proclaimed his son King of Great Britain, France and Ireland. The young Charles, however, was required to pledge allegiance to both the National Covenant and the Solemn League and Covenant, which, desperate for Scottish aid, he consented to do. So the Scots, under David Leslie, now found themselves in military support of Charles II against the English under Cromwell. Cromwell invaded Scotland, and utterly defeated Leslie's army at Dunbar on 3 September 1650. He went on to take Edinburgh and Leith and on 24 October he arrived at Glasgow, taking up his lodging at Silvercraigs House, which stood at the north corner of Steel Street and the Saltmarket. The magistrates and many leading citizens had already fled the city. Cromwell entertained Patrick Campbell, minister of the Outer High Kirk,* to a splendid meal, preceded by such an enormously long grace that Campbell was greatly impressed. On Sunday Cromwell and his staff marched in procession to the Cathedral, where Zachary Boyd, minister of the Barony and noted divine, author and versifier, preached a sermon boldly critical of the victorious English commander-in-chief. Cromwell responded by inviting him to spend the evening with him and the two sat arguing on theology until three o'clock the next morning: Boyd also, in spite of himself, was impressed. Cromwell behaved well in Glasgow. He visited the University and paid the £200 which Charles I had promised for the building fund, adding a personal donation of £500. He paid another visit to Glasgow the following April, when on a single Sunday he heard a sermon at the Inner High Kirk in the morning, and both a lecture and a sermon in the Outer High Kirk in the afternoon.

Opinion in Glasgow as elsewhere in Scotland was divided between moderate Presbyterians, known as 'Resolutioners', among whom Robert Baillie was the most notable figure, who retained a loyalty to the exiled young King together with Covenanting principles, and the extremist 'Protestors', led by Patrick Gillespie. In 1652, the English Parliament, having decided on the incorporation of Scotland

---

*After the Reformation the Cathedral was used for three separate parish churches, the Inner High, occupying the Choir, the Outer High (later St Paul's) occupying the Nave, and the Laigh, or Barony, occupying the Crypt.

into a united kingdom with England, announced an official 'Tender of Union', and representatives of the Scottish burghs met the commissioners sent by the English military government at Dalkeith. The Glasgow delegates on reporting back to their fellow citizens found great hostility to the Tender in the city. English soldiers were sent to Glasgow and more amenable delegates were sent by the commissioners. A declaration of a voluntary union of England and Scotland in one commonwealth was proclaimed at the market cross of Edinburgh on 21 April 1652, two weeks before the arrival in Scotland of the judges appointed by the English Parliament to administer justice in Scotland. These judges appointed a commission with power to change all Scottish laws concerning the universities and the ministry that were inconsistent with those of England, and announced their intention to remove from the Scottish universities and the ministry all persons who were 'either scandalous in their lives and conversations, or that shall oppose the authority of the Common-wealth of England' and replace them by persons considered more suitable. Protestors accepted this, while Resolutioners were strongly opposed, and the presbytery of Glasgow was riven by dissent. Patrick Gillespie, as leader of the Protestor minority, was *persona grata* with Cromwell's commissioners and at their instigation was appointed Principal of Glasgow University in 1653.

By the spring of 1654 Cromwell was Protector of England, Scotland and Ireland, and the countries were then united, with a single Parliament. A Council of State was appointed for Scotland, to sit in Edinburgh. It met there in September 1655 and, anxious to obtain the goodwill of the country, enacted a number of conciliatory measures, including restoring to the burghs their right to elect their own magistrates, which had been taken away in 1652. The only condition was that the name of the Protector should be substituted for that of the King in the oaths they took on entering office. We find, however, that on 29 September the Provost 'producit ane letter direct from his Highness the Lord Protector, quhairby his Hienes desyres the electione of the Magistratis of this burghe be deferred until he sall be mor fullie informed in that particular'. In 1657 Cromwell was pressed by some of his advisers to intervene in the choice of the Glasgow magistrates, but General Monck, his representative in Scotland, pointed out that the Scottish burghs had been the first to submit peacefully to the Commonwealth government 'and have ever since lived peaceably under us', and so firmly rejected the idea. But in January 1658 the Dean of Guild and others were appointed by the Town Council to appear on the Council's behalf before the committee appointed by the Council of State to prove the worthiness of 'the lyfe and conversatioune of the saidis Magistratis and Counsall', which suggests something other than a free election. And on 16 January 1658 the Town Council minutes report that there was no election of magistrates and Council made the previous Michaelmas. Other entries leave no doubt that the Council of State put pressure on the Town Council to exclude some duly elected magistrates and to include others and that this caused unhappiness among the Glasgow magistrates. On 13 March 1658 the Town Council appointed two bailies, the Dean of Guild and a James Polok 'to repair to Edinburgh for defence of the townes liberties now agitating before the Counsell of Stait, and for giving obedience to the citatioune given out thereanent.' The deputation were expressly instructed not to meddle 'with any capitulatioune whatsomever quilk in any wayes in the leist may infringe the townes liberties in its freedome of electioune of the Magistratis and Counsaill theirof, and uthers office bearers thereintill.'

So Glasgow, Puritan city though in many respects it was, was restless under the Commonwealth. The Glaswegians even appear to have resisted its coinage. On 9 July 1658 a proclamation was sent round the town, to the beat of a drum, commanding everybody to receive the Commonwealth silver currency 'without any exceptioune, the samyn being fand sufficient silver and weight'. But two months later Cromwell was dead, and in less than two years after that – on 26 May 1660 – the Town Council unanimously decided 'that ane address and applicatioune should be made to the KINGES Most Excellent Majestie, in name of this burghe'. Charles II was back on the throne of both England and Scotland. On 20 September the Town Council ordained that no person disaffected to His Majesty's Government should 'be admittit to any place of Magistracy, Counseill, or any office of Deaconrie within the burgh'. And on 2 October, 'being the first Tuesday after Michaelmas, and so the ordinarie day for electing the Magistratis of this burgh, for the year enshewing, ther was producit [in the Town Council] ane letter direct from the Right Noble the Earle of Glencairne, now High Chancellor of Scotland, wherin his Lordship desyres that, to the effect the towne show their wonted affectione to his Majesties service, theis Magistratis that wer most vnjustlie thrust from their places in Anno 1648, may be made use of as Magistratis for the year enshewing; and it being votted quether obedience should be given to the said letter or not, it was condeschendit that obedience should be given thairto'. Individuals who had been ejected in 1648 were sent for and asked to serve as bailies. Some were too 'waik and informe of bodie' to serve, one had 'depairted this life', but one who pleaded his age and infirmity

(Colin Campbell, who had been replaced as Provost) was eventually persuaded to agree. He was then chosen Provost 'for the year enshewing', and he duly served until succeeded by John Bell in 1662.

Throughout the years of religious and political turbulence the ordinary life of Glasgow went on with only a few interruptions. In July 1626 the Provost and bailies agreed to appoint James Sanders as city music teacher, and gave him a monopoly of such teaching. However, Sanders' music school did not flourish and in May 1638, seeing that it was 'altogider dekayit . . . to the grait discredit of this citie' and in view of the 'discontentment of sundrie honest men . . . who had bairnies whom they wold have instrictit in that art', Duncan Birnet was allowed to set up another music school. In February 1639 it was ordained that no more than four 'Inglisch scooles' together with one writing school should be maintained by the burgh. On 10 March 1640 preparations were made for building on the north side of the Trongate the hospital provided for in the will of the writer (lawyer) George Hutcheson. (The original Hutcheson's hospital supported twelve old men and twelve boys, the latter being educated at a school in the building. The original building was eventually pulled down to allow Hutcheson Street to open on to the Trongate, and a new building was erected in Ingram Street in 1805. The subsequent story is told in Chapter Seven.)

In 1638 Glasgow appointed George Anderson as city printer: he had come from Edinburgh and in January 1640 Glasgow Town Council voted to pay him a hundred pounds to cover the costs of his moving himself and his equipment from that city. In November 1647 the Council granted to Anderson's widow and children the right to continued payment by the city so long as they continued 'prenting in the toune'. Anderson's son, who was a printer in Edinburgh, came to Glasgow in 1657 to carry on his late father's business there, and he was succeeded by Robert Sanders in 1661, who was in turn succeeded by his son in 1696.

In February 1642 a tailor called Patrick Adam was imprisoned for eight days and fined £20 for vilipending and vilifying the magistrates in telling the burgh treasurer John Clark 'that he regardit not the provest, bailies and Counsall of the burghe ane fart of his erse'. On the same day that it sentenced Adam, the Town Council took note of 'the great increase of the poor, speciallie these that cum from Irland' and solicited contributions for their relief from the citizens. The Dean of Guild was appointed to look after 'the distressed people that com from Irland' by providing support for them out of the contributions collected, 'according to their necessitie'.

In October 1642 the Town Council enacted that no Provost should serve longer than two years consecutively. The following January the Council exercised its town planning function by ordering one Robert Rowan to take down a shop he had built in Rotten Row on the grounds that his neighbours had complained that it obstructed their view of the High Street. And so Glasgow life went on until the interruption caused by Montrose's campaign in 1645. The next crisis was caused by the plague in the autumn of 1646. On 5 November 1646 the Town Council appointed quarter-masters to 'tak up the names of everie famelie, and to visit everie famelie ilk day, and tak notice of thair healthe, to the effect that they may report to the Magistrats whair they find any seik persone'. Other regulations made the following February show that the plague was still raging: movement of citizens was restricted and the entry or re-entry into Glasgow by persons who had been in 'places suspect of the infectioune' was prohibited. On 13 March it was ordered that the graves of those who were suspected of having died of the plague should be specially marked.

On 17 June 1652 a serious fire destroyed 'neir fourscoir closses . . . estimate to about ane thousand families . . . the haill houssis, bak and foir, upon both sydis of the Saltmercat, with the houssis on the west syd of Wm. Lawsounis close in the Gallowgait; and the houssis on the west syd of Gilbert Merschellis close; with divers housses on the north syde of the Briggait'. About a third of the town was destroyed, and the Town Council appointed the Provost and another representative to go to Ayr to the English officers stationed there (who had 'seen the townis lamentable condition') in order to obtain from them letters of recommendation 'to suche officers and judges who sitts in Edinburgh, to the effect that the same may be recommendit be them to the Parliament of Ingland, that all helpe and supplie may be gotten therby that may be for supplie of such as has thair landis and guidis burnt'. The following September the Council sent one John Wilkie to London to petition Parliament for a contribution towards 'making up of the losses of the toune be fyre'. On 7 April 1653 Cromwell himself was one of the signatories of a document soliciting funds for the relief of Glasgow from 'pious and well disposed people'.

The Town Council were also concerned to prevent further fires. On 23 August 1656 they authorized discussions concerning 'the making of the ingyne for casting watter on land that is in fyre, as they have in Edinburghe' and paid James Colquhoun £23 14s. for his expenses in going to Edinburgh to see the Edinburgh engine. By the following June Colquhoun had constructed an engine on the Edinburgh model 'for the occasioune of suddent fyre, in spurting out of water thairon' and it was agreed that it should be kept 'near

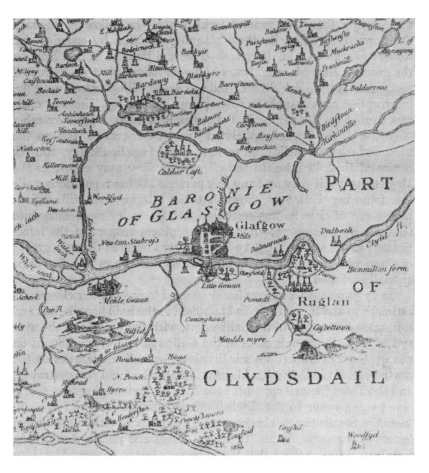

Detail from a map of the Glasgow region in 1654, in Blaeu's *Atlas*

himself'. This did not prevent another great fire on 3 November 1677.

On 17 February 1655 the Town Council expressed concern at the easy terms on which some persons were admitted to burgess-ship, and laid down rules concerning a minimum apprenticeship of four full years and other requirements. The following April they expressed their concern at the poor quality of the bread baked by Glasgow bakers 'to the great discredit of this burghe'. They noted that 'twa honest men baxters cume from Edinburgh' had offered their services to the town in baking bread of the Edinburgh quality, and unanimously agreed to ask the Provost and others to look into the matter of bread-baking in Glasgow and to settle things 'the best commodious

34

way they can for the townes credit, and to report'. Thus the first recorded examples of the rivalry between Glasgow and Edinburgh, later the subject of so many jokes, were about fire-engines and about bread and on these particular occasions Glasgow conceded Edinburgh's superiority.

In November 1659 orders were given for the removal of a familiar Glasgow landmark. The old market cross, which stood where Rotten Row and Drygate came into High Street, had become 'altogether defaced' through the building of a guard house 'about and wpone' it. The Town Council therefore gave orders for its removal, and appointed and ordained 'that pairt of the streit where the Croce did stand of befor, to be calsayed ("causewayed") in ane most comly and decent maner'. 'Through God's mercie our Toune, in its proportions, thryves above all the land', wrote Robert Baillie in 1656. 'The word of God is weell loved and regarded, albeit not as it ought and we desyre; yet in no toune of our land better. Our people has much more trade in comparison than any other: their buildings encrease strangely both for number and fairness: it's more than doubled in our tyme.'

CHAPTER 4

Before the Union

A GENTLEMAN from Cheshire called Sir William Brereton visited Glasgow in 1634 and was much impressed. He found the cathedral 'a brave and ancient piece', the tolbooth 'a very fair and high-built house', and the ale the best in Scotland. He described the town as made up of two streets built like a cross, with a cross placed at the intersection. A few years later another English visitor, Richard Frank, admired Glasgow's 'four large fair streets, modell'd, as it were, into a spacious quadrant, in the centre whereof their market-place is fixed' and he too was struck by the tolbooth, 'their western prodigy, infinitely excelling the model and usual build of town-halls': it was 'without exception, the paragon of beauty in the west'. The city's storehouses and warehouses were described as 'stuft with merchandize, as their shops swell big with foreign commodities and returns from France, and other remote parts'. There was abundance of good French wines to go with the native abundance of fish and fowl. He concludes: 'What to say of this eminent Glasgow I know not, except to fancy a smell of my native country. The very prospect of this flourishing city reminds me of the beautiful fabricks and the florid fields of England.' He had special praise for the Glasgow linen ('very neatly lapped up, and, to their praise be it spoken . . . lavendar-proof'), for the decency of the people's dress, and for the exemplary decorum in every rank of society.

In 1656, anxious to take stock of Scotland's economic potential in the now unified Commonwealth, Cromwell sent an Englishman called Thomas Tucker to Scotland to report 'upon the settlement of the revenues of Excise and Customs in Scotland'. His report contains a considerable amount of information about the economic state of Glasgow. 'This town,' he wrote, 'seated in a pleasant and fruitful soil, and consisting of four streets handsomely built in form of a cross, is one of the most considerable burghs of Scotland, as well for the structure as trade of it. The inhabitants, all but the students of the college which is here, are traders and dealers – some for

Ireland with small smiddy coales in open boats from four to ten tonnes, from whence they bring hoopes, ringes, barrell-staves, meale, oates, and butter; some for France with pladding, coals, and herring, of which there is a great fishing yearly in the western sea, for which they return salt, paper, rosin, and prunes; some to Norway for timber; and every one with theyr neighbours the Highlanders, who come hither from the Isles and Western parts.' Though he noted the beginnings of trade between the Clyde and the West Indies – 'Here hath likewise been some who have adventured as far as Barbadoes; but the losses they have sustained by reason of their going out and coming home late every year, have made them discontinue going there any more' – it was Leith that he saw as the great centre of Scotland's sea trade. He counted fourteen vessels belonging to Leith, the largest number in any Scottish port. The three ports next in order, possessing twelve ships each, were Montrose, Kirkcaldy and Glasgow. The great bulk of Scottish shipping, he noted, was from the east coast to Denmark, North Germany, Holland and France, with the Firth of Forth the great trading centre. The Clyde's date with destiny had not yet arrived. But Tucker realized that Glasgow's growth would be assured 'were she not checqued and kept under by the shallownesse of her river'.

We have already noted Cromwell's generosity towards Glasgow University: he was indeed well disposed towards all the Scottish universities, although, as we have seen, on his own terms. The English commissioners examining the Scottish universities had made Patrick Gillespie principal of Glasgow University: he had had a long record of staunch anti-royalist activity and devoted most of his time to ecclesiastical politics. As far as the University was concerned, however, he was more concerned with the buildings than with teaching. His appointment caused considerable dismay, and some students left the university and 'would no more return'. 'For the Colledge,' wrote Robert Baillie, Professor of Divinity, in 1658, 'we have no redresse of our discipline and teaching. Mr Gillespie's work is building and pleas; with the din of masons, wrights, carters, smiths, we are vexed every day. Mr Gillespie, alone for vanitie to make a new quarter in the Colledge, has cast downe my house to build up ane other of greater show, but farr worse accommodation... Mr Gillespie hes strange wayes of getting money for it, by his own industry alone; an order he got from the Protector of five hundred pounds sterling, (but for an ill-office to the countrie, his delation of so much concealed rent yearly of the Crown;) also the vacancy of all churches, wherein the Colledge had entres: this breeds clamour as the unjust spoill of churches and incumbents.' Gillespie was responsible for the Protector's ordinance of 8 August 1654, settling on Glasgow the lands of the late bishopric of Galloway and assigning to the universities of Glasgow and Aberdeen two hundred marks yearly out of the Customs of the town. In his building programme for Glasgow University – which included the completion of the south and west sides of the inner court by 1656, then the north and south sides of the outer court, and finally the pulling down and rebuilding of the whole front – Gillespie obtained a second grant from the Protector, bestowing on the University certain revenues that had belonged to the Dean and Chapter of Glasgow. This, however, was reversed at the Restoration before much practical benefit had been obtained, at which time Gillespie was deprived of his principalship and imprisoned.

The dissolution of the Commonwealth and the return to the throne of Charles II with the subsequent restoration of episcopacy in Scotland had their effect on the University and the ministry in Glasgow but did not at first hinder the city's progress. In 1662 the theological naturalist John Ray – whose book *The Wisdom of God Manifested in the Works of the Creation* was to be eagerly read by young Robert Burns over a hundred years later – visited Glasgow and found it 'fair, large, and well built, crosswise, somewhat like unto Oxford, the streets very broad and pleasant'. Seven years later another English divine, John Browne, gave his opinion of the city: 'Tis situated upon the River Glotta, or cluyd, over which is paved a very fair bridge, supported with eight arches, and for pleasantness of sight, sweetness of air and delightfulness of its gardens and orchards enriched with most delicious fruits, surpasseth all other places in this tract.'

It was not long, however, before the religious policies enforced by Charles II's commissioners in Scotland brought new conflict and violence. In November 1661 Andrew Fairfoul was appointed Archbishop of Glasgow, with power to choose the city magistrates. As a result of a complaint by him, the Scottish Privy Council met in Glasgow in a session known as the 'drunken meeting' because it was said that nearly everybody who attended was 'flustered with drink'. The Council passed an edict making acceptance of Episcopacy compulsory on both ministers and people under severe penalties. After two years Fairfoul was succeeded as Archbishop by Alexander Burnet, a high churchman who had taken Anglican orders and was bitterly opposed to the Covenanters and the whole Covenanting tradition. The policy of enforcing the edict of the 'drunken meeting' was strengthened. Ministers who refused to conform, including fourteen from Glasgow, were ousted from their livings and many were heavily fined. Two former Provosts of Glasgow, George Porterfield and John Graham, were banished from the country. The ousted clergy preached to their faithful flocks in open-air 'conventicles', which were declared illegal. The attempt to suppress coventicles and to keep the deprived clergy from their flocks provoked more and more bitterness. Harsh repression on the Government side faced religious bigotry on the side of the oppressed (Scott's *Old Mortality* is still the most satisfactory picture of this period), and the result was violence and cruelty. The murder of James Sharp, Archbishop of St Andrews, by a band of embittered Covenanters in 1679 was answered by torturings, executions and transportations on the Government side.

The Duke of Lauderdale, Charles's Commissioner in Scotland, decided to cow the Covenanters of the south-west of Scotland – where extreme Covenanting opinions flourished – and loosed an army of some 8,000 Highlanders on the area, allowing them to live off what they could take. Many were billeted on Glasgow citizens, to their great indignation and economic distress. The debonair James Graham of Claverhouse, scourge of the Covenanters, was now in command of a troop of Life Guards charged with watching for conventicles and enforcing the law. After a skirmish with an armed conventicle on 1 June 1679 on the farm of Drumclog some thirteen miles south of Glasgow, at which Claverhouse's dragoons got the worst of it, the conflict between Covenanters and Government forces blazed into open rebellion. Claverhouse fell back on Glasgow where the Covenanters followed, entering the city by the Gallowgate and the College Vennel, to be met by a hail of fire from Claverhouse's men sheltering in houses and behind specially constructed barricades. But the Covenanters temporarily prevailed and Claverhouse was forced to leave the city to them. It is significant of the bitterness of the conflict that while the Covenanting tradition asserted that Claverhouse gave orders that the dead bodies of the Covenanters who had been killed in Glasgow were not to be buried but were to be left to be eaten by butchers' dogs, the official indictment against the Covenanters later brought against them in the High Court of Justiciary in Edinburgh asserted that they occupied the house of the Archbishop of Glasgow (who was not in the city at the time), stripped it of its contents and set his cellar afloat with beer and wine, sacked the cathedral, and then entered the home of the Bishop of Argyll where they not only robbed and pillaged but dug up from their graves in the chapel the bodies of the Bishop's two recently buried children, broke open the coffins, and ran their swords through the bodies. On 22 June Claverhouse destroyed the Covenanting army at Bothwell Brig, up the Clyde from Glasgow, and that was the end of the rebellion. Several of Glasgow's citizens, notable among whom was

Donald Cargill, minister of the Barony parish, were executed in Edinburgh for their part in the rebellion. Cargill was not captured until July 1681. He kept up his defiance until the end.

The Presbyterian Church of Scotland, first set up in 1560 and consistently refused by the Stuart Kings, was re-established after the short reign of James VII of Scotland and II of England that ended with his expulsion from both thrones in 1688. It was the birth of a son to the Roman Catholic wife of this Roman Catholic monarch that precipitated the revolution that brought the Protestant William of Orange and his wife Mary to the throne, for the prospect of a permanent Catholic succession outraged both English and Scottish Protestants and was especially offensive to the Scottish Covenanters. Nevertheless, Glasgow Town Council ordered the city treasurer to spend a substantial sum of money to provide seven barrels of gun-powder and quantities of French wines 'to be made use of at the solemnitie for the birth of the Prince of Scotland and Waills, &c'. But less than six months later the Provost drew up an address 'to be presented to his Royall Highness the Prince of Orange, whilk was allowed be the Magistrats and Toune Counsell, and subscryvit be the most pairt'. On 16 August 1689 there was read in the Town Council a letter to be presented to King William and Queen Mary 'for getting the election of the Provest and Bailies of this city in their owne hands (bishopes now being abolished)', and on 18 January 1690 the Town Council's emissary returned from London with:

> ane Letter of Gift, granted be their Most Sacred Majesties King William and Queen Marie, whilk their Majesties ordaine to be made and passed under their Great Seall of the Kingdome of Scotland, not onlie ratifieing, approveing, and confirming the haill chartors, priviledges, grants, and concessions, from any of their Majesties Royall Predicessors, to and in favour of the communitie and city of Glasgow, to the Gildrie, Trades, and severall Incorporationes or Deacones therof, as effectuallie as if every severall erection, charter, or grant, were particularlie enumerated, or therein repeated; And likewayes, their Majesties being come in place of the Archbishop of Glasgow, for themselves, and for any other right competent to them of new, Give, grant, and dispone to, and in favours of, the said City of Glasgow and Towne Counsell thereof, full power, right and libertie to choise and elect their Proveist, Baillies, and haill other Magistrats, In the ordinar maner, and at the ordinar tyme, as freelie as any other royall burgh in the said kingdome doe or may choise their Proveist, Baillies, and Magistrats, beginning the first election at Michaelmas nixt, and so to continow in all tyme comeing.

The royal charter was confirmed by an Act of Parliament the same year, giving the Town Council power to choose the magistrates. By this time Glasgow's population had risen to nearly 12,000, rising to an estimated 12,766 in 1708. This made it the second largest burgh in Scotland, after Edinburgh. By the mid seventeenth century Glasgow was fourth in Scotland's 'stent roll', and by 1670 it was second, paying £12 out of every £100 of tax imposed on the burghs, after Edinburgh, which paid £33 6s. 8d. and above Aberdeen and Dundee which paid £7 and £6 2s. respectively.

The shallowness of the Clyde at Glasgow that had been noted by Thomas Tucker as restraining her growth provoked a variety of remedies. The first quay was built at the Broomielaw in 1662; more effective was the building of a seaport for Glasgow's sea-going ships at Newark Bay (Port Glasgow), some nineteen miles down river and three miles above Greenock, in 1668. The result was a rapid improvement in Glasgow's sea-going trade. Although the English Navigation Acts of 1660 and 1663 prohibited other countries, including Scotland, from trading with the English colonies, Glasgow ships found ways of evading the prohibition. In 1674 we find recorded the first cargo of tobacco from Virginia (forty hogsheads), together with 'cassnutt sugger', ginger and logwood; other such imports are recorded in 1677, 1681 and 1691. The Scots, wrote the Collector of Customs of Carolina in 1687, were able to undersell the English, 'their Goods being either much Courser and slighter, which will Serve for Servants weare and will be sure to go off, they being cheap so that an Englishman must go away unfreighted or sell to vast Disadvantage'. By the end of the century, despite the discriminatory Navigation Acts, ships from the Clyde were trading regularly with the American colonies. There was also much trade with England, in spite of the heavy tariffs on Scottish goods imposed by the English Parliament after the Restoration. The chief export to England from Glasgow was linen, 488,800 ells being sent overland from the city in 1672.

It was the discrimination by the English Parliament and merchants against Scottish sea-going trade and the specific attempts to prohibit any Scottish participation in England's profitable commerce with Asia, Africa and America, that led the Scots in 1695 to set up their 'Company of Scotland Trading to Africa and the Indies', a venture deliberately sabotaged by English interests, who prevented the Scots from raising money for the company outside Scotland. Forced to go it alone, the Scots thought up the idea of founding a trading colony of their own on the Isthmus of Darien, which connects North and South America and separates the Caribbean Sea from the Pacific Ocean, apparently a natural centre of world trade. A great deal of

Glasgow money went into this promising venture. When it ended in total disaster in 1701, with the evacuation of the colony and appalling losses both of men and of all the money invested (Glasgow citizens had subscribed £56,000 to the company and the Town Council had invested £3,000 on behalf of the burgh) there was both shock and anger in Glasgow as elsewhere in Scotland, and the English were blamed for deliberately sabotaging the scheme. The problem of Scotland's access to English colonial markets was finally solved by the Union of 1707, when Scotland joined England in an 'incorporating union', and though Glasgow's Member of Parliament voted against the Union and there were riots against it in the city, the Union immeasurably improved the prospects of Glasgow as a city trading across the Atlantic and opened a new chapter in its history. Before we turn to that chapter, let us take a look at Glasgow at the beginning of the eighteenth century.

It was a quietly busy city, with new commercial and industrial activities springing up regularly under the (on the whole) approving eye of the magistrates and Town Council, whose earlier habit of preserving traditional monopolies and trade restrictions gave way, as the seventeenth century drew to a close, to a more enlightened and progressive policy. There were cloth factories in the Drygate from 1638, coal-pits in the Gorbals from 1655 and candle factories established in the fields west of the city after the great fire of 1652 – hence the new street, Candleriggs, first mentioned in 1658. A company to cure fish was formed in 1667, and a soap factory using blubber supplied by whaling ships was built in 1673. The first of several sugar refineries was opened in 1675, which showed that Glasgow was able to trade with the West Indies even before the Union, and as a result Glasgow became the Scottish centre of the trade in duty-free rum. Rope works and glass works (for both bottles and window glass) were opened at the very end of the seventeenth century. Colonel Walter Whiteford was allowed to set up Glasgow's first coffee-house in 1673. On 29 July 1678 we find the Town Council minutes authorizing payment to William Hume, 'merchand in Edinburgh', for 'setting up and keeping' the stage-coach between Glasgow and Edinburgh: it ran to Edinburgh every Monday and returned on Saturday, at a fare of eight shillings sterling in summer and nine in winter. In October of the same year Alexander Thom was granted 'libertie and licence . . . to exerce his imployment and calling in architectorie or in measonrie' in the city.

Though the city fathers adjusted to the restored monarchy with a good enough grace and showed every evidence of loyalty to and affection for the monarch and his family – going so far in 1677 as to ask the Provost 'to use all dilligence to get the portratur of King Charles the First, that it may be hung in the Counsell-hous, with the rest now there', which was duly done, and a portrait was painted by John Hendry – Glasgow remained a Puritan city, combining a brisk interest in trade and commerce with a profound suspicion of the vanities of life. After the Glorious Revolution of 1688 the Town Council was able to indulge its Puritan inclinations. In February 1690 a proclamation against debauchery was made throughout the town, prohibiting any inhabitant or temporary resident from drinking in any tavern after ten o'clock at night on weekdays 'or in tyme of sermon, or therafter, on the Sabbath dayes', under penalty of a fine of forty shillings Scots to be paid by 'the furnisher of the drink' and twenty shillings by the drinker, half of the money to go to the informer. The proclamation also forbade all kinds of work on the Sabbath, including bringing water from wells, and prohibited the grazing of cattle on any of the city's fields on the Sabbath. In November 1701 'unnecessary walking abroad' and standing idly in the street or in the church yard or fields were equally forbidden on the Sabbath.

The Council was concerned with physical as well as moral cleanliness. An ordinance of 1685 prohibited the letting of midden-heaps and 'fulyie' (filth) lie in the street. Another 'against nestines' (nastiness) in January 1696 prohibited the casting 'out att their windows be day or night, either on fore or back streets, or in lanes, or closses, any excrement, dirt, or urine, or other filth, or water foul or clean' (Glasgow was much ahead of Edinburgh here, with its nightly 'gardyloo') and prohibited either voiding or laying down excrement or urine on any turnpike or stair or on the High Street or on any other street, lane, close, entry or passage. The same month the magistrates, taking note of 'the hazard, terror and amazement' caused by soot taking fire in chimneys through the negligence and carelessness of the inhabitants in not having them regularly swept, passed an act for the annual sweeping of 'lums' (chimneys), making the householder responsible if any fire broke out owing to his chimney not having been swept.

If they were strict, they were also compassionate. Glasgow pioneered a 'poor's rate' for looking after the poor and imposed a series of assessments for poor relief and the establishment of almshouses, as well as providing help for individual hard cases by special ordinance of the Town Council. Nor did the city fathers frown on all amusements. In November 1699 they appointed John Smith to 'teach danceing within this burgh', with the proviso 'that he shall behave himself soberly, teach at seasonable hours, keep no balls,

43

and that he shall so order his teaching that ther shall be noe promis-cuous danceing of young men and young women togither, bot that each sex shall be taught by themselves, and that the one sex shall be dismissed, and be out of his house before the other enter therin'. Music was not neglected either. In September 1691 Louis de France, 'musitian', was appointed 'to teach the inhabitants in toune to sing musick,' for fourteen shillings a month for one hour a day for those that came to the school and fourteen shillings 'for wryting the threttein comon tunes and some psalmes, the schollars furnishing bookes'; he also agreed to teach without charge such poor in the town as the magistrates recommended.

The standard of church music in Scotland had deteriorated rapidly in the seventeenth century. The psalter of 1635 contained over two hundred pieces, mostly metrical psalm tunes set in simple four-part harmony; the revised psalter of 1650 contained no music at all; the next psalter, John Forbes's 'Aberdeen psalter' of 1666, contained only twelve common-metre metrical-psalm tunes in simple harmony, together with a tune for Psalm 25 and only one example of choral polyphony, 'Bon Accord in reports'. Louis de France's 'threttein comon tunes' were thus the twelve common-metre tunes and the tune for Psalm 25. There was no instrumental music in the Church of Scotland.

Louis de France, who had originally come to Edinburgh in 1684 in search of work, was also granted £100 Scots paid yearly by the city 'dureing their pleasure and no longer' and given a monopoly of music teaching in the public schools in Glasgow 'dureing the tyme foresaid'. Music teaching in Glasgow as in several other Scottish cities at this time had only one function, namely, as Louis de France had put it in his letter to the magistrates of Edinburgh, to teach 'at least a competent number . . . to assist and bear up the true melodie in the four parts of the psalmes to the praise of God'.

In September 1701 the city of Glasgow was formally divided into six parishes, more or less equal in population. In October 1702 the shape of things to come was prefigured in the Town Clerk's note that 'her Majesty [Queen Anne] has been pleased to nominate and appoynt Hugh Montgomerie of Busbie, Provest of this burgh, to be one of the Commissioners to treat about the Union proposed betwixt the two kingdomes'. Four years later the Town Council was 'takeing to . . . serious consideratione the late tumults and uproars that has been in this city, and the indignitys and abuses done to the Magis-trats in the tumults, to the great scandall and opprobry of the place' – the citizens' response to news that the Scottish Parliament had passed the Act of Union, thus dissolving itself for ever and making Scotland part of Great Britain. The Merchants House, however, scenting commercial advantage in the new order, petitioned the council with suggestions for the stern repression of these anti-Union riots. The objection in Glasgow to the 'incorporating union' of Scotland with England was popular, spontaneous and emotional. Cooler mercantile heads in the city were less upset. They would have taken their stand with Scott's Bailie Nicol Jarvie in *Rob Roy* when he defended the Union a decade or so later:

> There's naething sae gude on this side o' time but it might have been better, and that may be said o' the Union. Nane were keener against it than the Glasgow folks, wi' their rabblings and their risings, and their mobs, as they ca' them now-a-days. But it's an ill wind blaws naebody gude – Let ilka ane roose the ford as they find it. – I say, let Glasgow flourish! whilk is judiciously and elegantly putten round the town's arms, by way of by-word. Now, since St. Mungo catched herrings in the Clyde, what was ever like to gar us flourish like the sugar and tobacco trade? Will onybody tell me that, and grumble at a treaty that opened us a road west-awa' yonder?

CHAPTER 5

'A road west awa' yonder'

I N August 1726 Daniel Defoe published the third volume of his *Tour Thro' the Whole Island of Great Britain*, which contained his account and description of Scotland, based on a close knowledge of and interest in Lowland Scotland in the years immediately before and after the Union, which he did so much to promote. The notes from which he wrote up this account were already some years old in 1726, but he made four short visits between 1724 and 1726 to check his earlier impressions. He had much to say about Glasgow, a city he greatly admired:

> Glasgow is, indeed, a very fine city; the four principal streets are the fairest for breadth, and the finest built that I have ever seen in one city together. The houses are all of stone, and generally equal and uniform in height, as well as in front; the lower story generally stands on vast square dorick columns, not round pillars, and arches between give passage into the shops, adding to the strength as well as beauty of the buildings; in a word, 'tis the cleanest and beautifullest, and best built city in Britain, London excepted . . .
>
> Where the streets meet, the crossing makes a spacious market-place by the nature of the thing, because the streets are so large of themselves. As you come down the hill, from the north gate to the said cross, the Tolbooth, with the Stadhouse or Guild-Hall, make the north east angle, or, in English, the right-hand corner of the street, the building very noble and very strong, ascending by large stone steps, with an iron balustrade. Here the town-council sit, and the magistrates try causes, such as come within their cognizance, and do all their publick business.
>
> On the left-hand of the same street is the university, the building is the best of any in Scotland of the kind . . . It is a very spacious building, contains two large squares, or courts, and the lodgings for the scholars, and for the professors, are very handsome; the whole building is of freestone, very high and very august . . .

The cathedral is an antient building, and has a square tower in the middle of the cross, with a very handsome spire upon it, the highest that I saw in Scotland, and, indeed, the only one that is to be call'd high . . .

Glasgow is a city of business; here is the face of trade, as well foreign as home trade; and, I may say, 'tis the only city in Scotland at this time, that apparently encreases and improves in both. The Union has answer'd its end to them more than to any other part of Scotland, for their trade is new form'd by it; and, as the Union open'd the door to the Scots in our American colonies, the Glasgow merchants presently fell in with the opportunity; and tho', when the Union was making, the rabble of Glasgow made the most formidable attempt to prevent it, yet, now they know better, for they have the greatest addition to their trade by it imaginable; and I am assur'd that they send near fifty sail of ships every year to Virginia, New England, and other English colonies in America, and are every year increasing . . .

The share they have in herring-fishing industry is very considerable, and they cure their herrings so well, and so much better than is done in any other part of Great Britain, that a Glasgow herring is esteem'd as good as a Dutch herring, which in England they cannot come up to.

Discussing the 'home trade of this city', Defoe singled out 'one or two very handsome sugar-baking houses, carried on by skilful persons, with large stocks, and to a very great degree', with 'a large distillery for distilling spirits from the molasses drawn from the sugars, which they call'd Glasgow brandy'; the 'manufacture of plaiding, a stuff cross-strip'd with yellow and red, and other mixtures for the plaids or vails, which the ladies in Scotland wear'; the manufacture of muslins, 'perhaps the only manufacture of its kind in Britain, if not in Europe', admirable in both quantity and quality; and the manufacture of linen, with a considerable export to the plantations.

Although in some respects Glasgow exporters were at a disadvantage compared with English, argued Defoe, the position of the city gave them a considerable advantage in the American trade, in spite of their having to carry their imported tobacco 'from fourteen to fifteen miles over land'. For:

if on the one hand it be calculated how much sooner the voyage is made from Glasgow to the capes of Virginia, than from London, take it one time with another, the difference will be found in the freight, and in the expence of the ships, and especially in time of war,

47

when the channel is throng'd with privateers, and when the ships wait to go in fleets for fear of enemies; whereas the Glasgow men are no sooner out of the Firth of Clyde, but they stretch away to the north west, are out of the wake of the privateers immediately, and are oftentimes at the capes of Virginia before the London ships get clear of the channel.

Captain Edward Burt, an English engineer officer, visited Glasgow in 1726 on his way to the north of Scotland, and left an account which agrees entirely with Defoe's:

GLASGOW is, to outward appearance, the prettiest and most uniform Town that I ever saw; and I believe there is nothing like it in Britain.

It has a spacious Carrifour, where stands the Cross; and going round it, you have, by Turns, the View of four Streets, that in regular Angles proceed from thence. The Houses of these Streets are faced with Ashler Stone, they are well sashed, all of one Model, and Piazzas run through them on either Side, which give a good Air to the Buildings.

Eleven years after Defoe's account Glasgow's Town House was begun in the Trongate next to the old Tolbooth. Its development, as Colin McWilliam has put it, 'showed the way towards the idea of continuous grandeur above, utility below, which is our highest conception of the formal city street.' By 1760 it had been enlarged from five to ten bays, its pattern continuing the motif of tenement above and arched passage below that had so struck Defoe.

A major factor in Glasgow's prosperity in the years after the Union was the spectacular increase in the tobacco trade. About 1715 Scotland's imports of tobacco – virtually all of it being shipped to the Clyde – had totalled about 2½ million lb.; by 1725 the figure was 4 million and by 1728 7¼ million. A lull followed, then the trade picked up again and in 1770 nearly 39 million lb. were imported. In 1771 the highest figure of all was reached – 47,268,873 lb. The Clyde was now importing more than half of all the tobacco that came to Britain, and it was the tobacco merchants of Glasgow who carried on the trade, with the cargoes coming in to Port Glasgow and Greenock (the Clyde was still too shallow for ships to come up as far as the city) and the great bulk of the tobacco then being re-exported to Europe, especially France. The Glasgow merchants were able to sell tobacco more cheaply than those in English ports for the reasons given by Defoe, and also because their ships sailed up the rivers directly to the plantation landings where they exchanged the goods

For NORFOLK in VIRGINIA, and to difcharge goods
at HAMPTON-ROAD,

THE Brigantine JANET, ———,
Mafter, will be ready to take on
board goods at Greenock by the 15th
of June next, and will be clear to fail
by the 10th of July at fartheft.
  The Janet is a fine Britifh built
veffel, about 170 tons burthen, quite
new, and has excellent accommodation for paffengers.
For freight or paffage apply to Robert Dunmore, Glafgow, or Francis Garden, Greenock.   May 12th, 1784.

For PHILADELPHIA,

THE Brigantine BETTY and
  MATTY, Archd. Moor,
Mafter, a ftout new veffel, has good
accommodation for paffengers, and will
fail pofitively on or before the 20th of
May inftant, wind and weather ferving.
  For paffage apply to Meffis. Alex-
ander Moubray, Edinburgh, William
Donald, Glafgow, and John Stewart, Greenock.

At LONDON, and begun to Load,
for CHARLESTOWN, SOUTH CAROLINA,

THE Ship CHRISTIANA,
  Hercules Angus. Mafter,
an excellent ftrong Britifh-built fhip,
of about 400 tons, to fail from London the firft day of June.
  For freight of goods, or for cabin-
paffage apply to John Cowan and Co.
at Borrowftounnefs, or Capt. Angus
at London.
  N. B. No room for fteerage-paf-
fengers.

Advertisements from the newspaper,
the *Glasgow Mercury,* in 1784

they brought for tobacco on the spot. Jealous English tobacco
merchants in Whitehaven, Lancaster, Liverpool and Bristol angrily
complained that the Glasgow importers' cheaper prices were the
result of their evasion of customs duties, but after an official inquiry
in 1721 the Lords of the Treasury rejected the complaints as arising
'from a spirit of envy, and not from a regard to the interests of trade
or of the King's revenue'. With the outbreak of the American War
of Independence tobacco imports dropped sharply – from 45,863,154
lb. in 1775 to 294,896 lb. in 1777. It picked up again in 1778, but
never again reached anything like the high figures of the early 1770s.
  At first the Glasgow merchants hired ships for the tobacco trade
from Whitehaven, for until 1718 they owned few ships capable of
making the long voyage to America. In 1692 there were just fifteen
locally owned ships, and only four of these were of 100 tons or over.

By 1735 Glasgow merchants had fifteen vessels of their own engaged in the Virginia trade alone, out of a total of over sixty; thereafter the number increased rapidly. The merchants filled their ships with manufactured goods bought from local shopkeepers – textiles, knitted stockings, linen tape, calico prints, shoes, saddles, gloves, glass – to be paid for when the ships returned from Virginia with their cargoes to Port Glasgow.

The Glasgow 'tobacco lords' were a close-knit group who formed both business and marital partnerships among themselves in such a way as to retain the control of the trade in the hands of a few important merchants. Among the most powerful was the firm of William Cunninghame and Co., composed of nine partners. Three of these partners worked for the company in Virginia as factors and storekeepers, for it was by operating the store system in the American tobacco-growing colonies that the Glasgow merchants were able to dominate the market. The store system involved buying the tobacco crop outright from the planters before shipping it to the Clyde. The Glasgow firms established stores in the colonies both to collect the tobacco crop and to provide the growers with consumer goods which they imported for this purpose. Tobacco planters could buy these goods on credit provided that they sold their tobacco to the company's factor. The credit was often extended over long periods, the merchants accepting tobacco in repayment at prices they were in a position to keep relatively low, so that it took a long time for the planters to pay off advances. This 'Glasgow store system' had a great practical advantage over the method largely used by English merchants who simply sold the tobacco on behalf of the planters on commission, and it was responsible for the outstanding commercial success of the Glasgow tobacco lords. It did have its risks and dangers. When trade with the American tobacco colonies was interrupted by the outbreak of the American War of Independence in 1775 Glasgow merchants found it impossible to collect their debts from the planters. The merchants themselves estimated the total amount owed them as over £1,300,000. Negotiations for repayment dragged on long after the war was over, and it was not until 1811 that a proportion was finally repaid as a result of a combination of legal action and diplomatic activity.

The other two dominant figures in the eighteenth-century Glasgow tobacco trade, besides William Cunninghame, were Alexander Speirs and John Glassford: the syndicates headed by these three merchants between them controlled over half the Glasgow tobacco trade in the peak years immediately preceding the outbreak of the American war. Other important Glasgow families involved in the tobacco trade

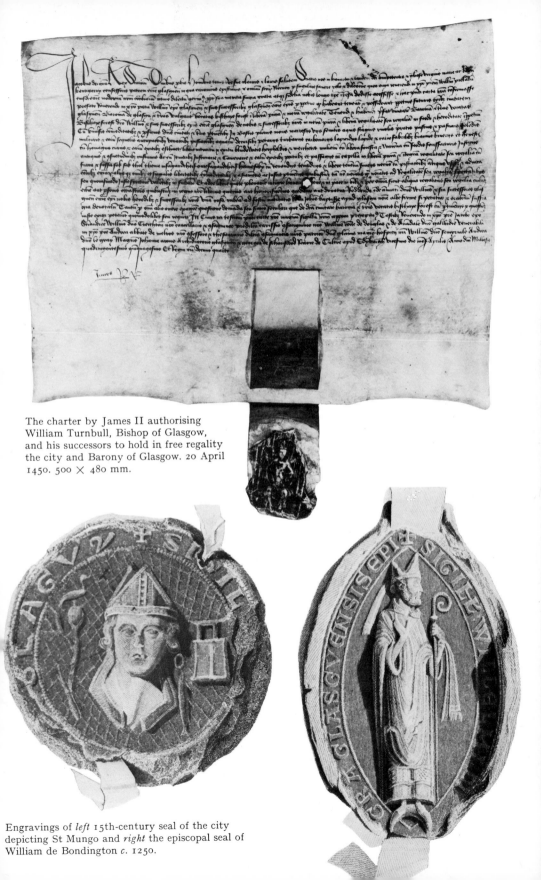

The charter by James II authorising
William Turnbull, Bishop of Glasgow,
and his successors to hold in free regality
the city and Barony of Glasgow. 20 April
1450. 500 × 480 mm.

Engravings of *left* 15th-century seal of the city
depicting St Mungo and *right* the episcopal seal of
William de Bondington *c.* 1250.

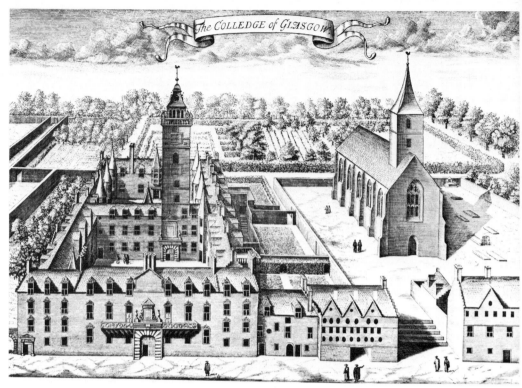

Late-17th-century engraving of the College on its original High Street site, which it occupied from 1460 to 1870, when the buildings were demolished and replaced by the College Goods Station.

Late-17th-century view from the NE; *left* to *right*, the Molendinar burn, the College, the Bishop's Palace and, next to it, the Cathedral.

in America were the Bogles, the Donalds, the Dunlops, the Murdochs, the Oswalds and the Ritchies. Many of the tobacco lords came from 'middling' merchant families and most were educated at the Grammar School and often also at the University. Some had been (or sent their sons) on the Grand Tour to improve their sophistication and general knowledge of the world. Some of the more socially pretentious joined the Scottish Episcopal Church rather than the Presbyterian Church of Scotland and a few sent their sons to be tutored in England by Church of England ministers. They played a self-consciously prominent part in the social as well as the economic life of the city. It was their re-deployment of capital that was responsible for the rise of banking in the West of Scotland: they founded the Glasgow Arms Bank, the Ship Bank and the Thistle Bank in the 1750s and 1760s. They used their profits from trade to buy country estates. It has been calculated that between 1770 and 1815 sixty-two America and West India merchants of Glasgow achieved the position of landed gentlemen, with property mostly in Lanarkshire, Renfrewshire, Stirlingshire and Ayrshire.

In their red cloaks, satin suits, powdered wigs, three-cornered hats and gold-topped canes, the tobacco lords would meet in small groups in the Trongate by King William's statue (presented to Glasgow in 1743 by James MacRae, a Glaswegian who rose to become Governor of Madras) or strut proudly along the Trongate 'plainstanes' (pavement) on which they claimed the exclusive right to walk. At first even the wealthiest of them lived on one floor of a tenement, reached by dark and narrow turnpike stairs, but gradually, as prosperity increased, they built themselves mansions to the west, some of them where St Enoch's Square now stands. Alexander Speirs (1714–82) built himself a mansion with splendid gardens nearer the centre of the city in Virginia Street, which had already been laid out by Andrew Buchanan (1670–1759), who traded in the Caribbean as well as with the tobacco colonies in America and bought the estate of Drumpellier in Lanarkshire. He was Provost of Glasgow in 1740–1; on his death his son George built a splendid residence called Virginia Mansion.

William Cunninghame not only bought himself an estate in Lainshaw, Ayrshire, but also built in 1778 a fine mansion in Cow Loan or Queen Street, the most magnificent in the city: in 1829, after the construction of a portico in front and other additions by David Hamilton, it became the Royal Exchange. Public outcry prevented its demolition in the 1840s in order to link Ingram Street and Gordon Street and, with additions by David Thomson in 1880, it still stands in what is today Royal Exchange Square. (It is now Stirling's Library.)

E

51

John Arthur's *Plan of the City of Glasgow*, 1778, clearly shows the town houses of the leading Glasgow merchants in the Argyle Street–Trongate area, marking those of 'J. Ritchie Esq.', 'Mr Cunningham', 'A. Speirs of Ellersley', 'J. Glasford of Dougalston', 'R. Bogle of Shettleston', and so on, calling many of them by the names of their estates. The tobacco lords enjoyed their position as both city merchants and landed gentry. Some were active in agricultural improvement, while others assisted the Industrial Revolution by exploiting the mineral and industrial resources of their land. A younger scion of the Buchanan family, Andrew Buchanan of Ardenconnal, and a number of other tobacco lords bought land in the mineral-rich parishes of Old and New Monkland in Lanarkshire towards the end of the century, and some bought shares in the Monkland Canal when it opened in 1793. Indeed, the tobacco lords seldom, if ever, confined their activities to the importing of tobacco, which was one reason why they were able to survive the decline of the tobacco trade resulting from the American war (though this was far from a total disaster, since several merchants found ways of importing American tobacco first from Canada, then from New York and Philadelphia while they were still in British hands and then, from 1779, clandestinely via the West Indies). Many tobacco lords invested in emergent industries as well as in factories designed to provide goods for their stores in America. There was considerable investment in textiles (both linen and cotton), coal mining and iron manufacture.

The effect of the American war on Glasgow was not confined to creating difficulties for the tobacco trade. American privateers attacked Clyde shipping and caused considerable losses. In 1777 Glasgow Town Council and the Convention of Royal Burghs petitioned the Admiralty for assistance against 'the alarming depradations made by rebel privateers', but their request was refused: 'it would be impossible for their lordships to station a ship for the protection of each port, more especially while so great a part of the fleet is stationed in America and the Indies'. Some assistance was sent in 1778, but it was not of much use. HMS *Satisfaction* was sent to the Clyde as 'guardship' but, as Provost Hugh Wylie complained, the American privateers which infested the Clyde estuary still escaped with impunity because the *Satisfaction* was slow and cumbersome. In 1781 HMS *Seaford* was sent to the Clyde, and was slightly more effective. More effective were the armed ships fitted out by the Glasgow merchants themselves, equipped with the Carron Company's famous carronades which were so light that they did not reduce the speed of the ship. One bonus for the Clyde during the American war was the Government's chartering of Glasgow-owned ships to transport troops across the Atlantic. Some Clyde ships armed themselves and acquired 'letters of marque' (at a price), giving them authority to attack and confiscate enemy merchantmen, and some Glasgow houses made a speciality of privateering (William Cunninghame and Co. owned three privateers and Robert Dunmore and Co. owned five) but, though there were a few spectacular captures, privateering did not prove a successful investment. Government use of the press gang on Clydeside to obtain crews for their warships made it difficult for Glasgow merchants to obtain crews for their own merchantmen, and this caused considerable frustration.

Sugar, its by-product molasses, and rum which was made from molasses, was the earliest to develop of Glasgow's three main sources of prosperity in the eighteenth century, and it was from sugar and rum that the first Glasgow fortunes were made. It was for the most part only after the American war that the tobacco merchants turned to cotton importing, although as early as 1743 a number of them imported cotton wool and gave it out to spinners in Glasgow. According to the report of a Government committee on the linen trade in 1773 and to Board of Trade returns and reports on the Scottish linen industry 1727–90, Glasgow's main textile manufactures were clear and long lawns, cambrics, checks and check handkerchiefs, and cotton and linen cloths. The growth of the tobacco trade and the development first of the fine linen industry and, later, of the cotton industry brought a surge of new population into Glasgow not only from the surrounding districts but also from the West Highlands. In 1708, as we saw in the last chapter, the population of Glasgow was calculated as 12,766. By 1740 it was 17,034, in 1780, with all the suburbs included, it was 42,832 and in 1801 it was 83,769. Growth in population brought with it expansion of the city from its original centre at the cross in the Trongate. We have noticed Andrew Buchanan's Virginia Street; he also gave his name to Buchanan Street, which was laid out for feuing in 1786. Miller Street, laid out by a merchant called Miller in co-operation with two well-known tobacco lords, Robert Hastie and Robert Bogle, was planned in 1762 and finally 'causewayed', after a successful petition to the Town Council to meet the cost, in 1773. Queen Street, between these two, dates from 1777. Jamaica Street, running down to the river well to the west of High Street, was opened in 1763: its name recalls one source of Glasgow's prosperity. St Enoch's Square was laid out in 1778 and opened in 1783. There was grass in the centre, where sheep grazed and volunteers paraded; on the east side was

Surgeons' Hall and the Custom House was on the west. Mansions of tobacco lords occupied other sites on the square. George Square was built in 1787 on a piece of marshy land called Meadowflats and was long regarded as the prime exhibit of Glasgow's elegant New Town. Here too, until well into the nineteenth century, sheep grazed in the grassy centre, which was surrounded by a four-foot railing with a gate facing Miller Street.

Glasgow was not directly involved in the Jacobite rising of 1715, but it contributed 500 men to the Duke of Argyll's army at Stirling in September of that year. On 29 October the magistrates 'represented that, in this tyme of common danger, the toun is put to vast charges and expenses in fortefying the toun, and many other ways which they cannot evite, and that it is the advyce of his Grace the Duke of Argyll, Generall and Commander in Chiefe of his Majestys Forces in North Brittan, the toun should be put in a better posture of defence by drawing lynes of intrinchment about the toun, in case of any attack against it by the rebells now in arms against his Majesty, and that the same be done with all expedition, which will be a furder charge upon the toun.' The Treasurer was authorized to borrow for this purpose to the extent of £500 sterling. After the defeat of the rising, 353 Jacobite prisoners were lodged in Glasgow castle, and on 12 December the magistrates wrote to the Duke of Argyll asking him to 'be pleased to give orders for removing of the 353 rebell prisoners, who are lying on the touns hand, and in custody in the Castle prison, and easing of the toun of the burden of them and of their maintenance.' In January 1718, through the good offices of its Member of Parliament Daniel Campbell of Shawfield, the city received from Parliament the sum of £736 13s. 5d. sterling for the cost of maintaining the Jacobite prisoners, but, as pages and pages of laboriously transcribed accounts in the Town Council minutes make clear, the rising cost the city more than this in 'expresses', carting of baggage, arms and ammunition, in trench works and barricades, strengthening of Kirkintulloch Bridge (this included £3 4s. 'for ale and buns to the workmen'), and many other items required for the defence of the city. In the event, the Earl of Mar's Jacobite army never came near Glasgow, and its anti-Jacobite citizens were, perhaps characteristically, involved in the struggle more financially than in any other way. It was probably a measure of their relief at the victory of the Hanoverian forces that the Town Council in September 1717 ordered the Treasurer to pay £15 sterling 'as the pryce of the picture of his Majesty King George, now put up in the Council house'.

Daniel Campbell was not in favour in Glasgow in 1725. The

Government had imposed a malt tax of 3d. on every barrel of beer, and popular wrath at this most unpopular of taxes was vented on their unfortunate Member of Parliament, who had voted for it. Campbell was also suspected of having betrayed Glasgow's tobacco secrets to the Government, so he was just as unpopular with the tobacco lords. A mob attacked his fine house, Shawfield Mansion (a pioneer work of Palladian architecture in Britain, built in 1712, standing at what is now the foot of Glassford Street – called after yet another tobacco lord, John Glassford, 1715–84), and proceeded to riot, undeterred by the efforts to prevent them of 'two companies of his Majesties forces . . . under the command of Capt. Bushel' (in the words of the Town Council's 'True and faithful account'). The mob threw stones at the soldiers, who eventually fired, killing two persons who, in the Council's version, 'had no way been concerned in the ryott'. The Provost, Charles Miller, seeing the incensed mob grow to formidable proportions, asked Captain Bushel to withdraw from the city with his men, believing that such a course 'would tend to the safety of the officer and the kings troops, and the quieting the present tumult'. 'The officer accordingly retired', continues the Town Council's account, 'and though there were no numbers pressing upon him, he continued fireing upon the streets, whereby, in all, there were nine persons killed, particularly one gentlewoman, out of a window, two stories high, some in the sides, and other crossing the streets, going about their lawfull affairs, and sixteen dangerously wounded, whereof not above five or six at most (so far as can yet be known) were in any way concerned in the mob. Upon the troops leaving the town, some of the mob followed after, and came up only with two of the souldiers, who, throw indisposition, had fallen behind. These two being brought back to the town, one of them was dismissed, and the other being hurt in the head, was carried to the Town-House to be taken care of, and in a few days, being fully recovered, was likeways sent off.'

The Government did not accept this version of events, and believed that the Provost and magistrates were in collusion with the mob. General Wade occupied the city; Provost Miller, the magistrates and nineteen other persons were arrested and taken to the Edinburgh Tolbooth. The Provost and magistrates were released the next day, to be received in Glasgow by cheering crowds and ringing bells. Of the others, a man and a woman were banished the city, eight were given prison sentences and nine were publicly whipped through the streets of Glasgow. Although the official Town Council account insisted that little damage had been done to Shawfield other than the breaking of some windows, Parliament, on Campbell's petitioning it for compensation for his losses, ordered Glasgow to pay him £6,080 sterling. In all, what became known as the Shawfield Riots cost the city over £10,000 and the bitter irony of it was that the Town Council had to impose a tax on ale and beer sold in the town in order to raise the money. Campbell bought land in the island of Islay with his compensation money (which suggests that he did not need to use it to restore Shawfield).* The city fathers tried hard to bring Captain Bushel to trial for murder, but the Government prevented this. It was long before Glasgow forgot the sense of grievance this affair produced.

The Jacobite rising of 1745–6 was an altogether more serious matter. Bonnie Prince Charlie had marched victoriously into Edinburgh immediately after his victory over Sir John Cope at the Battle of Prestonpans on 21 September 1745. From Holyrood House, where he took up residence, he sent a letter, dated 25 September, 'signed Charles P.R., direct to the Provost, Magistrats, and Town Council of the City of Glasgow, demanding complyance with the payment of the £15,000 sterling which he required by his former letter' [sent on 14 September]. In the end the sum agreed was £5,500; £5,000 was raised and the balance of £500 was paid in goods.

Worse was to come. After the Jacobite army's retreat from England Prince Charles and what the staunchly anti-Jacobite Glaswegians always called 'the rebels' entered the city on 25 December 1745, and there he decided to penalize the city for having raised troops in support of the Hanoverian government (the Glasgow Militia) by demanding '6000 short cloath coats, 12000 linen shirts, 6000 pairs of shoes, and the like number of pairs of tartan hose'. On 28 December the magistrates laid what they called 'this most exorbitant demand before a full meeting of the inhabitants, . . . who unanimously considering their then unhappy situation, agreed to comply with said unjust demand.' The Prince took up his residence in Shawfield Mansion and tried to impress the inhabitants by dressing with unusual elegance and dining publicly in front of the house. He had himself proclaimed Regent on behalf of his father at Glasgow Cross. On 2 January he reviewed his army on Glasgow Green, taking

*There is, however, an interesting footnote to this, provided by a minute of the Town Council of 6 May 1746, which records that the Magistrates had sent to London 'the broken necklace of diamonds, which several years ago were found among the rubbish of Daniel Campbell of Shawfields house, when mobbed by the crowd in the year 1725, and exposed by some of the mobb to sale, with a piece of gold coin, and that the same had been offered back to the Lady Shawfield, who refused to take it, in regaird Shawfield was satisfied by the Parliament as to his damages, and the town fyned upon that account, and that, accordingly, the said necklace was sold at £30 sterling, and the piece of gold at two pounds ten shillings.' The money was handed over to the city Treasurer.

his stand under a thorn tree afterwards known as 'Prince Charlie's Tree' and long protected by a wooden railing. But though the inhabitants preserved the tree they had no love at all for Bonnie Prince Charlie, who was bitterly disappointed in his hope of raising a substantial number of men in the city for his army. A mere sixty men joined up after the review, and a few ladies fell for him and his cause, but for the most part Glasgow looked on the Prince with a cold, Whiggish hostility. Nowhere, Charles bitterly complained, had he found so few friends as he had in Glasgow. It is said that he was only dissuaded from sacking and burning the city by Cameron of Lochiel. Charles and his army left the city for Stirling on 3 January taking with them Bailies Cameron and Coats as hostages for the balance of the goods, not all of which had been delivered, as well as a printing press, types, paper, three printers and as much arms and ammunition as could be found in the city. After the destruction of the Jacobite army at Culloden the following April the city rang its bells and lit bonfires to celebrate. It also took more practical measures to recover from the Government part at least of the financial loss it had suffered at the hands of the Jacobites. On 14 June 1749 the Town Council minutes record that 'the Parliament had granted to his Majesty the sum of £10,000 to reimburse the toun . . . and that the same was to be paid to the town by his Majesty's Exchequer, by his Majesty's warrant to the Commissioners of Treasury.' The two bailies who were taken as hostages received £13 15s. 8d. each to cover the costs of their enforced stay in the Jacobite camp.

Bonnie Prince Charlie had entered Glasgow by Back Cow Loan (the site of Ingram Street, opened in 1781, called after the Glasgow industrialist Archibald Ingram, Provost in 1762 and brother-in-law of John Glassford), then a country lane. At right angles to Back Cow Loan was Cow Loan; they were the old routes along which the city shepherd drove the city cows to pasture in the Cowcaddens. The name Cowcaddens, incidentally, found as Kowcawdennis in 1510 and as Kowkadens in 1521, derives from the Gaelic *cuil calldainn*, 'nook of hazels', but because of its association with the pasturing of cows the 'Kow-' became 'Cow-'. Glasgow in the middle of the eighteenth century slipped easily into the surrounding countryside. Shawfield Mansion, which established a vogue for its kind of detached town house as the city spread westward from the High Street, was described in the Town Council minute about the Shawfield Riots as 'situated in one of the extremeties of the town'. When George Buchanan's Virginia Mansion was built next door to Shawfield it was the most westerly house in Glasgow. Between here and Dumbarton to the north-west lay open countryside, through which ran the rough and muddy Common Loan and St Enoch's Gait. St Enoch's Square was the western boundary in the early 1780s. On the other side of the city, alongside the river, there was Glasgow Green – divided into Low Green, High Green and Gallowgate Green (later Calton Green). North of Trongate, Candleriggs was a path through corn fields until 1724, after which it was built up with plain frontages which, in Colin McWilliam's words, 'represent the bread-and-butter street architecture of eighteenth-century Glasgow'. Running south from Trongate opposite Candleriggs, King Street was also developed in 1724.

These developments were deliberately planned by the Town Council 'not only for beautifying the city, but also for the better accommodation of the inhabitants and the people resorting thereto, and for the more easie passage from one street to another'. Strict regulations were laid down about the height (three storeys), window size (six feet by three) and building style (facings of square hewn stones, or 'ashlar work'). Between the lines of Candleriggs–King Street and High Street–Saltmarket lay the heart of mid eighteenth-century Glasgow, with the tobacco-processing factory in King Street, the fishmarkets in Candleriggs, the Wester Sugar House at the corner of Candleriggs and Bell's Wynd (which joined Candleriggs and the High Street), and a variety of shops and business enterprises. Many prosperous merchants lived here too, for only a relatively few of the richer ones built themselves mansions to the west; many were content on one floor of a tenement in the centre of the city. But there were always gardens and orchards – not to say cow byres – nearby. In 1736 John M'Ure, the city's first historian, described Glasgow as 'surrounded with corn-fields, kitchen and flower gardens and beautiful orchyards, abounding with fruits of all sorts, which by reason of the open and large streets send furth a pleasant and odoriferus smell.' Many of the new houses to the west had their own large gardens and orchards.

The pleasant and odoriferous smell had to battle with the less desirable odours. Despite the Town Council's concern for cleanliness and its promulgation of ordinances designed to promote it and to prohibit 'nestiness' Glasgow was still, by modern standards, a most unhygienic city, and citizens regularly defied the Council's ordinances by emptying filth from windows and allowing stinking midden heaps to lie in the streets, particularly in closes and side streets, which the authorities tended to ignore. So although Glasgow prohibited the discharge of refuse from windows before Edinburgh it was Edinburgh which actually abandoned the practice first: as late as 1849 fifteen Glasgow women were summoned for the offence. There were, how-

58

ever, individual owners who made strenuous attempts to improve matters. One was Bailie John Shortridge, a great improver of Argyle Street – originally Westergait, leading westward out of the city from Trongate through the West Port, and called Argyle Street after the funeral procession of the fourth Duke of Argyll had passed along it in November 1770 – who insisted on his own tenants observing the special regulations he made about 1760. They were 'not to fix any boards or boxes without the kitchen windows, either for throwing out of water, or any nestiness, or dropping of bottles, the fowl water being to be conveyed from the kitchen, in the said tenement, by a lead pipe; no nestiness or water shall be thrown out of any of the windows, nor shall any carpets or floor-cloaths be shaken or cleaned over any of the fire-windows looking to Argyll Street, but shall be cleaned over the pass-windows, under the penalty of five shillings for each transgression. The dung or fulyie to be made in the tenement is to be carried to the midden-stand belonging to the land, and to be laid down thereon.' Then it was the responsibility of the bailie who 'undertakes to keep the midden decent, by carrying away the contents four times each year, or oftener, if needful'.

Water was obtained from the Clyde and from public wells. The affluent sent their servants to the wash-house on Glasgow Green. 'There is a singular conveniency here', wrote Bishop Pococke from Glasgow on visiting the city in 1760, 'which is a sort of portico built round a court for washing, with a large furnace in each corner. It is in the Green, and is farmed out by the city. Everyone pays for boiling water by the measure, and they lay the cloaths to dry on the Green, which grazes a hundred cattle, at twenty shillings a head.' Water for domestic use came from public wells, from which it had to be brought in buckets. A notable well was at the West Port, across the road from Shawfield Mansion; women with their buckets used to congregate here and gossip as they waited their turn, sometimes blocking the traffic. The West Port Well was eventually dismantled and replaced by a small iron pump at the foot of Glassford Street. 'In the city there is plenty of water,' wrote M'Ure in 1736, 'there being sweet water wells in several closses of the toun, besides sixteen public wells which serves the city night and day, as need requires, all with pumps in them for drawing the water.' At the beginning of the nineteenth century there were thirty public wells.

By the middle of the eighteenth century Glasgow's original centre towards the top of the High Street, by Rotten Row and Drygate, already had an air of historical decay. Many of the older buildings had housed ecclesiastical functionaries who disappeared after the Reformation. The Bishop's Castle was now in ruins. But the Cathedral, housing its three separate congregations, continued in good repair, as did the University, further down the High Street, with its seven acres of College Gardens and walled Physic Garden.

Across the river, the village and lands of Gorbals (formerly called Bridgend) had long interested Glasgow Town Council. In February 1648 the Council learned of 'ane bargane the towne micht halve of the Gorballs' (at that time the property of Sir Robert Douglas of Blakerston, who had inherited it from his uncle, Viscount Belhaven). The Council therefore chose commissioners to arrange its purchase, and the result was that the Council, the Trades House and Hutcheson's Hospital jointly acquired Gorbals village and several hundred acres of surrounding agricultural land. In October 1661 the Town Council intimated 'the annexing of the lands of Gorballes to the burgh'. According to the Reverend William Anderson, minister of the Parish of the Gorbals of Glasgow (as it was known) in 1793, this was done 'at the desire of the inhabitants of these lands'. The Gorbals of Glasgow was separated from the parish of Govan and erected into a parish in 1771. The greater part of the village of Gorbals was burned down in 1748, but it was rapidly rebuilt, with substantial houses of two or three storeys. The population in 1771 was 3,000, and it had risen to over 5,000 by 1790.

CHAPTER 6

Work and Play

Alexander ('Jupiter') Carlyle was a student at Glasgow University in 1743–4, and in his valuable *Autobiography* he provides a picture of the city as it was then. He had come from Edinburgh University, and though he conceded that Glasgow students applied themselves to their studies more diligently than their Edinburgh counterparts, he found Glaswegians inferior 'in knowledge of the world, and a certain manner of address that can only be attained in the capital'. He continued:

> It must be confessed that at this time they were far behind in Glasgow, not only in their manner of living, but in those accomplishments and that taste that belong to people of opulence, and much more to persons of education. There were only a few families of ancient citizens who pretended to be gentlemen; and a few others, who were recent settlers there, who had obtained wealth and consideration in trade. The rest were shopkeepers and mechanics, or successful pedlars, who occupied large warerooms full of manufactures of all sorts, to furnish a cargo to Virginia. It was usual for the sons of merchants to attend the College for one or two years, and a few of them completed their academical education. In this respect the females were still worse off, for at that period there was neither a teacher of French nor of music in the town. The consequence of this was twofold; first, the young ladies were entirely without accomplishments, and in general had nothing to recommend them but good looks and fine clothes, for their manners were ungainly. Secondly, the few who were distinguished drew all the young men of sense and taste about them; for, being void of frivolous accomplishments, which in some respects make all women equal, they trusted only to superior understanding and wit, to natural elegance and unaffected manners.
>
> There never was but one concert during the two winters I was at Glasgow, and that was given by Walter Scott, Esq. of Harden, who

was himself an eminent performer on the violin; and his band of assistants consisted of two dancing-school fiddlers and the town-waits.

The manner of living, too, at this time, was but coarse and vulgar. Very few of the wealthiest gave dinners to anybody but English riders, or their own relations at Christmas holidays. There were not half-a-dozen families in town who had men-servants; some of them were kept by the professors who had boarders. There were neither post-chaises nor hackney-coaches in the town, and only three or four sedan-chairs for carrying midwives about in the night, and old ladies to church, or to the dancing assemblies once a-fortnight.

The principal merchants, fatigued with the morning's business, took an early dinner with their families at home, and then resorted to the coffeehouse or tavern to read the newspapers, which they generally did in companies of four or five in a separate room, over a bottle of claret or a bowl of punch. But they never stayed supper, but always went home by nine o'clock, without company or further amusement. At last an arch fellow from Dublin, a Mr Cockaine, came to be master of the chief coffeehouse, who seduced them gradually to stay supper by placing a few nice cold things at first on the table, as relishers to the wine, till he gradually led them on to bespeak fine hot suppers, and to remain till midnight.

There was an order of women at that time in Glasgow, who, being either young widows not wealthy, or young women unprovided for, were set up in small grocery-shops in various parts of the town, and generally were protected and countenanced by some creditable merchants. In their back shops much time and money were consumed; for it being customary then to drink drams and white wine in the forenoon, the tipplers resorted much to those shops, where there were bedrooms; and the patron, with his friends, frequently passed the evening there also, as taverns were not frequented by persons who affected characters of strict decency.

Carlyle exaggerated somewhat when he said that taverns were not frequented by persons who affected characters of strict decency, for it was in taverns as well as coffee-houses that professional people often consulted their clients, and merchants often transacted business with their customers. Doctors and lawyers, having no accommodation for patients or clients in the flats where they lived, would advise them in a tavern over a chopine (half-pint) of twopenny (ale at twopence a quart) or a mutchkin (pint) of claret or a glass of rum and hot water ('three-waters rum' or 'five-waters rum' according to its strength and the amount of water to be added). Merchants similarly entertained their customers, and when the morning bargaining came to an end with the Tolbooth chimes ringing noon, a general partaking of a 'meridian' or noon drink (generally of rum) in tavern or coffee-house was a regular part of a Glasgow merchant's weekday routine. On more purely social occasions, in taverns or clubs, a company would indulge in what was now virtually Glasgow's civic drink, 'Glasgow punch', a mixture of lemon-juice-and-sugar ('sherbert') and rum, with a few limes run round the rim of the bowl to add the final touch of flavour. If the session of punch drinking took place after supper at home, the toast 'The trade of Glasgow and the outward bound' was given as the signal for the ladies to retire. Ladies stayed at home, and if they had social pretensions they entertained their female friends to tea in the bedroom at the 'four hours', using delicate china cups which the hostess would carefully wash herself after the guests had left.

Clubs for men began to appear in Glasgow in the 1740s. The Anderston Club was founded in 1750 by Robert Simson, Professor of Mathematics at Glasgow from 1712 until 1761, and it did not survive his death in 1768. The Club met on Saturdays in John Sharpe's hostelry in Anderston (just beyond the western extremity of Argyle Street and then still a separate village: the walk to Anderston and back was a favourite Saturday afternoon activity). The Hodge Podge Club was founded in May 1752 as a literary and debating society by a group of young men who met once a fortnight in Cruik-shank's tavern; but it was not long before the literary and debating activities gave way to sixpenny whist. Eating and drinking were a principal activity at the meetings of this as of other Glasgow clubs at this time. The Hodge Podge attracted some of the most influential merchants in Glasgow, many of them tobacco lords, but its member-ship from 1752 to 1802 included, as well as twenty-five merchants, two surgeons, a physician, a professor, a master at the Grammar School, an advocate, a general and a number of merchants who had moved into the ranks of the landed gentry. The Club survived to celebrate its centenary in May 1852. My Lord Ross's Club (Ross was no peer but the name of the landlord of the tavern in the High Street where the club met nightly except Sundays) was founded about 1780; its members drank twopenny ale and Jamaica rum, winding up with the tavern's speciality, rabbit, and they prided themselves on their ability to discuss literature and the fine arts. A few years later the Morning and Evening Club began to meet at a tavern in Currie's Close on the east side of the High Street; members would get out of bed when the early morning gun signalled the arrival of the Edinburgh mail, bringing newspapers from Edinburgh and from London, and hasten to the club where the newspapers would already be laid out for them. There they sat over the fire perhaps drinking a tankard of hot herb ale as a cure for a hangover, or, if this was not required, a rum, hot water and sugar mixture known as a 'baurie'. There were also evening meetings, largely devoted to drinking, beginning with 'mahogany' (port and lemon in a quart mug) and proceeding to a variety of other tipples. This was the most frankly convivial in objective of all the Glasgow clubs. The Gaelic Club was founded in 1780 for those of Highland birth, parentage or connections. It first met at Mrs Scheid's tavern in the Trongate and then moved to a variety of different hostelries. The Gaelic Club survived late into the next century and became an important social force in Glasgow.

Clubs proliferated as the eighteenth century drew to an end. The Accidental Club met at John Tait's in the Gallowgate, and seems to have specialized in producing and listening to humorous doggerel. The Face Club met at Lucky Black's tavern at the end of a long close at the head of the Gallowgate and specialized in the consumption of that traditional Scottish dish (favoured by Sir Walter Scott for breakfast), a sheep-head. The Camperdown Club was founded after the battle of Camperdown on 11 October 1797 by a group of patriotic Tories who met to damn the French and democracy. The Meridian Club consisted of employees of the Ship Bank (which closed between one and two) and other firms who took advantage of the break to consume spirits in the back parlour of a house in Stockwell Street. The Pig Club flourished from 1798 until 1807: it specialized in whist and betting (mostly on the outcome of political and military events) and numbered among its members some wealthy and influential Tory citizens. The Stockwell Beefsteak Club, later known as the Tinkler's Club, met in Bryce Davidson's tavern in Stockwell Street at a time when, in the words of John Strang, the mid nineteenth-century historian of Glasgow's clubs, 'the bloody consequences of the French Revolution had produced such a horror against *popular* rule, in the minds of the comfortable and wealthy in Glasgow, that, among the majority, the most common sentiment of liberality was sure to subject the individual who had the courage to offer it, to the opprobrious epithet of *democrat* or of *traitor*.' Its favourite toast, after 'the King', was 'may the Devil take the democrats'. Other clubs included the Coul Club (after 'Old King Coul'), the Gegg Club ('gegg' means a practical joke) and the Go-As-You-Please Club.

There were already some clubs in the city when Alexander Carlyle was there in 1743. He joined two, one of which was literary, and the members 'criticized books and wrote abridgements of them, with critical essays'; it was intended for serious university men and met at the porter's lodge in the College (as the University was known). 'The other club met in Mr Dugald's tavern near the Cross, weekly, and admitted a mixture of young gentlemen, who were not intended for the study of theology.' There students mingled with younger merchants to drink 'a little punch after our beefsteaks and pancakes, and the expense never exceeded 1s. 6d., seldom 1s.'

Meal times changed as the century advanced. The hour for dinner was put back from one o'clock to two o'clock, and after 1770 the more socially pretentious did not dine till three. Edinburgh led the way here, and Glasgow followed about ten years behind. In the 1780s the smart Edinburgh citizens were dining at four or five, and the habit of returning to work after dinner was given up. Glasgow duly followed, and by the early nineteenth century the fashionable world of the city was dining at six. The later dinner meant that instead of tea at the 'four hours' there was late supper in the evening.

Meals were not elaborate. A Glasgow merchant in mid century would breakfast off porridge, herring and ale and as likely as not dine on broth and either salt beef or boiled fowls or Clyde salmon. But later in the century Glasgow showed more culinary adventurousness. Indeed, as early as 1740 the Town Council agreed to pay £10 sterling annually to James Lochhead, 'teacher of cookery', who had petitioned the Council:

> mentioning that he being regularly educated by his Majesty's cooks, under whom he served in the art of cookery, pastry, confectioning, candying, preserving, and pickling, and of making of milks, creams, syllabubs, gellies, soups and broaths, of all sorts, and also taught to dress and order a table, and to make bills of fare for entertainments of all kinds, and that of late he has successfully taught severall young ladies, to their own and their parents satisfaction, and that for instruction of his scholars he is obliged to provide, on his own charge, flesh, fowles, fish, spiceries, and severall other ingredients, but when dresst, lye on his hand for want of sale, by which he is a loser, and will be obliged to lay aside his teaching unless he be assisted in carrying it on . . .

There are no recorded results of James Lochhead's teaching of cookery in Glasgow. Later in the century we hear of a 'pastry school' in Glasgow, where young ladies were taught 'all sorts of pastry and cookery'. About 1780 the head cooks of the Saracen's Head (the first hotel in Glasgow, opened in the Gallowgate in 1755 by Robert Tennent, the brewer) and the Black Bull Inn (in Argyle Street, designed especially for Highlanders; it was at the western boundary of the city as the Saracen's Head was at the eastern boundary) gave cooking lessons to Glasgow young ladies. Whenever a grand dinner was given at one of the inns, a crowd of eager learners watched the proceedings, and, for a fee of five shillings a head paid to the cook, were able to see how different dishes were prepared and how the dinners and dessert were placed on the table. On one notable occasion, when an important county dinner was being given at the Saracen's Head, the gentlemen guests were agreeably surprised to find some fifteen or sixteen attractive young ladies in white aprons helping to hand round dishes and place them on the table. When they learned that these were not menials but young gentlewomen there for instruction, some of the younger guests cheerfully began to flirt with them and ended by trooping down to the kitchen and helping to carry up the dishes themselves.

Yet even in the second half of the century eating habits were still modest compared with those of London and even with those of Edinburgh. It was noted with surprise in 1786 that an adventurous Glasgow hostess, influenced by the custom in Edinburgh, produced for her guests a dinner with two courses, an innovation regarded as highly extravagant even though the lady explained that she had simply divided the meal into two and given in two separate courses no more dishes than others provided in one. (It is clear from this that a course could consist of several dishes provided they were served simultaneously, so even a one-course meal need not have been spartan.)

As the century advanced, we hear more and more of heavy drinking by the men after the ladies had withdrawn to bed or to the drawing-room. This was after supper at about nine, after which the gentlemen would sit late over Glasgow punch or claret. In some houses a servant was given the special task of loosening the cravats of those guests who had drunk themselves into a stupor and were in danger of choking. (The most vivid account of how this operated comes, however, not from Glasgow but from Kilravock Castle near Nairn, where, according to Lord Cockburn, Henry Mackenzie once attended a feast and, in feigning a drunken doze to escape having to drink more, was alarmed to feel a hand at his throat; when he exclaimed, a voice said, 'Don't be feared, sir. A'm the lad that louses the craavats.') But Glasgow families kept fewer servants than those in Edinburgh. Henry Mackenzie recorded the innovation of men servants in Edinburgh at the end of the century and added, 'It is not so in Glasgow, where mercantile luxury is in eating and drinking, not in establishments.' Maids, however, were widely kept: board wages of maids in Glasgow in the latter part of the century were about £4 a year.

The Merchants' House, Bridgegate (1659). It was demolished in 1817, except for its fine steeple in the Dutch style.

Late-18th-century view from the s w across the Clyde. The towers from *left* to *right* are: Hutcheson's Hospital, the old Ramshorn Church, the Cathedral, the College, the Tron Church, the Tolbooth, the Merchants' House, St Andrew's Church.

The heart of 18th-century Glasgow: the Trongate seen from the east. *Left* to *right*, the tower of the Tron Church, King William's statue outside the Tontine Hotel, the Tolbooth steeple. The statue was a popular meeting place for the Glasgow merchants.

Although conservative Glaswegians might deplore the growth of swearing and of excessive drinking in the later part of the century, grace was nearly always pronounced over the most self-indulgent of meals and at the commencement of the severest bout of drinking. In the 1780s the Rev. John M'Leod was a regular diner out in Glasgow, and had a grace ready for every kind of meal. If, as he surveyed the table, he found that it gave promise of a particularly abundant meal, he would recite his top-category grace, which began 'Bountiful Jehovah'. At the bottom end of the scale was a grace which began 'We are not worthy, O Lord, of these, the least of Thy mercies'.

The Town Council's earlier disapproval of mixed dancing did not prevent the growing popularity of such dancing in the second half of the century. In the early 1780s we hear of dancing parties which began with tea (handed round by the men: no servants attended) before the dancing, which went on until ten o'clock with brief intervals for sucking sweets and drinking white wine negus or Glasgow punch. Supper was served between ten and eleven – fowls, hams, jellies, and more negus and punch. After supper, dancing to the music of the hired fiddlers would resume and continue until the small hours. In the last decade of the century public dances took place in the assembly hall of the Tontine Hotel at Glasgow Cross, but in 1796 the building of a New Assembly Hall in Ingram Street provided the principal locale. There was no great variety in the dances, which were confined 'almost to the walking of the minuet and *contredanse*, with Roger de Coverly, or bab-at-the-bolster and Highland fling'. 'The assemblies, during the winter session, are held weekly,' wrote James Denholm in his *History of Glasgow* (1797); 'the first, however, which is well attended, is generally that kept in honour of Her Majesty's birthday, on the 18th of January; upon that night the tickets sell at 5s., and on every other at 4s.' There was also 'an assembly of genteel people' who met to play cards once a fortnight 'in rotation with the dancing assembly'. Both the dancing and the card assemblies began at 8 o'clock. Ladies drew tickets for their places in the dances, and the regulations stated that no ladies should 'stand up in the Country Dances, except in the place to which their Ticket entitles them'. No gentleman was allowed 'to stand before the Ladies, so as to intercept their view' and, except for officers on duty, no gentleman was to be admitted in boots or half-boots. 'Those who have sticks are desired to leave them at the bar.' These public dances at the end of the century, as distinct from the earlier private dancing parties, did not go on after midnight: at least 'no Country Dance or Rubber at Cards' could be 'begun after twelve o'clock'.

F

The Tontine Hotel was originally the town hall, designed by Allan Dreghorn and built between 1737 and 1748 in an impressive neo-classical style influenced by Inigo Jones's piazzas at Covent Garden. Additions were made in the 1750s and in 1780 it was bought by the Tontine Society and remodelled by William Hamilton as a hotel with an assembly hall and a coffee room for subscribers, well stocked with newspapers and periodicals. The opening of the coffee room was celebrated in May 1784 with the most magnificent ball ever held in Glasgow. The Tontine served for many years as Glasgow's Exchange, and business was transacted either in the coffee room or on the causeway outside or underneath the arches of the piazza.

Among the more lowly pastimes of eighteenth-century Glasgow were the stone-throwing contests between the inhabitants of the north bank of the Clyde and those of the south (the Gorbalonians) for the possession of an island which then lay in the channel of the river between the old bridge and the new Jamaica Street Bridge opposite where Carlton Place now runs. The battles took place on Saturday evenings at the foot of Stockwell Street. Not only boys but also grown men took part, and considerable tactical manoeuvring took place, with stealthy reconnaissances, ambushes, and the judicious deployment of reserves. Sometimes the sides succeeded in creeping across the river unobserved, one by one bridge and another by the other, and sometimes they reached the island simultaneously and fought at close quarters. The authorities seemed incapable of stopping these fights, and it was only after the death of a boy who was hit by a stone that these traditional Saturday night encounters died away. Other stone-throwing contests were indulged in between college students and the less-educated youth of Glasgow and between the boys of the Grammar School and those of 'Wilson's Charity', a free school for poor boys founded by a man called Wilson in 1778.

There was no adequate police force to deal with such disturbances. In real emergencies the military were called upon, but in normal times the policing of the city was left to its own citizens, every one of whom between the age of eighteen and sixty who paid a yearly rent of at least £3 annually was required to take his turn at patrolling the streets. 'On tuck of drum,' wrote H. H. Graham, the historian of the social life of eighteenth-century Scotland, 'the gentlemen was at his post at ten o'clock at night, and strolled with weary tread and yawning gait along the Trongate and High Street, and up the pitch-dark lanes of winter nights, where not a lamp was burning, till three or four o'clock in the morning. After that hour, in the obscure and unprotected mornings, the city was without a police, and the tired and hungry guardians of the peace were snug and snoring in their box-beds.' A small police force was created in 1788, for which the sum of £135 2s. was paid to Richard Marshall, the superintendent, for himself and his officers; the force was armed, and seems to have assisted the citizen patrols at night. During the day the red-coated town officers, known as 'hornies', about twenty in number, were supposed to be in charge of keeping the peace, but their activities seem to have been largely ceremonial when they were not engaged in chasing idle boys and girls causing obstructions by congregating or dancing in the streets. Several attempts to provide an adequate police force for the city were made in the latter years of the century, but they failed because the citizens objected to the taxation involved. At last in 1800 a more realistic but still inadequate system was established by Act of Parliament, with a chief constable, a clerk, a treasurer, three sergeants, nine officers and sixty-eight watchmen, each of whom was provided with a sentry-box.

There was a special tradition of shooting cocks at Govan on New Year's Day. Men and boys would pour out from Glasgow to what was still the village of Govan and for a penny a shot try their hand at the not very demanding 'sport' of shooting at a cock that was tied to a stake. Whoever killed the bird could take it home for dinner. This was a working-class amusement, and was accompanied by a great deal of drinking and miscellaneous jollification. Wealthier and more respectable citizens played golf on Glasgow Green in the last decade of the century. At this time, too, the Duke of Hamilton encouraged an interest in horse-racing, which took place on the Duke's estate. Cock-fighting (as distinct from the vulgar cock-shooting) was also enjoyed by some of the most influential citizens, often under aristocratic patronage. Spectators bet on the cocks as they watched them fight to the death, just as they bet on the outcome of boxing matches, which were popular in the 1790s. In 1791 the great English pugilist Daniel Mendoza appeared in Glasgow in a fight against one Fawtrell.

In 1758 a mail coach drawn by four horses began the Glasgow–Edinburgh run, stopping at Falkirk en route. The post arrived from Edinburgh – first by horseback and then by coach – at six in the morning and after the mail had been sorted the postmaster fired a gun and the citizens came and collected their mail before returning to their homes for breakfast. The post from England came via Edinburgh until 1758 when the first regular wagon connection between Glasgow and London was established via Newcastle-upon-Tyne. The journey took seven days. In 1781 the Glasgow–Carlisle diligence began to run, connecting with London and other stages and claiming to be able to make the journey to London in four days. In 1789 the time taken for the London mail to reach Glasgow was reduced to sixty-six hours.

In spite of the passing of a number of Turnpike Acts, roads connecting Glasgow with the outside world remained pretty primitive throughout the eighteenth century. A canal linking the Clyde with the Forth seemed an obvious way to improve communications with the city. The idea was first mooted as early as the reign of Charles II but no action was taken. Several proposals were made and routes suggested in the eighteenth century before a petition was presented to Parliament in January 1767 praying leave to introduce a bill for a Forth and Clyde canal terminating in or near Glasgow. It would be four feet deep and twenty-four feet wide and would cost about £50,000. It was decided in Glasgow to raise £40,000 in £100 shares, which was quickly done, with John Glassford and John Ritchie raising over £24,200. Lord Frederick Campbell, Member of Parliament for Glasgow burghs, introduced the bill, but there was strong opposition in Edinburgh to such a small canal ('When a canal, big with general utility, was thus in agitation,' wrote the *Edinburgh Evening Courant*, 'it must be provoking to see a ditch proposed in place of it'). The Convention of Royal Burghs also agitated for a larger canal, and the agitation was taken up throughout the country. By the middle of May 1767 over £100,000 had been subscribed for the larger project, and in November the subscribers, meeting in London under the chairmanship of the Duke of Queensberry, decided to apply to Parliament for leave to bring in a Bill for the construction of a canal in accordance with a more ambitious scheme that had been drawn up by John Smeaton in 1764. After Smeaton had made a new survey and revised his estimates, an Act was passed in March 1768 for the construction of a canal eight feet deep and fifty-six feet wide, taking the route originally preferred by Smeaton, from Carron to the River Kelvin and thence to the Clyde by Yoker Burn. Operations started at the Forth end in July 1768 and by 1773 the canal was navigable as far west as Kirkintilloch, nine miles north-east of Glasgow. On 10 November 1775 the canal was opened from Kirkintilloch to Stockingfield and on 29 July 1790 the complete canal, thirty-five miles long, was ceremonially opened by Archibald Speirs of Elderslie, chairman of management, who poured a hogshead of Forth water into the Clyde at Bowling 'as a symbol of the junction of the eastern and western seas'. Private sources were not sufficient to provide funds for completing the canal, and in 1784 the Government had had to authorize a loan of £50,000 to the canal company from the proceeds of the estates forfeited in the 1745 rebellion. The terminus of the Glasgow branch was an enlarged basin made with the purchase of eight acres of land at Port Dundas, called after Lord Dundas, governor of the canal company. In August 1790 the sloop *Agnes* of 80 tons sailed from Leith to Greenock, inaugurating the new east–west passage. Two years later the much shorter but economically important Monkland Canal, linking Glasgow with the Lanarkshire coal-fields, was opened. It had been planned in 1770 and construction was commenced in that year under the direction of James Watt. But financial and other difficulties interrupted the work in 1772 and it was not resumed until more than ten years later. After the canal was finally completed and opened the Monkland company joined with the Forth and Clyde company in forming a junction between the terminus of the Monkland Canal and Port Dundas, thus enabling coal to be shipped direct from Lanarkshire coal-fields to both the Clyde and the Forth.

But the Clyde was more important to Glasgow than any canal, and it was in the second half of the eighteenth century that steps were at last successfully taken to make the river navigable for ocean-going ships up to the Broomielaw. In 1755 John Smeaton reported that the depth of the Clyde at Pointhouse was one foot three inches at low water and three feet eight inches at high water. On his suggestion an Act of Parliament was promoted and obtained for the construction of a lock, seventy feet long by eighty feet wide, at Marlin Ford, four miles down the river, but (fortunately, as it turned out) the project fell through. In 1768 the English expert John Golborne of Chester was called in and he advised the narrowing of the river by means of jetties eight miles below Glasgow and the dredging of sandbanks and shoals. His advice was accepted, an appropriate Parliamentary Act was obtained, and Golborne was given the contract for the work. The scheme was wholly successful. The jetties, confining the wide and shallow river, increased the speed of the current which was now able to carry away the loose material obtained by raking the river bed. At Dumbuck, twelve miles below Glasgow, the river was so shallow as to be fordable; after James Watt reported on the Dumbuck ford in 1769 Golborne contracted to deepen it and by 1775 had succeeded in deepening the channel at Dumbuck to six feet at low water. In 1781 he was able to report that the channel was now fourteen feet deep, and in some places as much as twenty-two feet, by the action of the river. The turning of the city of Glasgow itself into a deep-water port at the very time when the American War of Independence was threatening its commercial prosperity helped the city to weather that disaster. A grateful Town Council gave Golborne a present of £1,500 sterling and a silver cup. In 1799, on the advice of the distinguished engineer John Rennie,

Some 'Characters of Old Glasgow'

DAVID DALE.   BOB DREGHORN.

over 200 jetties were built between Glasgow Bridge and Bowling, and some old jetties were shortened; in this way the channel was made uniform and a considerable amount of land was reclaimed. A rapid increase followed in the number of ships coming up to Glasgow: in 1796, 1,326 vessels carrying 58,980 tons sailed to Glasgow Bridge, and in 1806 the number was 1,678 vessels carrying 83,683 tons.

Glasgow still had the old eight-arched fourteenth-century stone bridge, repaired in 1671 when the southern arch collapsed and widened by ten feet on the eastern side in 1777, when the two north arches were filled up. It survived until 1847. A second bridge over the Clyde, of seven arches – this is the Glasgow Bridge referred to above – was begun in 1768 and opened for traffic in 1772. It crossed the river from Jamaica Street on the north side to the division between Tradestown and Lauriston on the south. It lasted for sixty-five years.

LOWRIE COULTER.   WALLACE, of Kelly.

Linen and cotton manufacture and exports grew steadily more important to Glasgow's economy as the eighteenth century advanced. The linen industry in Scotland had been officially encouraged in Scotland by the Convention of Royal Burghs since early in the century. In 1727 the Convention appointed a Board of Commissioners to recommend steps for encouraging the industry, and the Board provided money to subsidize flax growing, set up spinning schools, provide improved looms, award prizes for yarn and cloth of especially good quality, and appoint inspectors to supervise the scheme and enforce standards. One of the first spinning schools set up was in Glasgow, whose manufacturers went on to specialize in high-quality cloths, as distinct from the coarse linen, called harns, which was the characteristic Scottish manufacture and had to compete with coarse cloth from Germany ('Osnaburghs') that English merchants imported and

73

then exported to the Plantations to compete with the Scottish exports there. Over a million yards of checkered handkerchiefs were produced in and around Glasgow in 1748, with 223,470 yards of muslin handkerchiefs and 37,202 yards of muslin or 'Glasgows': these also involved the use of cotton, which by the end of the century had become Scotland's major industry. In 1738 the first establishment for the printing of cotton-linen (as distinct from pure linen) was set up in Glasgow. Glasgow manufacturers imported fine yarns from France, Flanders and Holland for the production of lawns and cambrics.

The pioneer in the switch from linen to cotton was James Monteith who, after many years of manufacturing cambrics out of a fine, hard-spun cotton yarn mixed with linen yarn, devised in 1780 a cheap method of weaving a good-quality imitation Indian muslin purely out of cotton. James Monteith's six sons were all active in the cotton industry: of these Henry was the most notable. He broke the monopoly of the tobacco lords with respect to certain of their privileges and twice – in 1814 and 1818 – was elected Provost. Associated for a time with James Monteith was David Dale, the greatest name in the Scottish textile industry. Dale started as a weaver in Paisley, then became a dealer in linen yarns and an importer of French and Flemish yarns which he distributed to the numerous cambric and lawn weavers whom he employed. In conjunction with Richard Arkwright, who had already patented his carding machine and water-frame, he set up the famous cotton mills at New Lanark. By the last decade of the century cotton spinning flourished in nearly all the villages of Lanarkshire, Renfrewshire and Ayrshire. The 'several respectable inhabitants' of Glasgow who contributed the account of that city to Volume V of the first *Statistical Account of Scotland*, published in 1793, had this to say:

> The variety of manufactures now carried on in Glasgow, which have extended in almost every branch, are very great; but that which seems, for some years past, to have excited the most general attention, is the manufacture of cotton cloths of various kinds, together with the arts depending on it. For this purpose cotton mills, bleachfields, and printfields, have been erected on almost all the streams in the neighbourhood, affording water sufficient to move the machinery, besides many erected at a very considerable distance; and though the number of these mills have [sic] increased greatly of late, yet they are still unable to supply the necessary quantity of yarn, required by the increased manufactures, as a considerable quantity is still daily bought from England. This trade not only

employs a great number of persons in Glasgow, but is extended over
a very large tract of country in the neighbourhood, many weavers
being employed by the Glasgow manufacturers, 20 and 30 miles from
the city. In 1791, it was computed, that they employed 15,000 looms;
that each loom gave employment to nine persons at an average,
including women and children, in the different stages of the manufacture, from picking the cotton wool, until the goods were brought
to market, making in all 135,000 persons; and that each loom, at an
average, produced goods to the value of L. 100 *per ann.* making
L. 1,500,000 . . . This manufacture is not only important in itself,
but is productive of work to many thousands of bleachers, tam-
bourers [embroiderers on a tambour-frame], callico printers, &c.,
many of whom, being women and children, whose work was formerly
unproductive, renders it of still more importance to the country.
Though this great manufacture has, in some measure, supplanted
the linen trade, which used to be the staple manufacture of the west
of Scotland, there is yet, however, a very great quantity of linens,
lawns, cambrics, checks, diapers, &c. still made, though the demand
for cotton goods has much diminished the consumption of these
articles. There is also a considerable manufactory of carpets and
coarse woollens, for which no place seems better adapted, being in
the neighbourhood of a country where great quantities of sheep are
raised.

Among the other manufactures listed in this account are delft ware,
'in imitation of the Dutch', first begun in Glasgow in 1748, and a
variety of stoneware, pottery, bricks and tiles. Hats, both for the
home trade and for export to America and the West Indies, stockings,
gloves, ropes, cordage, soap and candles are also listed. Sugar
refining, the authors add, now long established, was still carried on
on a large scale, and type founding and bottle manufacture are also
cited. A 'very extensive brewery' was erected near Anderston about
1760, which exported large quantities of ale and porter to Ireland and
America, and a number of other breweries were built later in the
century. In spite of 'the many late inventions for abridging labour' –
and the coming of the Industrial Revolution to Glasgow is a subject
in itself, to be discussed below – there was still a greater demand for
labour than could be easily supplied. This helped to swell the number
of immigrants into the city – from Ireland, especially after the
unsuccessful rebellion of 1798, from the Highlands, as a result of the
Clearances, and from other parts of the Lowlands, where the reorganization of agriculture compelled many agricultural workers to migrate
to industrial centres.

In 1783 a society known as The Chamber of Commerce and Manufactures was founded, 'to unite the influence of the merchants and manufacturers . . . and, by establishing a public fund, to give strength and efficacy to the measures of those who should interest themselves in the public good.' Merchants of Glasgow, Paisley, Greenock and other neighbouring manufacturing towns subscribed to the society and succeeded in obtaining a royal charter. The leading spirit in the foundation of the Chamber of Commerce – the first of its kind in the British Isles – was Patrick Colquhoun (1745–1820), a second-generation tobacco lord who was active in raising troops in Glasgow to fight against the Americans during the American war (he knew that Glasgow trade would suffer if the Americans won) and was elected Provost of the city in 1782, after which he devoted most of his time to public affairs.

CHAPTER 7

Education and the Arts

THE ecclesiastical settlement in Scotland which followed the ousting of James VII and the accession of William and Mary abolished bishops and deprived of their positions those university professors and 'regents' who supported episcopacy. A commission consisting of noblemen, barons, judges and ministers was appointed by an Act of Parliament in 1690 to visit all universities, colleges and schools and remove 'scandalous, insufficient and disaffected persons'. The committee appointed to visit the University of Glasgow was much less harsh than that at St Andrews, and in the event only three men were dismissed for not complying with the provisions of the Act – Dr James Fall, the Principal; Dr James Wemyss, Professor of Divinity; and one of the regents. Even so, it affected the intellectual life of the University and the next thirty-five years were a fairly stagnant period. The system by which regents took their students throughout their whole course, teaching them in successive years Greek, ethics, 'pneumatics' ('the science that deals with the properties of air, or elastic fluids'), logic, mathematics and physics, while it had the advantage of enabling the teachers to get to know their students, had the disadvantage that the teachers could not be expected to be adequately qualified in all their subjects. It was only after the abolition of this system in 1727 (Edinburgh gave it up as early as 1708 but it survived at Aberdeen until the end of the century) that Glasgow University began to make itself a force in the intellectual life of the country.

At the beginning of the century the University was still governed under the constitution that had been promulgated in 1577, known as the *Nova Erectio*. Under this new system there were three regents, who during the seventeenth century were supported by a teacher of Latin ('Humanity') to make sure that the students understood the lectures, which were still delivered in Latin. A Chair of Mathematics was established in 1691, a Chair of Greek in 1704, a Chair of Humanity in 1706 (it had been decided to appoint a Professor of Humanity as early as 1683, at a salary of £20, but no funds were available), and with the abolition of the 'ambulatory' system of regents in 1727, the three regents were assigned to specific subjects, Logic, Moral Philosophy and Natural Philosophy (Physics). New Chairs in Oriental Languages and Ecclesiastical History followed, strengthening the Faculty of Theology, and these were followed by Chairs in Medicine, Law and Anatomy and the development of these faculties. The establishment of a Chair of Astronomy brought the number of professors to thirteen; they, together with the Principal, were known collectively as the 'Faculty'.

I have been talking of the 'University' although I might have said the 'College'. The *Nova Erectio* had provided for a College presided over by a Principal who was himself to teach theology and Greek and Hebrew (and also to preach in Govan on Sundays), with the three regents providing the teaching in arts. The University, whose officers were the Chancellor, the Rector and the Dean of Faculty, was to grant degrees. By 1760 the professors of the College, with their Principal, claimed and obtained the sole right to handle finance and in practice ran the institution. This arrangement persisted until 1858, when a completely new scheme was introduced by Act of Parliament: the finances of the University were put in charge of a University Court consisting of the Rector (still, as traditionally, elected by the students), the Principal, the Dean of Faculties and four assessors appointed by the Chancellor, the Rector, the General Council (representing the graduates) and the *Senatus Academicus*, which last body retained control of teaching and discipline. So if throughout the eighteenth century we hear of Glasgow College as often as Glasgow University the explanation lies in the primary position of the College as a teaching institution under the *Nova Erectio* and the powers eventually assumed by its professors and Principal.

The appointment of Francis Hutcheson as Professor of Moral Philosophy in 1729 marked the beginning of Glasgow's active part in the eighteenth-century Scottish Enlightenment. Hutcheson had already published, in 1725, his influential work, *An Inquiry into the Original of Our Ideas of Beauty and Virtue*, the classic exposition of the theory of 'moral sense' (which argues that our concept of virtue is analogous to our sense of beauty). His importance in the history of philosophy also lies in his foreshadowing, in this and other works, David Hume in introducing the inductive method into the discussion of morals and approaching the subject from an analysis of human nature. He was a pioneer, too, in giving his lectures in English rather than in Latin, a practice which was gradually followed by other professors. Together with his younger colleague William Leechman, who became Professor of Divinity in 1743 and Principal in 1761, he brought a new note of humane curiosity into the hitherto harsh discussions of religion and morality that had prevailed in this part of Scotland. 'It was, no doubt, owing to [Leechman] and his friend and colleague Mr Hutcheson, Professor of Moral Philosophy, that a better taste and greater liberality of sentiment were introduced among the clergy in the western provinces of Scotland,' wrote Alexander Carlyle when recollecting what the University was like in 1743. He went on:

> I attended Hutcheson's class this year with great satisfaction and improvement. He was a good-looking man, of an engaging countenance. He delivered his lectures without notes, walking backwards and forwards in the area of his room. As his elocution was good, and his voice and manner pleasing, he raised the attention of his hearers at all times; and when the subject led him to explain and enforce the moral virtues and duties, he displayed a fervent and persuasive eloquence which was irresistible . . .
>
> Besides Hutcheson and Leechman, there were at that period several eminent professors in that university; particularly Mr. Robert Simson, the great mathematician [Professor of Mathematics 1712–61, notable for his rediscovery of Greek mathematics], and Mr. Alexander Dunlop, the Professor of Greek [from 1706 to 1743] . . . I derived much pleasure, as well as enlargement of skill in the Greek language, from Mr. Dunlop's translations and criticisms of the great tragic writers in that language. I likewise attended the Professor of Hebrew, a Mr. Morthland [Charles Morthland, Professor from 1709 until his death in 1744], who was master of his business.

By 1759, when young James Boswell was sent for a year to Glasgow University to remove him from the temptations of Edinburgh, Glasgow College, except in the Faculty of Medicine, could claim to be the superior as well as the older institution, both architecturally (its two quadrangles and handsome tower in the 'Scottish baronial' style, dating from the seventeenth century, were in sharp contrast to the decaying Edinburgh college buildings) and intellectually. Adam Smith had been elected to the Chair of Logic in 1751 and transferred to the Chair of Moral Philosophy the following year. The year in which Boswell heard him lecture was the year of the publication of Smith's *Theory of the Moral Sentiments*; he was not to publish his more widely known *Wealth of Nations* until 1776, while his lectures on Rhetoric and Belles Letters were not printed until 1963. As Professor of Moral Philosophy, Smith lectured on theology, ethics, jurisprudence,

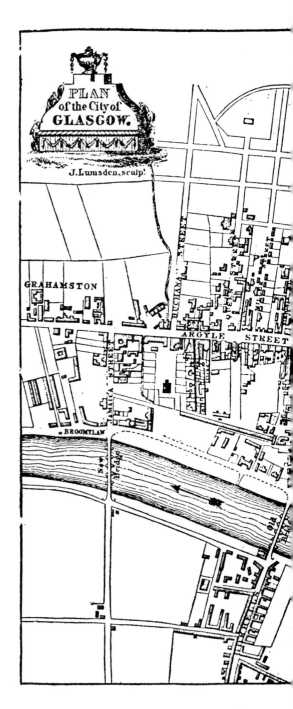

Glasgow in 1783, published by John Mennons. The western development is beginning, and the centre of the city has clearly moved from the Drygate/ High Street cross to the Gallowgate/Saltmarket Street cross, where the Tolbooth stands

and political institutions, but he also had a passionate interest in language and style and introduced this interest into his lectures. As Professor of Logic he found an opportunity of subsuming many of his interests in this subject. One of his most brilliant pupils, John Millar (who himself became Professor of Laws in Glasgow in 1761), later recollected his teacher's methods:

> In the Professorship of Logic, to which Mr. Smith was appointed on his first introduction into this University, he soon saw the necessity of departing widely from the plan that had been followed by his predecessors, and of directing the attention of his pupils to studies of a more interesting and useful nature than the logic and metaphysics of the schools. Accordingly, after exhibiting a general view of the powers of the mind, and explaining so much of the ancient logic as was requisite to gratify curiosity with respect to an artificial method of reasoning, which had once occupied the universal attention of the learned, he dedicated all the rest of his time to the delivery of a system of rhetoric and belles lettres. The best method of explaining and illustrating the powers of the human mind, the most useful part of metaphysics, arises from an examination of the several ways of communicating our thoughts by speech, and from an attention to the principles of those literary compositions which contribute to persuasion or entertainment. By these arts, everything we perceive or feel, every operation of our minds, is expressed in such a manner, that it may be clearly distinguished and remembered. There is, at the same time, no branch of literature more suited to youth at their first entrance upon philosophy than this, which lays hold of their taste and their feelings.

This brought a breath of fresh air to the students at Glasgow, and his lectures were immensely popular. John Millar had already completed his university education when he attended Smith's lectures in Glasgow, led there by Smith's great reputation. Millar went on to achieve a great reputation in his own right. His *Observations concerning the Distinction of Ranks in Society*, 1771, is a pioneering work in sociology, which ends with a reasoned attack on the institution of slavery as practised in the American colonies. (' . . . it affords a curious spectacle to observe, that the same people who talk in so high a strain of political liberty, and who consider the privilege of imposing their own taxes as one of the unalienable rights of mankind, should make no scruple of reducing a great proportion of the inhabitants into circumstances by which they are not only deprived of property, but almost of every right whatsoever.') It is not always remembered by historians of Glasgow that eighteenth-century

Steam and sail together: the Broomielaw in 1820.

English travellers frequently commented on the brazenness of the washing women. This picture was painted on the lid of a snuff box made in 1820 for the owner of the Washing House on the Green.

Drawing the salmon nets at Govan in the first half of the 19th century.

The view down St Vincent Street in the early 18th century, from Blythswood Place.

Glasgow ship-owners were often, like those of Liverpool, engaged in transporting slaves across the Atlantic and that some of the city's prosperity in the eighteenth century derived from the slave trade as well as from sugar, tobacco and textiles. Millar has a further claim to fame in that he was probably the first man to use the term 'constitutional history' (in his *Historical View of the English Government,* 1787).

Eighteenth-century Glasgow knew many other distinguished professors. Among philosophers, there was also Thomas Reid, a forceful and at one time influential opponent of David Hume, who was Professor of Moral Philosophy at Glasgow from 1764 to 1796. In the field of medicine Glasgow never equalled Edinburgh, but the great William Cullen was Professor of Medicine at Glasgow from 1751 to 1755 before going to Edinburgh to be first Professor of Chemistry, then of the 'Theory of Physic'; he was later President of the Edinburgh College of Physicians. And the great chemist Joseph Black, the discoverer of latent heat, was Professor of Medicine at Glasgow from 1756 to 1766 before going on to the Chair of Medicine and Chemistry at Edinburgh.

Glasgow University must take some credit for the achievement of James Watt, the Greenock-born inventor who, after having gone to London in 1755 at the age of nineteen to learn the business of a philosophical-instrument maker there, returned to Scotland a year later and worked for some of the Glasgow professors repairing astronomical instruments. He tried to set himself up as an instrument maker in Glasgow, but the city guilds would not let him do so as he had not served the full term of apprenticeship. The College, however, was interested in his work and set him up within its precincts with the title of Instrument Maker to the University. He became friendly with Professor Joseph Black and with John Robison, who was then a student but who lectured on Chemistry at the University in 1766 and became Professor of Natural Philosophy at Edinburgh in 1773, and he discussed with them the possibility of improving the steam-engine invented by John Newcomen. It was while repairing a model of Newcomen's engine in 1764 that he was able to discover the cause of the waste of power involved in its enormous consumption of steam. By a careful experimental study of the properties of steam he concluded that what an efficient steam-engine needed was as low as possible a temperature of condensed steam and a temperature in the cylinder as hot as that of the steam which entered it. These two conditions were incompatible in Newcomen's engine. While walking across Glasgow Green one Sunday morning early in 1765 Watt suddenly realized that if the steam were condensed in a vessel separate from the cylinder it would be possible to keep the temperature of condensation low while keeping the cylinder hot. He at once put his idea to the test by building a model with a separate condenser, and the result was the steam-engine which he patented in January 1769.

The establishment of the Carron Iron Works near Falkirk in 1759 had stimulated industrial invention and brought to Scotland the Birmingham chemist Dr John Roebuck (who had studied medicine and chemistry at Edinburgh and Leyden). Roebuck's concern was the chemistry of smelting and he also interested himself in Watt's experiments with the steam-engine, providing both capital and encouragement. Another Birmingham man, Matthew Boulton, was also interested in the industrial potentialities of the steam-engine, and he invited Watt to join him in partnership in his Soho Engineering Works at Birmingham, where Watt remained in fruitful activity from 1775 to 1800. Watt's design was first used in steam-engines constructed to drain tin and copper mines in Cornwall. In 1781 he invented the rotary engine, which made possible the working of forge-hammers by steam. He went on with further improvements and inventions, patenting his double-acting steam-engine in 1782 and his arrangement of 'parallel motion' in 1784, and carrying on with his researches almost until his death in 1819. He had left Glasgow long before to live at Heathfield Hall near Birmingham, but Glasgow has always regarded him as her own. The University awarded him the honorary LL.D. degree in 1806.

The influence of Glasgow University was significant in the New World. James McGill was born in Stockwell Street in 1744 and attended the University before emigrating to Canada where he made his fortune. On his death in 1813 he left property valued at £30,000 for the foundation of the university in Montreal which still bears his name. Glasgow cannot claim the same credit for Princeton University, New Jersey, although immigrants from the West of Scotland were partly responsible for its foundation in 1747 as an institution of higher learning largely devoted to training students for the Presbyterian ministry. One of its best-remembered Presidents was John Witherspoon who was called to that position from his church at Paisley in 1768.

Influential and highly esteemed though the University was, especially in the second half of the century, some considered that the kind of education it offered was not suited to a commercial city. Among them was William Thom, a Govan minister who in 1762 published the first of a series of pamphlets attacking the University, called *Letter to J—— M——, Esq., on the Defects of an University*

Education and its Unsuitableness to a Commercial People: with the Expedience and Necessity of erecting at Glasgow an Academy for the Instruction of Youth. Thom was indignant over the time wasted in studying logic and metaphysics and advocated the introduction of practical mathematics, 'universal history' and the history of Britain and her trading partners, geography, the history of commerce, and a course in 'practical morality'. Thom also attacked the snobbishness of the professors, who, he charged, 'loved rank and kept themselves at greater distance from their scholars than common schoolmasters do' and took no real interest in their progress. But, although an academy of the kind recommended by Thom was established at Perth in 1760, Glasgow Town Council ignored Thom's plea and no such institution was set up in the city. The professors, however, did in some degree respond to criticisms by setting up private classes in additional subjects, the fees for which they pocketed. These classes came to be regarded as more of a scandal than a reform, for they drew the professors away from the primary commitment to teach the university curriculum to the regular students, and were a major factor in provoking university reform in the following century.

Even without an academy of the kind recommended by Thom, eighteenth-century Glasgow had many schools and was proud of their variety. The 'several respectable inhabitants' of Glasgow who contributed the account of the city to Volume V of the *Statistical Account of Scotland* published in 1793 wrote with some complacency:

As Scotland has always been honourably distinguished, by the superior education of the lower classes of her inhabitants, so this important article has had considerable attention paid to it in Glasgow, by institutions of various kinds: many of which, at the same time that they provide for the instruction of the youth, also provide for their comfortable clothing . . .

Hutcheson's Hospital . . ., under the management of the Magistrates, Council, and Ministers, clothes and educates 48 boys, for a course of four years; during which time, 32 of them have an annual pension of L. 3 each, and all of them, at leaving the school, are completely clothed, and bound apprentices to different trades. – The *Town's Hospital* clothes and educates all the boys and girls who live in it, upwards of 100 in number, and, when at a proper age, binds them apprentices to trades, or gets them into service. The *Highland Society* clothe about 60 boys annually, binding them apprentices to trades, and attending to their education during their apprenticeship.

Mr *Wilson* of London, who formerly had gone from this city, impressed with the advantages of education to the lower class of people, in 1778, mortified L. 3000 for the purpose of educating and clothing boys. This fund has been augmented by sundry donations from other persons, and now educates 48 boys, who, at the end of 4 years, are also completely clothed, and bound apprentices to trades. – Besides these, *Crawford's School* gives education to 48 boys and girls, Tennent's to 96, and Baxter's to 48, though without clothing. – There are also, of late, some schools set apart for girls, such as Lennox's school which educates 48, and Peadie's, which educates about 30, in reading, sewing and knitting. – A fund of above L. 7000, has likewise been lately left by Mr Archibald Millar, for educating and clothing girls in a genteel way during a course of 5 years. – A neat school-house is now building for that purpose, where it is proposed to instruct them in every branch of education suited to their station.

The account goes on to list eleven Sunday Schools, begun in 1787 and supported by voluntary subscriptions, 'intended to preserve the education formerly given, to increase knowledge, and to form good habits'. 640 boys and girls attended such schools. There are also, the writers continue, about sixty fee-supported schools in the city, where the masters derive their income entirely from 'school wages, from 5s. to 1s. 6d. the quarter'. In most of these, however, the curriculum is restricted to 'reading English, the Catechism, and perhaps a little writing'. The writers emphasize the importance of persuading parents to send their children to school at six years of age, 'for if their education is then neglected, it is in great danger of being lost for ever'. A temptation for parents to take their children from school is provided by the fact that manufacturers 'find employment for children between 7 and 8 years of age, and even then their work will bring in from 1s. to 1s. 6d. per week' – a great temptation to poor families. 'The only method, therefore, by which the education of the poor can be secured, is by giving it early, and supporting the Sunday schools, which may prevent such education as they have got being lost.'

For the education of 'the higher classes' there were 'many public teachers of the living languages, Writing, Arithmetic, Book-keeping, Mathematics, &c. whose fees are generally from 5s. to 10s. 6d. the quarter, and some of them considerably higher.' The account continues:

Besides a considerable number of private schools, in which the Latin language is taught, a very elegant building has lately been erected [in 1789, on the north side of George Street] for the public grammar school, in which the course of education is 4 years, and is conducted by 4 masters, who each carry on their classes the whole time, having equal salaries of L. 25 each for the three first years, and L. 35 for the fourth year. Each scholar pays 5s. *per* quarter, besides a present at Candlemas; and for some years each of the classes has generally consisted of from 80 to 100 scholars. Great care has been taken in the choice of the masters, both as to their worth and professional abilities. To this, and to the great attention which has for some years been bestowed on it by the Town-council, is the flourishing state of the school to be ascribed. A committee of gentlemen of the Council are chosen annually, who take the superintendence of it, and who, with the advice of the Professors of the University, settle the plan of teaching, &c. in the different classes; and along with them the ministers, and other patrons of learning visit the school frequently, without giving any previous notice. At these visitations, the scholars go through their different exercises, and the particular standing of each boy in the class is marked down in a book; and at the end of each season, when there is a public examination, before the Magistrates, prizes are distributed to the boys, not according to the situation in which they may be accidentally found at that time, but according to the average of their places at the different examinations throughout the year; . . . Prizes are also given for good attendance, in order to form habits of attention, which may be useful to them in their after life, in whatever situation they may be placed.

The 'present at Candlemas' (2 February) referred to in this account was first presented to the Rector at a ceremony in the Common Hall, with each of the masters sitting at his 'pulpit' (desk). After each boy had gone up to give his offering to the Rector, he went to his class teacher with an offering for him. The amount of each offering was read out by the Rector. At an offering of five shillings the Rector cried '*Vivat*' and the boys stamped; for ten shillings he cried '*Floreat*' and the boys beat twice with their feet. For fifteen shillings the cry was '*Floreat bis*' (let him flourish twice) and three stamps; twenty shillings brought '*Floreat ter*' (let him flourish thrice) and four stamps; a guinea and over won the exclamation '*Gloriat*' and six stamps of the feet by the boys. The rich man's son or daughter who was able to produce the largest sum was hailed and crowned as 'Victor', 'King' or 'Queen'. This iniquitous custom went on until 1786, when the Town Council resolved that while the offerings ('Gifts', 'oblations' or 'free-will offerings' as they were ironically called) should be continued the public announcements and the cheering of the victor should be terminated.

Some of William Thom's objectives were achieved at the very end of the century, in 1796, with the foundation of Anderson's Institution with money bequeathed for the purpose by John Anderson. He was an irascible but public-spirited Glasgow man who had studied at the University and became successively Professor of Oriental Languages and Professor of Natural Philosophy (Physics) there. In his account of Glasgow written a few years later, Robert Forsyth wrote:

> Mr Anderson, during life, was known to be much attached to those branches of experimental philosophy which are most subservient to general utility, and to the operations of the different arts and manufactures to which the talents and arts of civilised nations have given birth. His property bequeathed to the institution consisted chiefly of a very valuable apparatus, which he had formed for illustrating the various branches of natural philosophy and chemistry; a museum, containing a well arranged collection of fossils, working models of different kinds of machinery; a complete apparatus for illustrating fortification and military tactics; together with a large library, consisting of the most scientific works in different languages.

Anderson's special interest was to provide training in applied science for mechanics and artisans, related to the manufacturing and architectural needs of the time. He himself wrote a special textbook for the type of student he had in mind ('Methods of making houses less subject to be burnt', 'Of instruments and machines for architecture and manufacture' are two typical chapter headings). Though the funds Anderson left were not sufficient to fulfil all his intentions, the trustees were able to appoint Dr Thomas Garnet to give evening lectures in two class-rooms in the new Grammar School in George Street and a twice-weekly popular course in the Trades Hall. By the time of the third session of lectures 'several public-spirited gentlemen, friends to the institution, [had] purchased and fitted up for its accommodation a very spacious and convenient hall, with adjoining rooms for containing the library, museum and apparatus' in Duke Street. Dr Garnet left for London in 1800 and was succeeded by Dr Birkbeck, who started a special class for mechanics 'with the beneficent view of diffusing philosophical information as extensively as possible . . . These lectures, delivered in a perspicacious style, in which every principle was illustrated by models and experiments, were at first given gratuitously, and afterwards for a trifling fee for each individual.' Anderson's Institution became Anderson's University in 1828, Anderson's College in 1877, and, after its regrouping

Anderson's Institution as seen in the 1820s
by the illustrated magazine, the *Northern Looking Glass*

with other institutions in Glasgow, The Glasgow and West of
Scotland Technical College in 1886. In 1912 it became The Royal
Technical College, Glasgow, to become the Royal College of Science
and Technology in 1956 and the University of Strathclyde in 1963.
So, in the end, Professor Anderson's intentions were more than
realized.

For much of the eighteenth century there was no recognition of
the part that a theatre could play in the intellectual and cultural
life of Glasgow. Clerical and mercantile opposition to the theatre was
strong. A wooden theatre built against the ruined wall of the Bishop's
Palace in 1752 was burned down in 1754 by a furious mob inspired
by the preaching of the Rev. George Whitefield, the Calvinistic
Methodist, in the High Churchyard. The first permanent Glasgow
theatre was built (like the first permanent theatre in Elizabethan
London) outside the city boundary, in the suburb of Grahamston
(where the Central Railway Station was later built). On the opening
night in 1764, when Mrs Bellamy was making her Glasgow debut, an
unsuccessful attempt was made to set fire to it by a crowd urged on
by an itinerant preacher, but they succeeded in destroying much of

the interior. It was repaired, but it finally burned down on 5 May 1780, officially by accident but perhaps deliberately by incendiaries. John Jackson, the manager, was not a man to give up easily, and he built a new theatre in Dunlop Street which was opened in January 1782. But it was not until the last fifteen years of the century, after the appearance of Mrs Siddons at the Dunlop Street Theatre in 1785, that Glasgow's citizens positively welcomed the theatre. With the opening of the Theatre Royal in Queen Street in 1805, the theatrical history of Glasgow becomes continuously lively and interesting.

Eighteenth-century Glasgow was not known for its musical life. Robert Forsyth, surveying the Glasgow scene at the beginning of the nineteenth century, noted curtly that 'a few years ago, an attempt was made to establish a subscription-concert after the nature of that which so long existed at Edinburgh; but it was soon abandoned.' He added: 'A society has been formed in Glasgow for the encouragement of sacred music . . . . Six public meetings are held during the winter, with weekly rehearsals.' Glasgow had a long way to go before it reached the position in our own time when it could upstage Edinburgh by building an opera house for the Scottish National Opera.

More directly concerned with the intellectual life of the city in the eighteenth century were the printers, most notably the brothers Robert and Andrew Foulis (1707–76 and 1712–75). Robert attended Francis Hutcheson's lectures while still a barber's apprentice and in 1738–40 the two brothers visited Oxford and France to collect rare books, for which they had a passion. Robert became printer to the University in 1743 while Hutcheson was still professor, and was later joined by his brother. His constant association with University scholars increased his appetite for scholarship and encouraged him to enter on a career of issuing editions of classical and modern authors which are landmarks in the history of fine printing and book production. In 1743 he printed for the University their first Greek book, and his famous 'immaculate' duodecimo edition of Horace (not, as it transpired, literally immaculate, for six errors were eventually discovered, though the sheets had been exposed at the University and a reward offered – which was never claimed – for the discovery of any errors) appeared in 1774. The brothers went into partnership and over about thirty years proceeded to issue accurately and beautifully printed editions of classical works in Latin, Greek, English, French and Italian. Their four volume Homer in folio which appeared between 1756 and 1758, is probably the best known of their numerous publications. In 1752 they decided to establish an 'Academy' for the encouragement of the fine arts, and persuaded the University to provide a large room in which to house pictures and sculptures. The brothers ruined themselves in collecting paintings, encouraging young artists and importing art teachers, and the Academy collapsed. But it was a remarkable effort, ante dating by over fifteen years the school of the Royal Academy in London. Andrew died in September 1775 and Robert went to London hoping to raise a large sum of money by the sale of their pictures. But they brought much less than he hoped for – under £400 – and he died broken hearted in Edinburgh in June 1776. The catalogue of the paintings lists thirty-eight Raphaels, thirty-five Rubenses, twenty-one Titians, eight Rembrandts, and many other great names, including Leonardo, Michelangelo, Correggio, Veronese, Tintoretto, Dürer, Van Dyck and Breugel; but none of the attributions proved correct. It was a sad end to a nobly conceived Glasgow venture. But the Foulis brothers' achievements in book production and fine printing remain.

Eighteenth-century Glasgow is also notable for the development of printing of a less exalted kind. Glasgow's first newspaper appeared on 14 November 1715. It called itself *The Glasgow Courant, Containing the Occurrences Both at Home and Abroad,* and it appeared three times a week, on Tuesdays, Thursdays and Saturdays, and cost three-halfpence. With the fourth issue the title was changed to *The West Country Intelligence.* Only sixty-seven numbers appeared. A weekly newspaper of more specialist interest ran throughout much of 1742, producing fifty-two numbers. This was the *Glasgow-Weekly-History Relating to the Late Progress of the Gospel at Home and Abroad; Being a collection of letters partly reprinted from the London-Weekly-History, and partly printed first at Glasgow,* printed by William Duncan and sold to subscribers only for one halfpenny. Its eight quarto pages were devoted to religious news from a strongly evangelistic point of view. It came out sometimes weekly and sometimes twice a week. The *Glasgow Journal* was founded by Andrew Stalker in 1741 as a weekly and ran until well into the next century. A second *Glasgow Courant,* another weekly, began publication on 21 October 1745, published by Matthew Simson, and printed by the Foulis brothers (who advertised their books in its columns): it soon outdid the *Journal* in popularity, partly because of the latter's refusal to print items that might be thought to be controversial or dangerous and partly because of the livelier nature both of its social news and of its advertisements. ('Mr James Johnstone married Miss Peggy Newall, a young lady of great merit and a fortune of £4,000.' 'James Hodge sells burying crapes ready-made, and his wife's niece, who lives with him, dresses dead corpses at as cheap a rate as was

THE

Glafgow Courant,

Containing the

OCCURRENCES

Both at Home and Abroad:

From *Friday November* 11, to *Monday November* 14. 1715.

Glafgow, Printed for *R. T.* and are to be Sold at the Printing Houfe in the Colledge, and at the Poft-Office. 1715.

formerly done by her aunt, having been educated by her and per-fected in Edinburgh, from whence she has lately arrived, and has all the newest and best fashions.') In spite of its enjoying greater popularity than the *Journal*, the *Courant* lasted only until 1760. Little is known of the *Glasgow Weekly Chronicle*, which ran from 1766 into the 1770s. The *Glasgow Mercury*, published by Alexander Duncan and Robert Chapman, ran from 1778 till 1796: it prided itself on its responsibility and respectability and on the fact that, being a weekly and thus allowing a whole week for news to be ruminated on, it contained 'articles mostly of authentic intelligence', while 'the editor, having leisure to distinguish truth from falsehood, imparts that information that seems to merit attention'. It came to an end on 27 September 1796 because, as the proprietor (Robert Chapman, nephew of the co-founder) explained in a notice, of 'the extensiveness of his printing business in general'.

More ambitious than any of these newspapers was the *Glasgow Advertiser*, founded, published and edited by John Mennons who, after experience of newspaper and magazine printing in Edinburgh, came to Glasgow to establish a paper worthy of the city's commercial greatness. The first number appeared on 27 January 1783. In it, under the Glasgow coat of arms and the motto 'Let Glasgow Flourish', he made a formal dedication to the Right Honourable Patrick Colquhoun, Lord Provost, and to the Town Council of Glasgow, and addressed the public about his intention: 'In the foremost com-mercial city of Scotland, the number of persons who are well-informed in the various departments of trade and manufacturers must be very considerable; and any communication on subjects so interesting to the nation in general, and to Glasgow in particular, shall be received with gratitude. The late institution of a Chamber of Commerce gives every reason to believe that topics of this kind will occasionally be discussed in such a manner as to lay the founda-tion for such general and comprehensive conclusions as may serve as guides in critical conjunctures both to the merchant and the manufacturer. . . .' He also announced that they had engaged the services of an 'eminent correspondent at London, not only to send him the latest and most authentic intelligence, but likewise the debates in the British Parliament on the day the post leaves London, which cannot appear even in the London papers till the next day'. The first issue contained a despatch from London dated 23 January, together with other news arranged under the headings, 'Thursday's Post', 'Saturday's Post', 'Sunday's Post', 'Tuesday's Post' and 'Monday's Post' (the paper was published weekly on Mondays). The paper also contained Lloyd's Marine Lists, notes of the rise and fall of stocks, and the report of the War Office, as well as a large number of advertisements (for, among other things, spirits, tea, rum, medicinal herbs, seeds, lands and books). Before the end of the century it had changed from a four-page weekly to an eight-page twice-weekly, and eventually it became a daily. On 29 June 1789 it expanded its title to the *Glasgow Advertiser and Evening Intelligencer*, and finally, on 23 August 1805, it adopted the name by which, after many changes of ownership, it is still known, the *Glasgow Herald*.

John Mennons also produced Glasgow's first monthly magazine, the *Glasgow Magazine and Review or Universal Miscellany*, in October 1783, an ambitious attempt to show 'the connection between commerce and the liberal arts' and to 'diffuse knowledge, excite the emulation of youth, and promote the liberality of sentiment and social intercourse which ought to be the characteristics of a commercial people'. But Mennons' mixture of long extracts from recently published serious books and varied articles on literature, history, biography and politics, does not seem to have appealed to the Glasgow taste of the time, for the magazine survived less than a year. There were also short-lived weekly magazines in eighteenth-century Glasgow, including the *Glasgow Museum or Weekly Instructor*, 1773, and the *Glasgow Universal Magazine of Knowledge and Pleasure*, 1772–3, but none was of any great merit or won any considerable support.

CHAPTER 8

Coal, Cotton and Iron

THE Industrial Revolution came to Scotland with the cotton industry which, unlike the linen industry, was in Scotland mechanized from the start. English inventors – Lewis Paul, John Wyatt, James Hargreaves and Samuel Crompton – developed the necessary technology, the first two of these originating the principle of spinning by rollers that was improved by Richard Arkwright, while Crompton invented the spinning mule in 1779. In 1775 Arkwright developed machinery for carding, roving and drawing, and a few years later the first effective cotton-spinning mill in the west of Scotland was established at Rothesay, soon followed by others in the neighbourhood of Glasgow – at Anderston, Barrhead and elsewhere – thanks to the numbers of fast-flowing streams in the region. As we saw in Chapter Six, the Glasgow manufacturer David Dale brought Arkwright to Glasgow in 1783 and together they founded the New Lanark cotton mills in 1786. In 1799 Dale's daughter married Robert Owen, whose pioneering schemes of social and industrial organization in the interests of the cotton workers owed a good deal to his father-in-law.

In the last years of the eighteenth and the early years of the nineteenth centuries Glasgow became the centre of a cotton-spinning region: the number of cotton-mills within a radius of twenty-five miles of Glasgow rose from nineteen to a hundred and thirty-four between 1787 and 1834. In the city itself, the tobacco lord had given way to the cotton king. The new communities established in the open countryside near the mills were at first integrated social units in which the mill owner took a close personal interest. But the introduction of the power-loom, invented by William Radcliffe and his mechanic Thomas Johnston in 1804, gradually changed the picture. Improvements to the machine and the increasing use of steam-engines in succeeding years altered the nature of the industry and the social conditions of its workers who, since the mills no longer needed to be by the sides of streams, could now be herded into the city. This had inevitable political repercussions and in 1820 Sir Walter Scott could write:

> Formerly obliged to seek the sides of rapid streams for driving their machinery, manufacturers established themselves in sequestered spots and lodged their working people in villages around them. Hence arose a mutual dependence on each other between the employer & employd for in bad times the Master had to provide these people sustenance else he could not have their service in good & the little establishment naturally looked up to him as their head. But this has ceased since manufacturers have been transferred to great towns where a Master calls together 100 workmen this week and pays them off the next with far less interest in their future than in that of as many worn-out shuttles.

The flourishing cotton industry stimulated the development of related industries such as bleaching, dyeing and fabric printing. The inventor and chemist Dr John Roebuck established a factory at Prestonpans in 1749 to manufacture sulphuric acid, whose bleaching properties were finally demonstrated by Dr Francis Home, Professor of Materia Medica at Edinburgh, in 1756. This reduced the bleaching period of textiles from eight to four months. Then followed the discovery in 1774 by the Swedish Carl Scheele of the use of chlorine as a bleaching agent and its successful employment in France ten years later by Claude Louis Berthollet whom James Watt met in Paris and from whom he learned the method. Watt's father-in-law was the Glasgow bleacher James McGregor, and it was on his bleachfields that Watt tried out Berthollet's method. By the end of the century further experimentation by Professor Patrick Copland of Aberdeen and Charles Tennent of St Rollox had led to the perfection of the chlorine method with the introduction of 'bleaching powder' (chloride of lime) and had reduced the whole bleaching process to a few hours, when it had originally taken months. Bleachfields were now no longer so necessary and many were returned to cultivation; the bleaching industry, now independent of weather and seasonal changes, could take its place as an industrial process in specially constructed bleachworks. The result was an enormous expansion of the bleaching industry in and around Glasgow, and hence of dyeing and printing. At the beginning of the nineteenth century there were over sixty bleachworks in the Clyde basin, all using chloride of lime; there were also thirty large print-fields in the neighbourhood of Glasgow. William Stirling had greatly encouraged the development of cloth printing when he set up his printing and bleaching works at Dalsholm on the Kelvin in the middle of the eighteenth century, moving later to the Vale of Leven to establish works at Cordale. The firm of Crum and Co., equally active in cotton spinning, weaving, calico printing and bleaching, began in the Gallowgate in 1779 and moved to Thornliebank in Renfrewshire, some four miles south of the city, as its business expanded. Renfrewshire and the Vale of Leven attracted textile printworks partly because of the suitability of the water, but partly also because the undeveloped countryside offered a steady supply of cheap labour, unlike Glasgow itself, where wages were relatively high.

Robert Forsyth, observing Glasgow in 1805, summed the whole matter up:

> The cotton manufacture . . . together with the various arts dependent upon it, is now become the staple of the west of Scotland, and is here carried on to a greater extent than in any town in Britain, except Manchester. In order to carry this manufacture through all its branches, cotton-mills, bleachfields, and printfields, have been erected, not only on all the streams in the neighbourhood, but even in situations more remote; and such is its prosperous state, that though the number of spinning mills has of late greatly increased, they are still unable to supply the necessary quantity of yarn which the trade requires; so that daily that article, to a considerable amount, is brought from England. Neither is this trade confined to the workmen in the city: the manufacturers of Glasgow employ several thousand weavers who live in the district of the country around it, and even to the distance of thirty or forty miles . . . This manufacture is not only important of itself, but is productive of work to many thousands of bleachers, tambourers, calico-printers, &c.: many of whom being women and children, whose work was formerly unproductive, renders it of still more general interest.

The great development of manufacturing in Glasgow towards the end of the eighteenth century went together with a recovery of trade after the sharp set-back caused by the American War of Independence and a resulting increase in shipping. 'In 1783,' noted Forsyth, 'the number of ships belonging to Clyde were only 386, and their tonnage 22,896; whereas in 1790 their number was 476, and their tonnage 46,581. In two years thereafter, the registered vessels belonging to Glasgow, Port Glasgow, and Greenock, were 464, and their tonnage 46,806 tons.' By 1810 the tonnage at Glasgow was 2,600, at Port Glasgow 13,100 and at Greenock 40,000. Greenock, where important improvements in port facilities culminated in the opening of a splendid new Custom House in 1818, had by now surpassed Port Glasgow in the number and size of ships registered there, but some of the largest were in fact owned by Glasgow firms, such as the textile firms of Stirling, Gordon & Co. (not connected with the Walter Stirling who left money, books and property to found Glasgow's first public library in 1791) and Buchanan, Steven & Co. Robert Forsyth noted in 1805 the cargoes of these ships:

> The principal articles of exportation from Glasgow and the ports farther down the river, to America and the West Indies, are British manufactures, also coals, fish, &c.; to the continent of Europe, and the ports in the Baltic, besides British manufactures, raw and refined sugars, coffee, rum, and other productions of the western hemisphere. Glasgow imports from the West Indies and America the principal articles of growth or manufacture there; such as coffee, cotton, sugars, rum, mahogany, wheat and flour, staves, pearl and wood ashes, fruits, &c.; and from Spain and Portugal, wines and other productions of these countries; from the Baltic, wood, iron, flax, hemp, pitch, tar, Russia linens, and wheat. To Ireland Glasgow sends manufactures, and in return receives hides, grain, salted beef, butter, and meal, &c.
>
> Of all the articles imported, however, the chief are sugar, rum, coffee, and cotton. Of this last article, between forty and fifty thousand bags are imported annually into the Clyde; and, upon the whole, this river is now justly considered as having at least the third trade in the island, admitting London and Liverpool to have the two first.

Meanwhile, efforts to improve the navigability of the Clyde at Glasgow continued; the original dykes were improved and parallel dykes were built down the river. Port Dundas, at the Glasgow end of the Forth–Clyde canal, was increasingly used to bring European trade into Glasgow and in 1808, partly as a result of this, Glasgow was admitted as a port of registry, many of the first ships registered in Glasgow plying between Port Dundas and European ports. In 1815 Glasgow became a head-port, no longer subordinate to Greenock, which had by now replaced Port Glasgow as the customs head-port. In 1822, 482 feet were added to the quay at Broomielaw, and the Custom House was built at Broomielaw in 1837. And, most significant of all, after William Symington's experiments with a paddle steamer on Dalswinton Loch in 1788, Henry Bell, who had begun as a millwright in Helensburgh and had been brooding over the possibilities of steam navigation since 1786, finally produced the first practical steamboat to appear on any European river, the *Comet*, which plied on the Clyde (Glasgow–Greenock–Helensburgh) between 1812 and 1820. Though the *Comet* took five hours to get

David Hamilton's St Enoch's Church seen from Buchanan Street, *c.* 1885.
It was demolished in 1926.

Left The Theatre Royal, Dunlop Street, which
burned down in 1863; the site is now occupied
by the derelict St Enoch's Station.
Right Queen's Park Terrace, 355–429
Eglinton Street, (*c.* 1850) a splendid
example of Alexander 'Greek' Thomson's
tenement architecture.

Sir George Gilbert Scott's Glasgow University (1866–70) stands on the hill overlooking the Kelvin.

The entrance to the Botanic Gardens in Great Western Road, 1905. The domes mark the Botanic Gardens Station of the Glasgow Central Railway, opened in 1896.

from Glasgow to Greenock, its introduction of a regular steamboat passenger service was to mark the beginning of a remarkable chapter in the history of Glasgow.

The development of steam tugs and dredgers followed, freeing the sailing of ships up the Clyde to Glasgow from the mercy of the wind and also making it possible to maintain a channel both wide and deep, so that really large vessels could come to Glasgow. By 1836 the Trustees of the Clyde Navigation heard from their engineer David Logan that there were seven to eight feet of water at ebb tide, twelve feet at neap tide, and fifteen feet at spring tides at the Broomielaw. An Act of Parliament of 1840 approved a proposal put forward by Logan for a three-hundred-foot channel with a minimum depth of twenty feet, and this eventually led to the enlargement of the Clyde to its present dimensions, at the cost of massive dredging and excavating and the acquisition and demolition of various factories (including Parkholm printing works, Wingate's engine works, and the large Springfield cotton mill) by the riverside. This took place largely in the fourth and fifth decades of the nineteenth century, which found the increasing numbers of ships straining even the enlarged capacity of the quays. Even more enlargement was demanded, until there were 4,400 yards of quays in 1858. But Logan's ideal of a minimum depth of twenty feet proved difficult to attain, and where the channel at Elderslie reached solid rock,* the Clyde Trustees had to be content with a minimum depth of eleven feet at low tide. The later development of a method of underwater blasting enabled a depth of twenty feet at low tide to be reached, but not until 1886.

Bell's *Comet* (officially described on registration as 'a square stemmed carvel full-built passage boat with a Cock Pit, being furnished with a steam engine by which she sails') was, like the other early steamers that followed her, built of wood. Gradually these steamers extended their range, plying to Rothesay in 1815, Campbeltown in 1816, Belfast in 1818 (as a result of David Napier's successful adaption of the steamship for deep-sea traffic) and Liverpool in 1819. The *Comet*'s original three-horse-power engine, made by the Glasgow mechanic John Robertson, was eventually replaced by one more powerful to enable her to inaugurate a service to Fort William via the Crinan Canal in 1819. David Napier, who built engines for his ships in his own works at Camlachie, designed the *Ivanhoe* in 1820: it was built by Scott's of Greenock and plied between Holyhead and Dublin. By 1820 there were over forty wooden paddle-steamers

---

*The existence of the 'Elderslie Rock' was first discovered when the steamer *Glasgow*, one of the first steamers trading between Glasgow and New York, was grounded on it in 1854.

plying on the Clyde on regular services and there were forty-eight others under construction on Clydeside.

A new tradition of Clyde shipbuilding was springing up. Before the American war, Clyde ships had been built mostly in North American or English ports, but after the war there was a surge of shipbuilding on Clydeside, with 3,400 tons of shipping on the Clyde out of a total of 16,800 tons owned on the Clyde in 1787. But this phase was short-lived: the new surge of shipbuilding set off by the coming of the steamship was to last much longer and prove more important in Glasgow's history. The *Comet* was still in service when Clyde-built steamers appeared on the Thames and the Mersey. James Nasmyth (engineer son of the painter Alexander Nasmyth) patented his improved steam-engine in 1830, thus giving a further boost to the development of the steamship. By 1835, 560 tons of the total United Kingdom merchant steamship tonnage of 1,180 were built on the Clyde, and by 1851 Clydeside's share was 5,300 out of a total of 6,270 tons. Because of the development of the Clyde Valley iron industry the Clyde was also a pioneer in the building of iron ships. As early as 1818 Thomas Wilson launched his iron boat, the *Vulcan*, on the Monkland Canal, and in 1831 the iron steamship the *Fairy Queen*, designed by J. B. Neilson, the inventor of the hot blast in iron manufacture, was launched in Glasgow. The Clyde also took the lead in the development of screw propulsion: in 1851, 4,360 of the total United Kingdom screw propulsion tonnage of 4,870 was built on Clydeside. While wooden sailing ships were also built on the Clyde – many in Glasgow itself – it was with the development of new building methods for new types of steamship that the Clyde made shipbuilding history. In 1839 Robert Napier, cousin of David and also a marine engineer, with his partners George Burns of Glasgow and David McIver of Liverpool, joined with the Nova Scotia-born shipowner Samuel Cunard to form the Cunard Company to provide a regular steamship service to North America. Napier himself got the contract for the hulls and engines of the first four vessels (the hulls were of wood: Cunard adopted the iron hull in 1855 and screw propulsion for passenger ships in 1862). With the arrival of the Cunarder *Britannia* at Boston on 4 July 1840, having taken fourteen days and eight hours from Liverpool, a new era in trans-Atlantic communications opened. The success of the early Cunarders established the Clyde as the river able to provide the necessary shipbuilding facilities for this new era.

Coal mining was an established though primitive industry in the Clyde valley by the seventeenth century, and in the eighteenth the use of coal in the local iron, pottery and glass manufacturing (which provided exports to the American colonies) increased demand and production. The opening of the Monkland Canal in 1792 facilitated the transport of coal from the Lanarkshire coalfields to Glasgow and reduced coal prices there; in the immediately preceding decades complaints had been made (including a petition to the House of Commons) about the increasing price of coal in the city as a result of the high cost of land transport. The coal industry fuelled the growing iron industry. In 1759 the Carron Company set up its furnaces just south of Falkirk, thus beginning Scotland's modern iron industry. 'This was an event of capital importance in the economic history of Scotland,' Henry Hamilton, the economic historian, has written, 'for the [Carron Iron] works was the first in this country to use ironstone from the carboniferous formation of central Scotland and to employ coal in its furnaces.' The Carron Works supplied iron goods to Glasgow merchants. They also supplied guns to the Government, for the country was now in the midst of the Seven Years War. It was not, however, until twelve years after the war had ended that the company succeeded (by adopting without permission a method invented by John Wilkinson) in perfecting the process of gun casting to produce a readily saleable cannon; it became universally known and esteemed, so much so that the company's name gave rise to the term 'carronade' for the short large-calibre cannon they produced. In 1759 the three Carron partners (William Cadell, Dr John Roebuck and Samuel Garbett) acquired the nail-making mills at Cramond on the Forth; in 1787 Thomas Edington and John MacKenzie established the Clyde Iron Works, with blast furnaces and forges on the Clyde at Tollcross on the outskirts of Glasgow.

Expansion of the iron industry in Scotland at the end of the eighteenth century was the result of the invention of new ways of applying steam power to the furnaces, forges and mills. The local availability of coal and ironstone led in 1787 to proposals by John Gillies (of the Dalnotter Iron Works), William Robertson (of the Smithfield Iron Co.) and John Grieve (of Bo'ness) for the setting up of iron-furnaces and forges in Muirkirk, some twenty miles south of Glasgow in the hills on the Lanarkshire–Ayrshire border. These three were joined in 1788 by Thomas Edington, manager of Cadells of Cramond (for by now the Cadell family had bought the Cramond Iron Works from the Carron Company) with the result that the following year saw the establishment of the Muirkirk Iron Works. Important developments followed J. B. Neilson's discovery of the true nature of 'blackband ironstone' (hitherto regarded as useless 'wild coal') in 1828 and his subsequent discovery of the 'hot blast' technique of smelting it. Early in the nineteenth century the Dixons of Govan, who owned both the Dumbarton glassworks and coal-mines in Govan, set up the Calder Ironworks near Coatbridge. In 1837 William Dixon established the Govan Iron Works (popularly known as 'Dixon's Blazes') at the head of Crown Street just south of the river – one of the developments, incidentally, which eventually led to an area originally conceived of as a choice residential district turning into a mixture of piecemeal industrial proliferation and city slum. But that story belongs to a later chapter.

Members of distinguished Glasgow merchant families who had made fortunes in tobacco and in textiles were far from indifferent to developments in coal-mining and iron production; many moved easily from commercial to industrial interests. Much of the invest-ment in iron companies and coal-mines came from these families. In some cases they played a part more active than investing: Andrew Buchanan, for example, was a proprietor of the large and successful coal-mine at Faskine, while John Glassford leased from Cadell the Banton Ironstone Mines near Falkirk. So the sequence was tobacco lords – cotton kings – captains of industry. The further expansion of iron, steel and shipbuilding in the second half of the nineteenth century completed the transformation of Glasgow from a com-mercial centre to a great modern industrial city with the concomitant prosperity and the problems that such cities seem always to generate.

Some of these problems were already manifest in the eighteenth century. In 1779 Glasgow weavers rioted in protest against the introduction of a Bill to remit the duties on French cambrics: the Bill was eventually withdrawn. More serious were the Calton weavers' riots of 1787, as a result of the employers' refusal to raise wages. The rioters wrecked looms and stoned the magistrates and town officers when they tried to interfere. The military were called in and when they in turn were attacked by the rioters the Riot Act was read in Duke Street. The soldiers fired, and three of the rioters were killed and several wounded.

Hand-loom weavers wove into cloth the cotton yarn spun by the power-mills, but when the factories began manufacturing their own cloth domestic hand-loom weaving was threatened and the wages fell. From 1815 the position of these weavers deteriorated rapidly: from earning thirty to forty shillings a week at the turn of the century they were reduced to a wage of about seven shillings and sixpence for top quality muslin weavers and four shillings and six-pence for the less skilled. Indeed, hand-loom weavers survived, though in surprisingly large numbers, only at the extreme ends of the industry – for weaving very high quality specialized articles such as Paisley shawls or for low-grade work where sometimes a weaver's wages were so low that his work cost the manufacturer less than the same work done by machine. With the introduction of cheap printed imitations of the Paisley shawl even the specialized weaver found his living disappearing. But, paradoxically, hand-loom weavers continued to increase in numbers until after 1840, with their wages falling steadily. 'This continued inrush into a collapsing trade', comments T. C. Smout, 'was the symptom of the plight of an adult male immigration into the towns after the Napoleonic Wars.'

Natural disasters exacerbated those made by man. In November 1795 a great flood brought the Clyde into the Bridgegate, the Saltmarket, the Gorbals and Stockwell and Jamaica Streets for five days; the Hutchesontown Bridge, then being built (on the site of the present Albert Bridge) after a generous subscription by Hutcheson's Hospital to provide a bridge connecting their new suburb south of the Clyde with Glasgow Green on the north, was swept away and a little boy was drowned. The crops failed in both 1799 and 1800 and there were bread riots on 15 February 1800. The magistrates raised a public subscription to provide the poor, who were literally starving, with grain under cost price, but the whole sum required was never raised, partly because of the loss of several cargoes of grain and partly because of the failure of the underwriters. The fund was left with a deficit of £4,000, and an attempt to raise this by local taxation had to be abandoned because of the hostility of the ratepayers.

The French Revolution and the Napoleonic Wars that followed brought a new political dimension to Glasgow's social unrest. Discontented weavers readily joined secret societies with alleged revolutionary opinions, and the Government regarded Glasgow as a centre of suspect revolutionary activity. In 1792 Glasgow sent a subscription of £1,200 to the French National Assembly. But it was after the War was ended, with the victory of Waterloo in 1815, that the soldiers, returning to Glasgow to find high prices, little prospect of employment (because of the introduction of machinery) and low wages for such employment as there was, swelled the discontent to proportions that seriously alarmed the Government. Increased immigration from Ireland exacerbated the problem. Unemployed and ill-paid weavers and cotton-spinners turned to political agitation, under the leadership of Alexander Richmond, originally himself a weaver in what was then the small village of Pollokshaws. In 1811 Richmond had petitioned the magistrates of Glasgow to fix fair rates for weavers, after a disastrous fall in wages resulting from the blockade imposed in Napoleon's Continental System and the counter-measure of the British Orders in Council. The petition was made under the terms of a Scottish act of 1661, and the magistrates had to grant it, though with reluctance. But the employers appealed to the Court of Session, and though they lost their case the employers ignored the Court's decision and the Court apparently had no power to enforce it. The result was that the weavers went on strike in 1812.

After holding out for nine weeks the leaders of the strike were arrested and their conviction put an end to the weavers' union formed the year before. The Government scandalously repealed the Act on which the Court of Session's decision had been based and Richmond, on the advice of Francis Jeffrey and Henry Cockburn, the distinguished Whig advocates who had pleaded the weavers' case, disappeared. After a while he gave himself up, and was imprisoned for a month. He then seems to have been influenced by Kirkman Finlay, Member of Parliament for the Clyde burghs, a wealthy cotton manufacturer who was terrified at the prospect of revolution in Britain. In 1816 Finlay established himself as the Government's agent for collecting intelligence about the radical movement in Glasgow and he sought out Richmond, who took the opportunity of persuading him to raise a relief fund for the Glasgow poor. But Richmond, perhaps in good faith, was prevailed upon to reveal information about the activities of specific weavers in the radical movement, and several were arrested. Whether Richmond was the unscrupulous informer that many nineteenth-century historians assume him to have been or a well-meaning man misled by Kirkman Finlay, as some modern historians now believe, his story is evidence of the profound unrest among Glasgow weavers at the end of the Napoleonic Wars.

Richmond was involved in providing information about an oath taken by a group of conspirators at a meeting in Glasgow on 29 October 1816. The oath now seems innocent enough – it was to work for universal adult franchise at the age of twenty-one and for annual Parliaments, and not to inform on or give evidence against any other member of the group – but news of it caused panic in the Government, which proceeded to suspend the Habeas Corpus Act and to bring to trial for high treason a weaver called Andrew M'Kinlay (he was acquitted). Other 'state trials' for sedition in Scotland in 1817 ended less happily for the accused. Alexander M'Laren, a weaver, and Thomas Baird, a shopkeeper, were accused, the former of making a speech at a public meeting at Kilmarnock and the latter of publishing it, 'wickedly and feloniously' in order 'to degrade and bring into contempt the Government and Legislature, and to withdraw therefrom the confidence and affections of the people, and to fill the realm with trouble and dissension.' They were found guilty, but they were ably defended and clearly the Court could not bring itself to believe that the men were seriously seditious, for they were sentenced, not to transportation which was the normal penalty, but to six months' imprisonment.

By 1819 the situation was even worse. The wages of Glasgow hand-loom weavers had now dropped to half of what they had been in 1816, and the streets of Glasgow, as of other British cities, were full of discharged soldiers and sailors begging from passers-by. The Tory Government of Lord Liverpool was in a state of panic, which was not lessened by the 'Peterloo Massacre' of August 1819 and the discovery of the Cato Street Conspiracy (to murder the whole Cabinet) the following February. Others panicked besides the Government. Sir Walter Scott wrote melodramatically in December 1819 about the prospect of civil war and told his brother Tom the improbable story that 'upwards of 50,000 blackguards are ready to rise between Tyne and Wear'. Cockburn, who had defended several of the accused radical weavers, took a calmer view. Looking back later on the close of the year, he recorded that 'the whole island was suffering from great agricultural and industrial distress' and that 'the usual advantage' was taken of this by demagogues. 'The Mid-Lothian Yeomanry Cavalry was marched in the middle of a winter night, to Glasgow; remained in that district a few days; did nothing, having nothing to do; and returned, as proud and as praised, as if fresh from Waterloo.' He continued:

> Some people, however, were clear that a great blow would be struck by the Radical army – by an army, much talked of but never seen, on the last night of the year. The perfect facility with which a party of forty or fifty thousand weavers could march from Glasgow, and seize the Castle of Edinburgh, without ever being heard of till they appeared in our streets, was demonstrated. Our magistrates [in Edinburgh] therefore invited all loyal citizens to congregate, with such arms as they had, at various assigned posts. I repaired to the Assembly Rooms in George Street, with a stick, about eight in the evening. The streets were as quiet as on an ordinary Sunday; but their silence was only held by the excited to forebode the coming storm . . . At last, about ten p.m. the horn of the coach from Glasgow was heard, and the Lord Provost sent us word that we might retire for the night. We never met again.

Nevertheless, there were groups in the manufacturing counties of the west of Scotland, with a central committee in Glasgow, who were involved in some kind of a plot. On 1 April 1820 posters appeared all over Glasgow appealing for armed struggle to regenerate the country and signed by 'the Committee of Organization for forming a Provisional Government'. This may well have been the work of an *agent provocateur*, but some weavers took it seriously and after a strike some (again perhaps, induced by Government agents) actually took up arms. An old radical called James Wilson, a weaver at Strathaven in Lanarkshire, was among those induced to march on Glasgow, but he and the others returned home when they found no one on the outskirts of the city to join them, as they had been promised. Some Calton weavers also marched eastward to join a non-existent group of English rebels who, they were told, were about to seize the Carron Ironworks, but they were easily overcome by a troop of the 7th Regiment of Hussars reinforced by some of the Stirlingshire Yeomanry. Forty-seven prisoners were put on trial for treason, and three – Wilson, who was arrested at his home, John Baird and Andrew Hardie who jointly led the march of the Calton weavers towards Falkirk – were convicted and executed. Wilson's trial took place in Glasgow on 20 July 1820 and he was hanged and then beheaded (the special procedure for those convicted of treason) on Glasgow Green on 30 August. Hardie and Baird were tried at Stirling on 13 July and hanged and beheaded on 8 September. After this savage retaliation, panic among Government and civic authorities subsided and the demand for electoral reform – which had played an important part in the radical weavers' programme – became an increasingly respectable middle-class objective.

In 1822 Richard Campbell, also an impoverished weaver, was whipped through the streets of Glasgow by the public hangman – the last man to be publicly whipped in the city – for an attack on John Provand's paint factory in Great Clyde Street. Provand had come under the quite unjustified suspicion of being a 'resurrectionist' – digger-up of dead bodies to supply to medical students for dissection – and a mob led by Campbell and others attacked his factory. A serious riot developed, the military was called out and the Riot Act was read; five rioters were transported for their part in the affair. In 1823 power-loom workers went on strike, and the manufacturers dismissed them and engaged new workers. The strikers attempted to intimidate the new employees, and had to be quelled by the military.

The spinners of Glasgow faced similar problems. After 1800 most yarn was spun in industrial towns, where there was none of the paternalism found in the rural factories. The spinners did not have to live in a community near the factory, but found accommodation in tenements put up and sub-divided by speculative builders. They early formed their own trade union, to resist any reduction of wages and restrict entry into their trade of unskilled workmen in a time of deflation and unemployment. The result was terrible violence in the 1820s and 1830s, brought about by the employers bringing in blackleg labour to break the union's power and their deliberate parading of the non-union workers in the face of the organized spinners. Non-union workers were killed, or blinded by having vitriol thrown in their faces. In 1837, after a cotton spinners' strike, the importing of blackleg labour, and a resulting riot in which mills were wrecked and one man was shot in Anderston, several of the ringleaders were transported for five years after a trial at the High Court of Justiciary.

An altogether less serious matter (on the surface at least) was the involvement of highly respectable young professional men in agitation in favour of Queen Caroline, George IV's neglected Queen whom he was bringing to trial. Addresses of support for the Queen and public meetings in her favour were proceeded with in spite of stern disapproval from the civic authorities, and when in November 1820 news reached Glasgow that the Bill of Pains and Penalties against the Queen had been abandoned in the House of Lords the citizens celebrated with illuminations, to the great annoyance of the city fathers. This was not simply a matter of gallantry. The pro-Caroline faction were in fact those members of the middle classes who were in favour of parliamentary reform, and the underlying purpose of the demonstrations was to bring together Whig politicians and middle-class democrats to form a new political base. The election of Francis Jeffrey, liberal Whig editor of the *Edinburgh Review*, as Rector of Glasgow University in 1820, showed the way the wind was blowing in the city, in spite of the fierce opposition of the city fathers to reform. The fact that Lord Archibald Hamilton came out strongly in favour of electoral reform in 1823, was another indication of the way opinion was moving. Writing in 1865, the elderly and garrulous Peter Mackenzie (who as a young man had been active in support of the Queen) explained Lord Archibald's position: 'His Lordship was then the popular representative of this great County of Lanark, in Parliament; for although we call it a great and mighty county, as so it is, and still prodigiously on the increase, there were then only about 160 *Electors*, or paper free-holders, in it altogether: and out of that small number, Lord Archibald and his friends could only reckon on the very slender majority of some *ten* or *twenty* individuals. . . . The city of Glasgow itself . . . was a mere nonentity at that time, as regarded the political representation, having only, in common with Rutherglen, Renfrew, and Dumbarton, the one-fourth share of a member,* and that member was a keen *Tory* – dead set against the Queen: whereas, Lord Archibald Hamilton from his eminent position and well-known liberal principles, and cherished regard publicly expressed by him in favour of the Queen,' was the best person to turn to for support in their endeavours on her behalf. Lord Archibald, a leading Scottish Whig member, had sat for Lanarkshire since 1802, and made no bones about the fact that under the existing system he had only been able to hold the seat in the last election of 1820 by creating or buying more fictitious freeholds than his rival. His motion for Scottish electoral reform was defeated by thirty-five votes. But henceforth electoral reform was a serious political issue and it was the co-operation of the Whigs and the working-class radicals that was eventually to achieve it. Glasgow played a significant part in this process.

*The Member of Parliament was elected indirectly by four delegates from the four councils and Glasgow's delegate was chosen by the votes of thirty-two members of her town council.

CHAPTER 9

Into the Nineteenth Century

THE Glasgow Police Act of 1800 divided the city into twenty-four wards, which, the 1801 census revealed, had a total population of 48,256 (20,913 males and 27,343 females; with 11,780 families). What sort of a town did these people inhabit? This is the account of Robert Forsyth, describing Glasgow a couple of years after the census:

> The most ancient part of this city is in the vicinity of the High Church or Cathedral; and the street leading from thence to the Cross and the river is still denominated . . . the High Street . . . In the neighbourhood of the Cathedral the buildings exhibit abundant marks of antiquity, from the gloomy appearance of many of the houses, and the meanness and decayed state of the rest. Here the residences are still pointed out of the ancient prebends, and likewise the site, and only the site, of the Bishop's Castle, . . . Advancing southwards from the Cathedral towards the river, at a trifling distance, is the summit of the high ridge . . . Two streets intersect each other, forming a cross . . . The Rottenrow runs precisely along the summit of the ridge, and is undoubtedly the most elevated and best aired situation in Glasgow. Having been occupied, however, at an early period, and being at a distance from the river, it consists of very mean buildings . . .
>
> From the point at which the Drygate and Rottenrow, at their junction, intersect the High Street, the latter continues to descend southward towards the river. For some length it is extremely steep, . . . The buildings here continue to demonstrate their antiquity by the rudeness of their aspect. At the bottom of the steepest part of the ascent, the High Street is crossed by the finest of all the new streets of Glasgow, called George Street. Being nearly at right angles with the High Street, it is parallel to the river, and to the principal street of Glasgow, which runs from east to west. Proceeding downward from George Street along the High Street, some new streets have been

opened towards the east; and on the same side, forming a part of the High Street, are the buildings of the College or University. Here the High Street assumes a fine appearance, and the buildings towards the Cross are lofty; the descent is gradual; lanes or streets proceed on both sides towards the Molendinar Burn on the east, or towards the New Town on the west. At the Cross the territory is level; and the aspect of the city, consisting of the junction of four streets, with several public buildings, the while in general supported by arcades in front, is very magnificent . . . Proceeding down the Salt Market Street or continuation of the High Street, besides a variety of lanes, the front-entry to which is covered, an open lane, called Prince's Street, proceeds off to the right; and afterwards a handsome street, called St Andrew Street, proceeds to the left eastward, terminating in a square, called St Andrew Square, and church . . . At some distance southwards [of the Salt Market], the Mollendinar Burn, crossing the street, forms the termination of it. Beyond the rivulet, the western corner of what is called the Green of Glasgow, intervenes betwixt the lowest part of the street and the river.

Having thus traced the High Street from the Cathedral . . . downwards to its termination at the banks of the Clyde on the south, we next proceed to attend to the still more important and much longer street, by which it is traversed at the Cross of Glasgow, and which runs from east to west. Beginning at the east on the road towards Edinburgh, a considerable length of suburbs stretches towards the country. The street is called the Gallowgate; and though its direction is towards the west it is by no means rectilineal. The first important object is the Barracks, which were built during the late war on the northern side of the street. Thereafter, at some distance, on the south, is the principal entry to the very populous suburb called the Calton. Proceeding westward, some new streets have been opened, but which are of no great extent, such as Campbell Street, Kent Street, Suffolk Street, and Charlotte Street, containing many handsome buildings, which form a striking contrast to many of the more ancient buildings which front the principal street or Gallowgate . . . The Gallowgate thereafter descends towards its lowest point, which is the bridge across the Mollendinar Burn; after which it gives off towards the left a street or passage towards St Andrew Square, the principal entry to which, however, is that already noticed from the Salt Market by St Andrew Street. The Gallowgate now proceeds between lofty buildings towards the Cross. Here the same line of streets assumes a different name, being first called the Trongate, and afterwards Argyle Street. Standing at the Cross of Glasgow, the appearance of the buildings . . . is very magnificent. This is particularly the case when the eye is directed westward along the Trongate. On the right or northern side the angle is filled by the Prison, five stories in height, beyond which are the Townhouse and Exchange; all which have a very splendid appearance. The houses are supported, to a certain length, on both sides of the street, by Doric pillars, forming piazzas. An equestrian statue of King William the Third stands opposite to the Exchange; and at some distance is seen, on the south side of the street, the spire of the Tron Church [rebuilt by James Adam in 1793 after the main body of the church had been accidentally set on fire by members of the Hell Fire Club; the original church was a collegiate church dedicated to St Mary and St Michael, dating from 1540 and extensively repaired in 1592: the steeple, which survives, dates from 1637]; the whole forming a street-scene which is scarcely surpassed in any other city. Proceeding westward along the Trongate, the first great street by which it is crossed is called King Street towards the south, and Candleriggs towards the north. The former communicated with the Bridgegate, and contains some of the principal markets; the latter communicates with Bell Street, which enters it on the right, and forms the communication between it and the High Street. On the west the Candleriggs Street is connected with Wilson Street and Ingram Street, and terminates at a church called the Ram's Horn or North-West [completed in 1724 and replaced by a new building in 1824: it is said to have been called Ram's Horn because of a miracle St Mungo performed on its site in turning a stolen ram's head into stone]. Proceeding westward, the Trongate, after giving out different streets to the right and left, is crossed by a long street, leading from the river on the south to Ingram Street on the north. The southern part of this street is called the Stockwell; the northern part is called Glassford Street, leading to the middle of the newest buildings of the city. Westward from Stockwell and Glassford Streets, the principal street of the city, leading from east to west, once more changes its name, and is called Argyle Street. It gives off towards the right or north a variety of new streets, containing uncommonly elegant buildings, particularly Virginia Street, Millar Street, Queen Street, Buchanan Street. This last, as well as Queen Street, leads northward towards Port Dundas. The houses of Millar Street and Buchanan Street are inhabited by single families from top to bottom, and have been finished with uncommon care and elegance. On its western side, Argyle Street gives off a considerable number of streets towards the river, particularly Dunlop Street, Maxwell Street, and St Enoch's Square, containing very fine houses. Jamaica Street is the next on the same side, leading down to the quay called the Broomielaw; and opposite to Jamaica Street, on the north, is a street called Union Place, not finished, but which contains lofty and elegant buildings. Proceeding further west, many streets have been laid out, and a considerable number of buildings erected; but they can only be considered as suburbs of the city, terminating still further west in the populous suburbs called Anderston, Finniestown, &c. situated at the distance of about a mile and a half from the centre of the city.

On the northern side of Argyle Street and the Trongate are the buildings of the Extended Royalty or New Town of Glasgow. Of these the principal street is George Street, running from east to west parallel to Argyle Street, and crossing the High Street on the east, at some distance northward from the buildings of the University. Beyond the High Street, eastward, it is called Duke Street. Between George Street, Argyle Street, and the Trongate, the space is occupied by a succession of beautiful streets intersecting each other at right angles. Of these we have already mentioned Wilson Street, Great Glassford Street, Millar Street, Queen Street, Buchanan Street, and Ingram Street. Besides these, are Cochran Street, John Street, Glassford Street, George Square, Gordon Street, and Camperdown Place; in all of which the buildings vie with each other in the expensive and elegant manner in which they have been executed. To the northward of George Street various new streets have also been opened, under the names of Hanover Street, Frederick Street, Montrose Street, upon the declivity or slope of the ridge of the western part of which the Rottenrow stands.

It unfortunately happened that the rapid increase of the wealth of Glasgow was not entirely foreseen, and hence care was not taken, at a sufficiently early period, as in Edinburgh, to form one great plan of a new town from which the whole might have derived uniformity. Hence we are under the necessity, to avoid minuteness or confusion, of passing unnoticed a variety of short but elegant streets, formed upon such plans as the proprietors of the soil judged most advantageous to their interest.

Forsyth is clearly right to point to the difference between Edinburgh's New Town, product of a long-matured plan, and that of Glasgow, which developed unplanned. It is, none the less, true that the westward development of Glasgow, once the fashion of detached town mansions started by the Shawfield Mansion had caught on, developed in a grid pattern from the old High Street, although that pattern has often been obscured by subsequent developments. This gridiron development continued during the first three decades of the nineteenth century, and, to quote Colin McWilliam again, 'in the late 'thirties, when Edinburgh was still recovering from her Georgian exertions, Glasgow was developing and enriching the idea of the Georgian terrace'. The grid pattern stopped at Woodlands Hill in 1839, and in the plan of Glasgow in 1847 in James Pagan's *Sketches of the History of Glasgow* Woodlands can still be seen as quite clearly the end of the westward development.

Forsyth does not mention Sauchiehall Street, for the line of Sauchiehall ('willow meadow') was not yet built on, though it was shortly to become an elegant street much praised for its 'sylvan charms' and hailed in the 1830s as having long been 'the favourite promenade of the beauty and fashion of the city'. In 1820 it was halfway between the willow meadow and the fashionable promenade:

> This was then a quiet, pleasant road, far removed from the noise and bustle of the City, having here and there a few rustic cottages placed by the roadside, where refreshments could be got. These houses were very much frequented at holiday and other times by families and youths from the City, who travelled out to enjoy 'Curds and cream and fruits in their seasons', which were to be had there . . . Some years previous to this time (1820) it was the usual custom for genteel families residing in and around Stockwell Street to have their summer quarters out in this direction, and a little farther to the north, about the end of Dobbie's Loan.

Forsyth noted the special nature of Glaswegians' pride in their city:

> As the rise of Glasgow has been very rapid, its inhabitants have not yet entirely lost the sentiment usually found among those who reside in small towns, of a great fondness for their own town, and a patriotic zeal for its respectability, and for the frame of whatever is connected with it. Hence the people of Glasgow seem much more anxious than those of the more ancient city of Edinburgh, to exhibit to strangers their public buildings and the beauties of their city, and are much more anxious that it should obtain applause. When the enumeration of the people was going on under the population-act, while the inhabitants of more ancient towns were perfectly indifferent about the matter, and either suffered it to be conducted in the most slovenly way, or even concealed their numbers, to avoid the inconvenience of militia levies and other public burdens, the leading inhabitants of Glasgow displayed a very pointed anxiety that no defect in the enumeration of their people should take place, and that their town should be reputed extremely populous and extensive.

William Wordsworth and his sister Dorothy made a tour in Scotland in 1803, and Dorothy kept a lively journal during their travels. They arrived in Glasgow on 22 August and stayed at a 'quiet and tolerably cheap' inn, 'a new building', the Saracen's Head.

> Having dined, William and I walked to the post-office, and after much seeking found out a quiet timber-yard wherein to sit down and read our letter. We then walked a considerable time in the streets, which are perhaps as handsome as streets can be, which derive no particular effect from their situation in connexion with natural advantages, such as rivers, sea, or hills . . . One thing must strike every stranger in his first walk through Glasgow – an appearance of business and bustle, but no coaches or gentlemen's carriages; during all the time we walked in the streets I only saw three carriages, and these were travelling chaises. I also could not but observe a want of cleanliness in the appearance of the lower orders of the people, and a dulness in the dress and outside of the whole mass, as they moved along.

The next morning they walked to Glasgow Green and Dorothy recorded their impressions there before going on to talk about the shops:

> Walked to the bleaching ground, a large field bordering on the Clyde, the banks of which are perfectly flat, and the general face of the country is nearly so in the neighbourhood of Glasgow. This field, the whole summer through, is covered with women of all ages, children, and young girls spreading out their linen, and watching it while it bleaches. The scene must be very cheerful on a fine day, but it rained when we were there, and though there was linen spread out in all parts, and great numbers of women and girls were at work, yet there would have been many more on a fine day, and they would have appeared happy, instead of stupid and cheerless. In the middle of the field is a wash-house, whither the inhabitants of this large town, rich and poor, send or carry their linen to be washed. There are two very large rooms, with each a cistern in the middle for hot water; and all round the rooms are benches for the women to set their tubs upon. Both the rooms were crowded with washers; there might be a hundred, or two, or even three; for it is not easy to form an accurate notion of so great a number; however, the rooms were large, and they were both full. It was amusing to see so many women, arms, head, and face all in motion, all busy in an ordinary household employment, in which we are accustomed to see, at the most, only three or four women employed in one place. The women were very civil. I learnt from them the regulations of the house; but I have forgotten the parti-

Frontispiece by
George Cruikshank.

John Burnet's Italian
Gothic Stock
Exchange in
Buchanan Street
(1875). It retains its
original exterior but
has been re-structured
inside.

The Clyde seen from the Sailors' Home *c.* 1891

The Barony Church (1886–90) by James Burnet and J. L. Pearson, photographed some ten years after it was built.

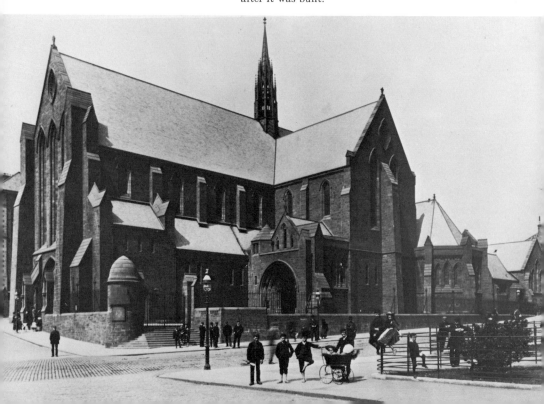

culars. The substance of them is, that 'so much' is to be paid for each tub of water, 'so much' for a tub, and the privilege of washing for a day, and, 'so much' to the general overlookers of the linen, when it is left to be bleached. An old man and woman have this office, who were walking about, two melancholy figures.

The shops at Glasgow are large, and like London shops, and we passed by the largest coffee-room I ever saw. You look across the piazza of the Exchange, and see to the end of the coffee-room, where there is a circular window, the width of the room. Perhaps there might be thirty gentlemen sitting on the circular bench of the window, each reading a newspaper. They had the appearance of figures in a fantoccine [fantoccini, puppet show], or men seen at the extremity of the opera-house, diminished into puppets.

One is struck, in reading the reminiscences of mid-nineteenth-century Glasgow writers, at the recurring expression of some kind of nostalgia for an old Glasgow that had been suppressed by the prosperity of the new. Old Peter Mackenzie, writing in 1865, recalled the shooting of partridges in Buchanan Street and '*hay stacks* standing up on the western side of Glassford Street, with the plum trees waving over the long brick wall near Robin Carrick's celebrated Bank, viz., the old "Ship Bank of Glasgow", now merged with others in the Union Bank of Scotland'. He comforts himself with thoughts of progress: 'But see now the busy hives of human beings in the said Buchanan Street! – the gorgeous shops – the displays of gold and silver plate – the pretty silken attires, fit for *Venus* herself, but shaming the worsted and home-spun linen of former times – with the delicious viands, of our Thynes, Forresters, and Fergusons, all redolent now of that street, with everything, in short, which wealth seeking for luxury can produce. There is, in fact, no other street like Buchanan Street, at this moment in Glasgow, save the Trongate and Argyle Street, to which, we protest, our old associations must ever cling.' It was Peter Mackenzie, too, who recalled seeing with his own eyes 'as many as twenty or thirty fine salmon taken out of that stream [the Clyde], by net and cobble, near the very steps of the stairs where the Custom House of Glasgow presently stands; while further down the river, at Finlaystone – nearly opposite Dumbarton Castle – we have also taken from the *stake-nets*, which then dotted the Clyde in that quarter, as many as one hundred and twenty fine clean salmon, on a Monday morning.'

Robert Reid, who wrote on the history of Glasgow under the pen-name 'Senex', recalled in 1843 what he had been told in his youth by his grandmother, born in 1715:

I   115

In speaking of Candleriggs Street, the old lady mentioned that, in her younger days, it was a corn field let in Riggs; that at the northern extremity of this field (near to the present site of St David's church [the same as the Ramshorn church]) there stood a candle work, to which a foot-path led to the Trongate; but the main entry was from the High street by Canon street . . .

The ground between the Candleriggs and Cowlone (Queen street) formerly consisted of a long range of narrow stripes of back garden ground, attached to the front properties in Trongate and Argyle streets . . . The different stripes of back garden ground, betwixt Candleriggs and Queen street, gradually came to be formed into streets running northward from Trongate and Argyle streets to Ingram street . . .

The Glasgow remembered by Robert Reid's grandmother was very different from that revealed by the investigations of the local statistician James Cleland, Superintendent of Public Works, in 1831. By this time Glasgow was the third largest city in the United Kingdom, exceeded only by London and Manchester. Out of a total population of 202,426 and an occupied population of about 94,500 Cleland found that no fewer than 30,600 were engaged in textile manufacture, and of these a high proportion were still hand-loom weavers in spite of the growing number of machine minders. 27,300 were engaged in various trades, with 8,200 in the clothing trades (tailors, clothiers, hatters, haberdashers, mercers, drapers, hosiers, glovers, milliners, shoemakers, &c.); 6,400 in trades associated with food and drink (grocers and victuallers, greengrocers, bakers, butchers and fishmongers, distillers, brewers, &c.); 5,900 in construction trades; 3,300 in metal trades; 3,500 in other miscellaneous trades (including compositors and printers, potters and glass-cutters, booksellers and binders, coopers and turners, coachmakers and wheelwrights, jewellers and clockmakers, flaxdressers and rope-makers). There were 3,800 professional people (mostly clergy, professors, teachers and students, but including 500 surgeons, druggists and chemists); 2,200 in the mercantile world as merchants, bankers, agents and accountants; 1,800 clerks and commercial travellers. T. C. Smout, who has conveniently tabulated the results of Cleland's researches, has noted that 'the very considerable number of people grouped under "trades" suggests something of the abiding vitality and strength of the traditional occupations of the city, though not by any means all were carried on in a perfectly traditional way'. Smout points out that 'many of the 2,900 people in the drink trade were wage earners in the city's distilleries and breweries, and no longer merely publicans and home-brewers as their ancestors would have been. Hardly any of the 3,100 milliners and seamstresses were tradespeople in the old sense: they were all out-workers making up hats and clothes at very low piece-rates for small independent capitalists. The same must have been true of many of the tailors and shoemakers, working under conditions more akin to the sweatshop than the guild.' It would appear that there was roughly only one shop to every seven or eight 'tradesmen', a term which became steadily down-graded, while 'the expression "shopkeeper" was beginning to be used instead to denote the minority that would come to own a shop'.

Between 1783 and 1791 over 417 children per thousand in Glasgow died before they reached the age of two and over 119,000 died between the ages of five and ten. Vaccination against smallpox, introduced in England by Edward Jenner in 1796 and quickly brought to Scotland, made a great difference. Between 1793 and 1802 thirty-six per cent of the deaths of Glasgow children were attributable to smallpox, and between 1803 and 1812 the percentage fell to nine. Between 1783 and 1800 nineteen per cent of all deaths in Glasgow were due to smallpox, but the percentage fell to four between 1807 and 1812 and it was under two between 1813 and 1819. The city introduced free vaccination for children in 1801 and by 1822 25,000 children had been vaccinated. In spite of the rise of smallpox deaths in the 1830s as a result of the immigration of unvaccinated children the disease became increasingly unimportant as a significant cause of death after 1800 and it may well be that the acceleration of Glasgow's rate of population growth between 1801 and 1821 was the simple result of the decline of the threat from smallpox. But the decline of smallpox often meant that children survived only to succumb a few years later to other diseases. Measles, for example, accounted for one per cent of deaths in Glasgow between 1783 and 1788 but for over ten per cent between 1807 and 1812; diphtheria ('croup') was a terrible killer of children; and tuberculosis was common among young industrial workers in the early years of the nineteenth century. Cleland calculated that in 1821 half the population still died under the age of ten, which was virtually no improvement on the figures for 1783–91 as given in the Statistical Account in 1793.

For the middle classes, however, life grew steadily more comfortable as the eighteenth century gave way to the nineteenth. John Strang, looking back in 1855 on the years 1795 to 1815, recorded his approval of social changes and documented the improvements that took place in the period:

The *Northern Looking Glass*, in the 1820s, depicts a perennial topic

As a leading improvement, it may be stated, that every class lived
in a better house, and, what is more, had their houses better furnished than formerly. Receptions in bed-rooms, by any pretending to
keep company, were abandoned entirely; while dinner parties, to
which ladies were invited, became more frequent. The drawing-room
ceased to be disgraced, as it was wont too frequently to be, with the
presence of intoxicated men; nor were such any longer seen stagger-
ing from the dining-room, with 'tongues unable to take up the
cumbrous word', when called upon by the hostess to declare whether
they preferred tea or coffee! . . . If we would indeed contrast the
drinking socialities of the close of the last century with those which
prevailed after the peace purchased by Waterloo, the improvement
would appear most striking. Instead of the great mass of the shopkeepers and other tradesmen of the City . . . invariably settling their
business matters over forenoon potations, the thing became almost
unknown, or was at least outwardly unpractised; while the open

exhibition of intemperance on the part of men in respectable stations
. . . was not only abandoned, but, if met with, was looked upon as an
offence against good manners, and was invariably visited by certain
banishment from all reputable society.

The softening of middle-class manners, symbolized by the decline of
hard drinking and swearing and, as Strang put it, the substitution of
the pianoforte for the punchbowl in evening entertainment, was a
feature of urban society all over Britain during this period. But
Glasgow was to develop its own special problem of excessive drinking, once it ceased to be an accepted middle- and upper-class habit
and became a feature of certain areas of working-class life and a
chief comforter of the hopeless. This is the concern of a later chapter;
but here it might be noted, as a formal recognition that drunkenness
or catering for it was no longer acceptable among the respectable,
that on 12 November 1812 the Town Council of Glasgow resolved
that 'no council-officer, town-officer, water-officer, harbour-master,
or officer connected with the Corporation, shall, in future, be allowed
to keep a tavern or public-house.'

CHAPTER 10

Reform

BEFORE the Union of 1707 Glasgow was represented in the Scottish Parliament by a member elected by the Town Council of the city, always a member of the Town Council and often the Provost. The first recorded member for Glasgow in the Scottish Parliament was Provost Andrew Hamilton, elected in 1546. Between the Union and the Scottish Reform Act of 1832 Glasgow itself sent no members to the House of Commons, but joined with the three royal burghs of Rutherglen, Renfrew and Dumbarton that chose the Member of Parliament for the Clyde burghs. Thus a total of some one hundred and twenty people chose between them four delegates who in turn chose their Member of Parliament, as Peter Mackenzie indignantly put it, 'by the mere puffs of their own four mouths'. The actual choice of the member took place in each of the four burghs in rotation, and in the case of a two–two split among the delegates the delegate representing the host burgh had a casting vote. Peter Mackenzie could not restrain his emotion on looking back to those unreformed days:

> Is not that on the face of it a rich farce, viz., that in those olden times the great city of Glasgow could be kicked and cuffed by the Dumbarton delegate and the Renfrew delegate, with perfect impunity, they dwelling in burghs, with not more than a population of some 5000 souls, whereas Glasgow, independent of Rutherglen, could swallow them all up in other respects fifty times over. We have no hesitation whatever in saying – and we could prove it if necessary – that the grossest bribery and corruption took place to secure the all-important *casting vote* of that one delegate. Fortunes were won and lost by it. Drinking and carousing went on to an extent hardly credible.

The General Election of August 1830 provided a characteristic example of how things were done before the Reform Act. The two candidates for the Clyde burghs were Archibald Campbell of

Blythswood, 'a decided and well-known Tory', who had the support of Renfrew and Dumbarton, and Kirkman Finlay, a former Provost of Glasgow, who relied on Glasgow support as well as on the support of the Whiggish burgh of Rutherglen. Both men had previously represented the constituency, and Campbell was the member when the dissolution of Parliament took place in June 1830. Glasgow Town Council was equally divided between choosing a delegate who favoured Campbell and choosing one who favoured Finlay. Alexander Garden, the Provost, insisted that as Provost he had a casting vote, and gave it for himself as a Campbell supporter, despite the protest of Robert Dalglish (who was to succeed him as Provost) who denied that the Provost had the right to give a casting vote. It was Glasgow's turn to host the election, which took place in the Justiciary Court House facing Glasgow Green (built by William Stark in 1807–14 and remodelled by J. H. Craigie in 1910–13). The four delegates proceeded to vote: Glasgow, represented by Provost Garden, voted for Campbell; then Dumbarton for Finlay; then Renfrew for Campbell; finally Rutherglen for Finlay. Garden, representing the host burgh, then gave his casting vote for Campbell. But Bailie Robertson of Glasgow came forward and, protesting that he and not Garden was the legal representative of Glasgow Town Council, gave his vote for Finlay. Uproar ensued, and at one stage it was suggested that the names of both candidates be written on the back of the election writ, leaving the House of Commons to decide which one they wanted. But eventually the Town Clerks ruled that Provost Garden did have a legal casting vote, so his status as Glasgow's delegate was confirmed and Campbell was therefore elected. Kirkman Finlay presented a petition to the House of Commons against Campbell's election, but it was unsuccessful. On 23 August 1830 'Mr. Campbell invited his friends and supporters to a splendid banquet in the Black Bull Ball Room, while Mr. Finlay entertained his in the Tontine Hotel.'

It is no wonder that enthusiasm for electoral reform mounted rapidly, and was especially violent throughout 1831 when the English Reform Bill was a central issue at Westminster. Public meetings and processions were held in the Town Hall, the Trades Hall, Glasgow Green and in the streets of the city: the citizens followed with eager excitement the progress of the Reform Bill through Parliament, celebrating its passing the House of Commons and demonstrating against its defeat in the Lords. In March 1831 the second reading of the Reform Bill was carried in the Commons, and when news of this reached Glasgow a general illumination of the city was ordered. The enthusiasm for the illumination was such that

Glasgow was cleaned out of candles and candlesticks in spite of their being sold at greatly inflated prices.* But the Bill was then defeated in committee and the Government resigned and appealed to the country. The ensuing General Election brought a great majority for the Whig Government and for Reform, and the Bill passed the Commons in September, only to be rejected by the Lords in October. When the Lords rejected the Bill a second time in May 1832 the Government again resigned, but Wellington was unable to form a Government for the Tories and on 15 May Lord Grey was back in office and, with King William IV exerting his influence on the peers, the Reform Bill became law on 4 June. Three weeks later, the Scottish Reform Bill – largely the work of Henry Cockburn, Francis Jeffrey and T. F. Kennedy of Dunure, the Whig member for Ayr Burghs – was read a third time and on 17 July 1832 it received the royal assent.

The election of May 1831, which returned a large majority for the Whig Government and for reform, was the last held under the old system, and as far as the Clyde burghs were concerned it was in some ways the most absurd. As Campbell of Blythswood had voted against the Reform Bill, Kirkman Finlay, who was mildly in support of it, was pretty sure that this time he would win. But a third candidate entered the field – Joseph Dixon, son of the Provost of Dumbarton and member of the wealthy ironworks and coal-mining family, was put forward by his father as a whole-hearted supporter of electoral reform beside whom Finlay's moderate and hesitant support was considered faint-hearted. But Finlay was sure of Glasgow, and he thought he was sure of Rutherglen until he discovered that Dixon's agents had been conducting highly successful propaganda there and had secured pledges to support Dixon from fourteen out of the eighteen Town Councillors. Finlay then sent his agents to Rutherglen to try and persuade the fourteen to change their minds: all sorts of promises were made and the councillors' wives were tempted with visions of 'fine new gowns and silken garments' (in Mackenzie's phrase). Alarmed and disturbed at the continual pressure brought to bear on them by Finlay's agents, the fourteen Rutherglen councillors decided to withdraw secretly to Dumbarton. They rowed across Loch Lomond from Luss to Rowerdennan and then proceeded to hold a convivial meeting at the top of Ben Lomond in which they renewed their pledges to the Dixon

---

*The illuminations also gave a boost to the increasing use of gas in Glasgow for lighting purposes. There were many extra orders for 'jetts and jettees'. Provost Dalglish's house in St Vincent Place had 3,000 'gas jettees' in front, with those in the centre arranged to spell out the motto 'Let Glasgow Flourish'.

interest. They then proceeded to take a leisurely trip through that corner of Scotland, visiting Tarbert, Arrochar and Helensburgh, then going on to Drymen, Aberfoyle and Stirling. They stayed at the best inns and indulged themselves in unlimited food and drink, all at the expense of Provost Jacob Dixon of Dumbarton, their candidate's father, who was determined to keep the Rutherglen councillors in a proper frame of mind. Meanwhile, Kirkman Finlay and his agents sought in vain to find the councillors in order to renew their persuasions.

The fourteen councillors were still absent from Rutherglen when the day arrived for the burgh to choose its delegate. The meeting was arranged for seven o'clock in the evening, and at six o'clock the wandering councillors had still not arrived. As the clock moved on towards seven Finlay and his agents and friends began to believe that Providence had contrived to save them. Provost John Gray of Rutherglen, a Finlay supporter, was prepared to convene the meeting with the rump of councillors, all Finlay supporters, alone present, when, on the very verge of seven o'clock, the errant fourteen arrived with music and drums from a splendid feast to which they had been entertained by William Dixon of Govanhill, a relative of Joseph Dixon. With them were hundreds of miners from the Dixon coalmines who were assembled to demonstrate for Dixon. Dixon's election was now assured: he had Rutherglen and Dumbarton, and since it was Dumbarton's turn to host the election this time, he had the casting vote of Dumbarton's Dixon-committed delegate. So on 23 May 1831, Joseph Dixon was duly declared the Member of Parliament for the Clyde burghs (sometimes also known as the Glasgow group of burghs). Finlay, who had by now heard of the strange goings-on on the top of Ben Lomond and elsewhere, petitioned Parliament asking for the unseating of Dixon on the grounds of bribery and corruption. A committee of the House of Commons heard the petition and examined witnesses in an attempt to discover the truth. Among the witnesses were some of the Rutherglen councillors, whose account of their somewhat alcoholic meeting on the top of Ben Lomond and of their subsequent festivities convulsed the committee. Joseph Dixon admitted that his father had paid for these festivities, but argued that this was a filial duty on his father's part which it would have been improper for him to refuse. Somewhat unexpectedly, the committee dismissed Finlay's petition and confirmed Dixon in his seat.

The coronation of William IV and Queen Adelaide took place on 8 September 1831, and, as the King was known to be in favour of electoral reform, Glasgow celebrated with a vast procession representing all the trades of the city, each walking 'with their count-less emblems, flags, and banners, through the principal streets and the Green of Glasgow, where, with one heart and voice, they set up their shouts for Reform – the Bill, the whole Bill, and nothing but the Bill'. Peter Mackenzie, whose words these are, was present, and made a note of the order in which the procession moved: first the carters, to clear the streets and lead the way; then the goldsmiths and watchmakers; then the brush makers; then the brewers; then the iron moulders; and so on down the ranks of glass makers, ship-wrights, coopers, tailors, plasterers, potters, hammermen, masons, warehousemen and warpers, cork-cutters, cloth-lappers, ropemakers and flax dressers, framework knitters, bricklayers, shoemakers, bakers, slaters, cabinet and pianoforte makers, dyers, labourers and quarriers, carvers and gilders, letterpress printers, bookbinders, engineers, smiths, calico printers and fleshers. The fleshers (butchers) were preceded by a large live ox, bearing on its front a board with the words 'I am Reformed – the patriotic spirit roused; all dangers scorn, and take corruption's monster by the horns'. Most of the other groups carried banners and emblems with slogans in favour of reform. The same evening, adds Mackenzie, 'the Magistrates dined together, and contributed to a splendid display of fire-works on the Green – with blue and red flames, sky rockets and other things – which reflected most amazingly on the dense mass of upturned human faces "glowering at them" – not less than eighty or ninety thousand people – and every one from the oldest to the youngest more delighted than another. Not so much as a black eye or a broken head was visible in Glasgow that day or that night.'

A more sophisticated route to reform was that chosen by the Glasgow Political Union, founded at a public meeting in the Trades' Hall on 16 November 1831 and meeting subsequently almost weekly at the Lyceum Rooms. The Union corresponded with important political figures in England and transmitted a petition in favour of reform to the House of Lords through the Duke of Hamilton. It ceased to exist after the Reform Bill was finally passed.

With the passing of the Scottish Reform Bill the Town Councils of the Scottish burghs were deprived of their electoral privileges and the franchise was conferred on householders occupying premises with an annual rental value of at least £10. Glasgow, like Edinburgh, was given two seats. 7,024 Glasgow electors registered under the new Act, as opposed to the thirty-three Town Councillors who had previously the sole power to choose a delegate to vote along with the delegates of the other burghs for a single member. The first election under the reformed system took place in December 1832, with two days allowed for voting. There were six candidates, all professing support for the Reform Act, and each elector had two votes. Joseph Dixon, the previous member for Clyde burghs, came bottom of the poll with 995 votes. The elected members were James Ewing of Strathleven, Provost of Glasgow, who topped the poll with 3,214 votes, and James Oswald of Shieldhall, who came second with 2,838. The result was part of the triumph of the Whigs and the rout of the Tories throughout the Scottish burghs, even though the principles of the successful members were never very clearly defined in the excited and confused debates that preceded the election. John Strang, who took part in the election, later recalled the atmosphere in which it was conducted:

> In consequence of the great disunion which . . . took place among the constituency, and the great ignorance which prevailed among the electors and their leaders on matters connected with an election where each had a double vote, it soon became absolutely impossible, amid the canvassing of hostile committees, to know, until the very last hour, what was the real will of the constituency; or to speculate, with any degree of probability, to whom, in the contest for split votes, the majority would ultimately fall. In this state of matters, it may be easily conceived into what a political turmoil the whole town was thrown for nearly six months. While candidates, with their various leading supporters, were holding district and central meetings without end or even object, and there declaring everything in favour of themselves, and everything they could tell or imagine against their opponents, there was at the same hour scarcely a social circle into which one might enter, where the demon of political discord was not evoked by some untoward allusion in regard to one or other of the Parliamentary aspirants.

Municipal reform followed hard on national electoral reform. Reform of the burghs had been agitated since 1784, when delegates from the Scottish burghs met in Edinburgh to consider appropriate measures, but the French Revolution put an end to further developments. The matter was not raised again until 1818, and in 1819 Lord Archibald Hamilton, member for Lanarkshire, managed to obtain a committee of inquiry into the condition of the Scottish burghs. Its report in 1822 showed the existence of many abuses, of which the primary one was the self-election of magistrates, but a Tory government consistently refused to take action. Finally, in March 1833 Francis Jeffrey, now Lord Advocate, introduced into the Reform Parliament proposals for Scottish burgh reform and on 28 August Parliament voted a complex measure, making different provisions for burghs with different constitutions, but in general granting to the burgesses the right to elect their own Town Councils. All those who had a vote in a parliamentary election in royal burghs were also given a municipal vote. Glasgow was divided into five wards, each with six representatives: these, together with a representative each from the Merchants' and Trades' Houses, made the Council number thirty-two. The first Glasgow municipal election under this system took place in November 1833.

These reforms entrenched middle-class interests in Scottish cities and satisfied the merchants, industrialists and shopkeepers. But the social picture was changing with extraordinary rapidity, and other needs were left increasingly unsatisfied. Glasgow's population continued to grow apace, partly as a result of immigration from Ireland. It has been calculated that from about 1820 a large number of the city's new residents were Irish-born: by 1841 the Irish-born constituted five per cent of Scotland's population, most of these being concentrated in Glasgow and the western coalfields, with others in Edinburgh and Dundee. The Irish provided heavy labour for all kinds of construction work, notably canals and later railways, and they also provided a reserve of cheap labour which employers could use to break strikes. Their presence caused resentment in the Lanarkshire coalfields and also in the countryside where they tended to replace native seasonal workers. The fact that the Irish were Roman Catholics while Glasgow was traditionally a Whig Presbyterian city produced further tensions that were to play a considerable part in the subsequent social history of the city.

Parliamentary and burgh reform had little relevance to these and similar problems, and the triumphant Whigs who rejoiced in the belief that the reforms of 1832 and 1833 represented a happy solution of Scotland's social and political problems were deluding themselves, none more so than in Glasgow. Henry Cockburn, who was jointly responsible for drafting the Scottish Reform Bill, looked forward to its consequences as a Scottish Millennium. But at the same time he was uneasily aware that the triumph of the Whigs, his party, would turn them into the defenders of the *status quo* against a new party of reform. In August 1832 he wrote triumphantly in his Journal: 'The regeneration of Scotland is now secured! Our Reform Bill has become law. . . . Nobody who did not see it could believe the orderly joy with which the people have received their emancipation, or the judgment with which they seem inclined to use it.' But later in the same paragraph he predicted: 'In a few years the Whigs will be the Tories, and the Radicals the Whigs.' Something like this in fact happened in Glasgow, for to the majority of those who walked in the great coronation procession of 8 September 1831 displaying their banners in support of Reform, neither parliamentary nor burgh reform was to make the slightest difference. It took some time for people to realize this. When they did, the political pattern in Glasgow changed.

The Price of Progress

As the nineteenth century progressed, the population of Glasgow expanded at an unprecedented rate. Indeed, the urban population of the whole Clyde basin increased faster during this century than anywhere else in Britain. In 1801 Glasgow contained five per cent of the population of Scotland, and London contained ten per cent of the population of England and Wales; by 1851 Glasgow contained twelve per cent of the population of Scotland compared with London's thirteen per cent of the population of England and Wales. By 1931 the percentages were twenty-two and eleven respectively.

This rapid increase produced the inevitable social consequences. Already in 1839 a report to Parliament on housing in Great Britain commented vividly on the overcrowding and squalor in some parts of the city. 'I have seen human degradation in some of the worst places, both in England and abroad, but I did not believe until I had visited the wynds of Glasgow that so large an amount of filth, crime, misery and disease existed in one spot in any civilized country.' Edwin Chadwick's *Report on the Sanitary Condition of the Labouring Population of Great Britain*, 1842, described Glasgow as 'possibly the filthiest and unhealthiest of all the British towns of this period'. 'In the courts of Argyle Street there were no privies or drains, and the dung heaps received all the filth which the swarms of wretched inhabitants could give. . . . The picture is so shocking that without ocular proof one would be disposed to doubt the possibility of the facts.' Such conditions pushed up infant mortality rates: in 1850 one half of all the children born in Glasgow died before their fifth birthday (as compared with one third for Paris, which was regarded as having a bad record in public health). While in England, stimulated by Chadwick, reformers concentrated on improving sanitary conditions in order to reduce disease, in Scotland reformers concentrated on relieving actual poverty rather than on improving the hygiene, which ensured that poverty bred such diseases as cholera and typhus which could and did spread to the elegant suburbs. It was not until 1855, after twenty years of opposition by private interests, that an Act of Parliament was passed allowing Glasgow to provide for its citizens an adequate water supply from Loch Katrine. The scheme took four years to complete, and involved not only thirty-four miles of tunnelling and the forming of a reservoir at Mugdock near Milngavie but also the buying out of landowners and the acquiring of water rights; the total cost was one and a half million pounds. It provided Glasgow with fifty million gallons of water a day. Queen Victoria, who was staying at Balmoral at the time of the scheme's completion, agreed to perform the opening ceremony, which she duly did on 14 October 1859. The new water supply naturally raised the standard of hygiene in the city, but as it was not immediately accompanied by any significant measures to improve public health, squalor and disease continued to take their toll.

The conditions described by J. C. Symons in 1839 were not easily improved:

> . . . In the lower lodging-houses [of the wynds of Glasgow], ten, twelve and sometimes twenty persons, of both sexes, and all ages, sleep promiscuously on the floor, in different degrees of nakedness. These places are generally, as regards dirt, damp, and decay, such as no person of common humanity . . . would stable his horse in . . . The population of all these districts is probably 30,000; it certainly exceeds 20,000; they consist in great proportion of the Irish and of Highlanders. Many of the younger girls, and there are a multitude of them who frequent these places, appear to have been driven there from sheer want, and apply to Captain Muller, (head of the Glasgow police), to be rescued from misery, in great numbers. No efficient aid can be afforded them under existing institutions, and hundreds in a year become inured to crime, and pass through the rapid career of prostitution, drunkenness, and disease, to an early grave.

Whisky was a readily available comfort. Ever since the Distillery Act of 1823 – aimed primarily at eliminating illicit distilling, and in the process reducing the duty on whisky – legal whisky had been relatively cheap (from 1825 duty was 2s. 10d. on the newly introduced imperial gallon) and there was still a lot of illicit whisky about at even lower prices. Dr John Dunlop, a strong campaigner for teetotalism, estimated that over £450,000 was spent annually on drink in Glasgow in the early 1830s and that this represented a high proportion of the wages of the lower paid. Reformers took note of the association of drink and squalor, of the ruining of families by the ready granting of credit by licensed grocers, of the decline in church-going and in moral standards as a result of excessive drinking, and a movement grew up advocating total abstinence from alcoholic drinks. A total abstinence society had been formed in Glasgow as early as 1829, as a result of Dr Dunlop's active propagandizing. One branch of the Chartist movement advocated total abstinence as a means of strengthening the character and power of working men: a Chartist total abstinence society was formed in Greenock in January 1840 while on 1 May at their monthly meeting the directors and delegates of the Lanarkshire Universal Suffrage Association recorded their approval in principle of total abstinence. Glasgow Chartists supported temperance coffee-houses which sprang up in the city.

There was a depression in the second half of the 1820s followed by a boom which continued until the late 1830s, followed in turn by a bad ten years after which came a period of steady expansion that lasted until the late 1870s. It soon became clear that the electoral reform of 1832, so enthusiastically supported by Glasgow workers, had done them no good at all. The result was a loss of faith in Whig reforms and in middle-class radicalism by the still unenfranchised working class. In the middle 1830s demonstrations took place at Glasgow Green and elsewhere in the city, and the National Radical Association was formed. In 1837 a strike of cotton spinners, protest-ing against the reduction of wages and of the numbers of those employed as a result of a temporary commercial crisis which reduced the price of manufactured goods by nearly a half, lasted fourteen weeks in a mood of great bitterness. Riots took place, mills were wrecked and one man was shot in Anderston. Five of the ringleaders were prosecuted at the High Court of Justiciary for illegal combina-tion, assault, fire-raising and murder, and four were found guilty and sentenced to seven years' transportation. All this encouraged support in Glasgow for the People's Charter, which was originally drawn up in 1838 by the London Working Men's Association to demand annual parliaments, universal male suffrage, equal electoral districts, the removal of the property qualification for membership of Parlia-ment, the secret ballot, and the payment of Members of Parliament.

The development of a radical press and of political and trade unions are features of Glasgow life in the immediate post-Reform Act period of disillusionment. The *Liberator* was founded by the Glasgow trades in November 1832 and for the next six years voiced the views of the Radicals and the trade unionists. The Glasgow Chartist weekly, the *Scottish Patriot*, first appeared on 6 July 1839. Another weekly, the *Chartist Circular*, was financed by George Ross, a well-to-do Glasgow shoemaker, and first appeared on 28 September

A typical back court at Calton, photographed in 1890 just before the area was re-developed. These two-storey houses of brick and pantiles from the local potteries were built between 1790 and 1810.

A common sight: taking the temperance pledge on Glasgow Green c. 1910, from the collection of the anarchist leader Guy Aldred. Both religious and political reformers were involved in the movement.

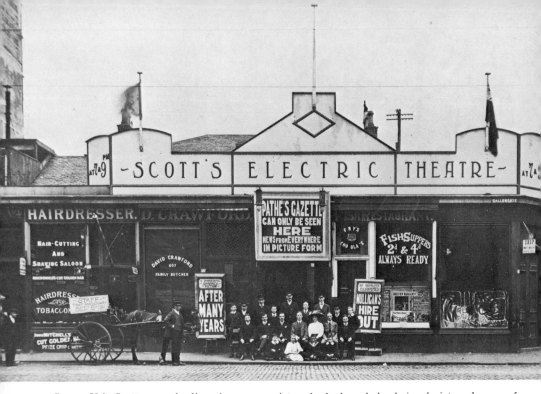

George Urie Scott was a leading cinema proprietor; he had a whole chain of picture houses of which this was one of the first. By 1917 there were well over 100 cinemas in the city.

Glasgow Corporation took over the running of the trams from a private company, in 1894.

1839. These were only some of the many indications of the important political force Chartism had become in Glasgow and in Scotland generally by 1839.

Glasgow Chartists were well represented at the General Confederation of the Industrial Classes which met in London in February 1839, and when a deputation from the adjourned Convention toured Scotland the following June a large Chartist demonstration took place on Glasgow Green. This was followed by the foundation of the *Scottish Patriot* whose owner and editor, Robert Malcolm, already ran the *Scots Times*, 1825–41, which, while not specifically Chartist, was sympathetic to the cause. (Glasgow had pioneered earlier in the century newspapers advocating liberal causes. The *Glasgow Chronicle* was founded in 1811, 'the first devoted advocate of liberal opinions in the west of Scotland', as John Strang called it, and this was followed by the *Free Press* and others. The *Glasgow Argus*, not a Chartist paper but a valuable source for the details of Chartist activity in Glasgow, was founded in 1833.) The Glasgow Universal Suffrage Association was formed at the end of August 1838. Chartist sabbath services were encouraged by this Association, which had its Preaching Committee, and there was even a plan to collect a thousand Chartists to form a Church with twenty-four elders and a preacher who would be, in the words of the *Chartist Circular* of 21 March 1840, 'an honest, wise, intelligent, temperate, prudent, zealous and well-educated Chartist . . . duly trained in religion, politics and philosophy'. Although this Utopian ideal was never realized, at least four Chartist churches were established in Glasgow, emphasizing the social and humanitarian aspects of Christianity and endeavouring to wean the working classes away from the 'pie in the sky' attitude to religion so often presented to them by both the Established and Dissenting Churches. Church of Scotland ministers were mostly strongly against Chartism; the Rev. Patrick Brewster, who held second charge of Paisley Abbey, was an eloquent Chartist who took the side of moral force in the inter-Chartist dispute between advocates of moral force only and those who believed in the use of physical force if necessary, and he had a stormy relationship with his colleagues of the Established Church. After the decline of Chartism the Chartist Churches disappeared, some of their elements being absorbed in the Free Church that emerged after the Disruption of 1843.

By 1840 the Glasgow Chartists had become a powerful force in the city, no longer content with organizing petitions but (in spite of internal dissensions and differences of opinion on such matters as how far they should be actively associated with the movement for repeal of the Corn Laws) confronting the middle classes with independence and confidence. Indeed, Peter Mackenzie, who had been so ardent in support of the Reform Bill of 1832, denounced them in panic as 'the veriest pests of society' and demanded their summary imprisonment. A Chartist anniversary meeting on Glasgow Green on 21 May 1840 was followed by a massive demonstration on the Green on Monday 21 September, with eighteen trade unions marching in procession with the upper ward of Renfrewshire and twenty-two districts of Glasgow. The *Scots Times* hailed the demonstration as proof of the revival of the 'old Radical spirit' and exclaimed: 'Chartism is supreme in Glasgow – Monday has settled that.'

The Chartist leader Feargus O'Connor toured Scotland in October and November 1841 and presided over a huge demonstration on Glasgow Green on 11 October. This was followed by a soirée attended by 3,000 people, where a sister of James Moir, the Glasgow Chartist leader, presented O'Connor with a diamond ring from the female Chartists of Glasgow. This was followed by (in O'Connor's words) 'a week of agitation such as I have never experienced in the course of my life'. O'Connor was back in Glasgow again in January 1842, but by now he had clearly emerged as the leader of one faction only, concentrating his energies on the National Petition while others, including Brewster, wished to associate the movement with Corn Law Repeal and other political questions. There were other causes of dispute, but a severe commercial depression beginning in the latter part of 1841 and continuing throughout 1842 dealt powerful blows to the movement by destroying the financial position of the Chartist press as well as by displaying the movement's impotence in the face of unemployment and hunger. The unemployed assembled in large numbers on Glasgow Green to demand relief, and there was a strike of colliers and iron miners in Lanarkshire and elsewhere. A meeting of Glasgow Chartists on 22 August 1842 to petition the Queen 'to recall Parliament to enact measures to ensure the permanent tranquillity of the country' was poorly attended and only gave further evidence of Chartist powerlessness. But the Chartists did their best. They organized meetings in Glasgow to draw attention to the plight of the unemployed and criticized the unsatisfactory administration of poor relief on the city. (Poor law reform was now being widely discussed in Scotland, and some Chartists directed their energies towards this question.) Chartists' churches took up collections for the relief of the distressed. In February 1843 there were an estimated 7,529 unemployed in Glasgow and the suburbs and 18,516 in a state of helpless destitution.

The economic position improved in the summer of 1843, and the Glasgow Chartists reverted to quarrelling on such issues as whether they should concentrate wholly on the National Charter or join the Anti-Corn Law agitation. But increased unemployment at the end of 1847 and in 1848 brought renewed misery and poverty and revived Chartist activity. 'The new year is ushered in, not amidst mirth and gladness, but with gloom and fearful foreboding,' wrote the *Glasgow Examiner* at the beginning of 1847, and went on to express a foreboding that it would be a year 'in which the inhabitants of the wealthiest and most powerful nation which was ever existed were on the borders of starvation'. By 1848 the situation was even worse. In February there were 13,000 to 15,000 unemployed in Glasgow, while the power-loom workers were on strike in protest against wage reductions of between seventeen and twenty-eight per cent. Once again masses of unemployed demonstrated on Glasgow Green, and these were less political demonstrations than simply cries of protest and appeals for help.

The demonstration of 6 March was the most serious. A large crowd collected on Glasgow Green, claiming that they were starving, and from there proceeded to march through the main streets of the city, entering and looting shops as they went. The police were unable to cope, and the military were called in to disperse the rioters. However, they gathered again the following day in the East End, and it took the joint efforts of the police and the militia to disperse them – but not before the militia had fired into the crowd, killing six and wounding several others, some of them innocent bystanders. Sixty-four people were arrested after the riots, and twenty were convicted and sentenced. In sentencing George Smith to eighteen years' transportation for mobbing, rioting and theft, Lord Medwyn expressed the hope that it would be 'a sufficient warning to the operative classes of this great city, whenever there occurs any depression in trade, and a consequent failure of employment, and the distress which accompanies such a state of things, that they should not listen to the bad advice of designing men, preaching to them about their rights'. They should, he added, trust to the benevolence of the rich, which 'they should receive thankfully and gratefully, patiently enduring what is so inevitable, till the state of trade again admits of their full employment'. Whatever educational effect the Chartists in Glasgow had had, clearly none of it had rubbed off on Lord Medwyn.

£7,000 worth of damage was done, for which the ratepayers were assessed. Ironically, both the casualties and the amount of damage done were far exceeded in October of the following year, when fourteen people died and £15,000 worth of damage was done in a fire that destroyed Wilson and Son's sugar house in Alston Street (which later became part of the site of Central Station). There was even greater loss of life on 17 February 1849 when a false cry of fire at the Theatre Royal in Dunlop Street produced a stampede in which sixty-five people were trampled to death and many injured.

On the arrest of two Chartist printers in Glasgow on 11 April 1848, following their publication the previous day of a poster entitled 'THREATENED REVOLUTION IN LONDON', there was a packed Chartist meeting in the City Hall on 12 April to protest against the 'unconstitutional infringement of liberties' involved in the proposed Sedition Bill. On 17 April a huge crowd mustered at a Chartist demonstration on Glasgow Green, the numbers swollen by the fine weather, and marched through the Green (they were not allowed to go through the streets) with a police escort and bands playing, displaying banners reading PEACE, LAW, ORDER; LIBERTY, EQUALITY, FRATERNITY; and THE CHARTER AND REPEAL. But it was little more than shadow-boxing. James Moir, who took the chair when the speeches came to be made, thanked Captain Miller of the police for his courtesy and, in the words of the *Glasgow Herald,* the 'best order and feeling was shown throughout the proceedings'. A demonstration on Glasgow Green on 10 June brought out something over 6,000 people, but was deemed a failure: by the time of the actual meeting and speeches, it was calculated that there were more police than Chartists present. Thereafter the Chartist movement declined rapidly.

Feargus O'Connor was in Scotland again in 1850, trying to revive the movement, and attended a riotous meeting in the Glasgow City Hall in June, when divisions between different factions brought about such bitter controversy that the police had to assist in dissolving the meeting. Economic conditions improved in the 1850s, with many unemployed Glaswegians emigrating (sometimes under assisted schemes) to America and the colonies and those that remained enjoying the advantages of industrial expansion on Clydeside. But with continuing acute poverty in the city, there were many protests against a system of poor relief that denied assistance to the able-bodied and their families. The Chartist movement as such, however, was not involved; it had now been superseded by or subsumed into the Parliamentary Reform Association. In September 1852 a meeting of the Glasgow Reform Association voted to adopt a programme of household suffrage, triennial parliaments and vote by ballot. Workers and reforming elements among the middle classes drew together as they had done to work for the Reform Act of 1832, to campaign not only for an improved electoral system but for a variety of humanitarian causes. Glasgow Chartist leaders entered municipal politics as civic reformers, James Moir being outstanding among these: he worked for improved hospitals and prisons, improving slum property in central Glasgow, preserving Glasgow Green, and the increase of civic amenities generally, including the erection of public urinals in George Square. But though Chartism as a movement had now withered away, its influence in Glasgow and Clydeside proved permanent. It had clarified the aims and ambitions of the working classes, given them self confidence and powers of organization and expression, and founded a tradition of working-class political activism that was to be revived at a later period with remarkable effect.

In 1863 Glasgow appointed its first Medical Officer of Health, and this marked the beginning of active concern with public health; but overcrowding in the deteriorating slums continued to present intractable problems. While the well-to-do moved into comfortable houses to the west, south-west and north, the poorest sections of the population remained in the increasingly overcrowded older areas of the city. The distinction was acknowledged even by those Glaswegians who were most proud of their city. Tweed's *Guide to Glasgow and the Clyde*, published in 1872 for the information and edification of tourists, made the distinction in its opening pages:

As to the situation of Glasgow, it lies pleasantly on both banks of the River Clyde, about sixty miles below the source of the river in Upper Lanarkshire, . . . Like London, the bulk of the city lies on the northern or right bank, which gradually ascends from the line of the bridges, till, at about 300 yards from the river, it covers the slopes and crowns the summits of a succession of ridges running irregularly east and west. The ridges, now rising, now dipping, give to that portion of the city embraced between the High Street on the east, and the fashionable terraces on the west, and the line of St Vincent and George Streets on the south, and Sauchiehall Street and Hill Street on the north, an irregular though picturesque appearance. Towards the west, some of the finest streets of the city are formed either along the backs of these heights, or in the hollows running parallel with them – among which are St Vincent Street, West George Street, West Regent Street, Bath Street, Sauchiehall Street, and Hill Street. While the north side contains the most fashionable dwellings, and is favoured with the most picturesque situation, it is on the same side that a low class of houses, and a gigantic system of overcrowding, swell from year to year the appalling mortality bills of Glasgow. Within that northern portion lies the old town, dirty, over-populated, closely built, and intersected in every direction by dark and filthy closes, the abodes of the poor, the wretched, and the criminal . . . In these regions the mortality is, in fact, nearly double what it is in the more elevated quarters north-west.

It was the growth of the textile industry that first stimulated the rapid growth of population in and around Glasgow, but as the nineteenth century advanced the development of iron production and the consequent increased demand for coal and expansion of the Lanarkshire coalfields (which in turn encouraged the building of new railways to make the coalfields more accessible) kept up the pace of population growth. The iron and coal industries developed together on Clydeside between 1830 and 1850. From 1870, when the first steel furnace was built by the newly formed Steel Company of Scotland at Newton, near Cambuslang, a few miles south-east of the centre of Glasgow, the production of steel began rapidly to take over from that of wrought iron. Shipbuilding and marine engineering benefited from the proximity of supplies of iron and steel and expanded rapidly throughout the second half of the century. This all promoted the growth of the population of Glasgow from just over 77,000 in 1801 to just under half a million in 1871 (over that figure if we include the suburbs) to 565,714 in 1891 (656,185 including the population taken in by the enlarging of the city boundaries that year), and though, as we have seen, grave social problems accompanied this rapid growth, it was at the same time an index of Glasgow's economic progress. The growth took place throughout what by the end of the century had become the Clydeside conurbation; new developments in steel ships and marine engineering in the 1870s and 1880s and the accompanying emergence of Clydeside as the centre of Britain's shipbuilding industry are reflected in the population statistics for this whole area. Govan, Partick and Renfrew each doubled its population between 1881 and 1891, while Clydebank on the right or north-west bank of the Clyde some six miles from Glasgow rapidly developed towards the end of the century from a sparsely populated rural area to a flourishing shipbuilding and engineering centre with a population of over 40,000 in the present day.

Glasgow's rapid growth of population in the nineteenth century depended on a steady flow of immigrants, from both the Scottish Highlands and Ireland. It was the cotton industry that first attracted Irish labour, on which by the middle of the century the industry in Scotland was dependent. The peak of Irish immigration was reached by 1851, when there were 207,400 Irish-born living in Scotland,

Irish nationalists at a
meeting in the City Hall
on 5 November 1883,
from *Quiz*, a weekly
magazine which ran in
the 1880s and '90s

including 43,100 in Lanarkshire, 12,400 in Renfrewshire and 68,200
in West Central Scotland generally. The figures were still higher in
1881 – 194,800, 52,600, 13,900 and 76,800 respectively – but by the
1891 census they were down a little though they were up again,
slightly above the 1871 level, in the census of 1901. Thereafter the
figures began to show a steady decline in Irish-born inhabitants of
Scotland.

The thousands of Irish who were driven by hunger to emigrate to
the west of Scotland as a result of the potato famine in the 'hungry
forties' arrived exhausted and penniless. It was cheap and easy to
come from Irish ports to the Clyde – fourpence to sixpence per head
for the Belfast–Glasgow passage – and those with least resources,

unable to make the passage to America as so many others did, landed in Scotland at the rate of some 50,000 annually. In December 1847 and the first three months of 1848 nearly 43,000 hungry and impoverished Irish arrived in Glasgow. Although the supply of cheap labour was welcomed by employers, it was not welcomed by other workers, while a city that was already having trouble in accommodating the Highlanders displaced by the Clearances was in no position to provide adequate housing for the newcomers from Ireland.

Though the majority of the Irish immigrants were Catholics, there were also Protestant Ulstermen, and to the traditional suspicion of Roman Catholics shown by a Presbyterian city there was added the imported orange-versus-green feuding among the Irish themselves. The Glaswegians naturally preferred the Protestant Ulstermen, not only for their religion but also because they were more likely to have learned a trade before arrival. A vicious circle was thus set up: the poor Irish Catholic immigrant started and most often continued his new life in Glasgow or elsewhere on Clydeside at the very bottom of the social and economic scale, available not only as cheap labour but also as blackleg labour in times of industrial dispute. The prejudice thus bred was religious, economic and also political. Even the employers who benefited from the cheap and blackleg labour looked down on those they so employed. And while the prejudice tended to keep the Irish at the bottom of the social scale, this simply exacerbated the conditions that had bred the prejudice in the first place and so ensured its perpetuation. The image of the violent, shiftless, drunken, fanatical Irishman was projected in all sorts of ways, from outright abuse to music-hall humour. This did not prevent many of the children and grandchildren of Irish immigrants from making important contributions to Glasgow life and culture.

Of the many examples of polarization of feeling about the Irish in the nineteenth century, the following two are characteristic. A celebration by Glasgow Irish of the hundredth anniversary of the birth of the Irish patriot Daniel O'Connell (1775–1847) on 5 August 1875, which took the form of a procession through Partick, provoked violence from bystanders that developed into a riot in which many people were injured though none was killed. The Riot Act was read and the police called in. The other incident occurred in 1878 after the restoration of the Roman Catholic Hierarchy in Britain and the appointment of the Most Rev. Charles Eyre as the first Roman Catholic Archbishop of Glasgow since James Beaton. A copy of the Pope's allocutionary letter confirming the appointment was burned on Glasgow Green on 13 April in the presence of several thousand protestors against 'papal aggression'. The authorities were apprehensive of a riot, and had the military standing by, but no intervention was necessary.

In the second decade of the nineteenth century another and much smaller community of immigrants, differing in religious faith even more radically from the majority of Glaswegians than the Catholic Irish, began to settle in the city to meet, surprisingly perhaps, with no discrimination and considerable sympathy. These were Jews, whose first synagogue in Glasgow was consecrated in 1823, on the first floor of a building on the west side of the High Street, very near the Trongate. Jews were to play a significant part in the commercial and later the professional life of the city, as the community grew to about 1,000 at the end of the nineteenth century and then rapidly to nearly 20,000 by the middle of this century. They play an unexpected part in the history of Glasgow: the first person to be buried in the Glasgow Necropolis was a Jew. The Necropolis, described by George Blair in 1857 as 'the first necropolis in order of time, not only in Glasgow, but in Scotland, and which, from its peculiar position and circumstances, seems to be selected, by general consent, as the hallowed depository of the ashes of our most distinguished citizens', lay immediately to the east of the Cathedral, on the other side of the Molendinar Burn, and was originally known as the Fir Park or the Merchants' Park, belonging to the Merchants' House of Glasgow. The idea of turning this park into a formal burial garden was first put forward by John Strang, the historian of Glasgow, in his book *Necropolis Glasguensis* published in 1831 and two years later, the city having acquired the land from the Merchants' House, the Necropolis was formally opened. However, it was in the year before the formal opening that the first interment took place, that of the Jew Joseph Levi, on 12 September 1832. Levi, a quill merchant, had died of cholera. How he came to be the first person buried in the Necropolis is made clear in a note appended to its first annual report:

> The Chief of the Synagogue sent, offering to purchase possession of a burial-place before any arrangements were completed or prices fixed, stating frankly that they had a specific sum raised and laid aside for the purpose, and their desire to have such accommodation as could be given for it. There was a corner with a few trees in the end of the park next the burn, where freestone had been wrought, and which seemed peculiarly adapted for the purpose, and least likely to interfere with any future operations. The request was accordingly complied with, although the price, when calculated, according to what was afterwards obtained from others, has proved

a trifle under the average. The payment of tribute upon interments was considered inconsistent with their religious ideas; and their mode of interment being peculiar, and such as the Committee would certainly wish to see generally introduced, of preserving the spot where any remains have ever been deposited from being again used, the fees which were not then fixed were also agreed to be given up in their case.

The purchase of this Jewish burying ground within what was soon to become the larger area of the Glasgow Necropolis took place in 1830, and the sum paid was one hundred guineas.

The comments of George Blair give some indication of how mid-nineteenth-century Glaswegians regarded the city's Jewish immigrants:

> Some allowance must be made for olden prejudices, even though they do not rest on any valid principle, and therefore it is perhaps well that the burying-ground of the Jews has been placed in this sequestered corner, which may be regarded as a suburb of the beautiful city of the dead. Although the position is a partial separation, it is not an exclusion, and perhaps the arrangement is equally satisfactory to both Jew and Christian.
>
> A beautiful gateway and ornamental column, erected at the expense of the Merchants' House, mark the spot where the children of Abraham are interred. . . .
>
> . . . Here, in this northern section of a remote island, mingling with the people of whom it was once said, '*penitos toto divisos orbe Britannos*' ['Britons totally divided from the whole world'], these descendants of the Mesopotamian patriarch actually slumber in a quiet place of sepulture near a magnificent Cathedral devoted to Christian worship, and not far from a monument erected to the memory of John Knox. Everything is Christian around them, and here, in a corner of the city of the dead, is a little group of Jews, slumbering peacefully together in a place of rest at last, after being strangers and sojourners in a land to which they have given a religion, and from which they receive only a grave.

The first reference to a Jew in Glasgow is to a hatter called Isaac Cohen, who was admitted a burgess of the city 'at far hand' (not related to any freeman of the city) on 22 September 1812. The *Glasgow Chronicle* of 28 January 1817 carried an advertisement of P. Levy, furrier. Other Jewish names then start to appear in the Glasgow directories. These early Glasgow Jews engaged in a variety of trades – there were hatters, furriers, cabinet-makers, auctioneers, optical instrument makers, and at least one family of dentists. Very small in numbers compared with the huge number of Irish immigrants, they threatened no one and took work from no one; so they were quietly accepted. They were not involved in the industrial progress of nineteenth-century Glasgow but provided services increasingly demanded by those to whom that progress brought prosperity.

In spite of ups and downs in the trade cycle and periods of working-class restlessness, Glasgow's progress as an industrial city and centre of an important industrial region continued steadily. A significant index of that progress was the development of railways, a central part of the general improvement of communications that was urgently needed in the first instance by the growing coal and iron industries. We have already seen the significance of the Forth–Clyde and Monkland Canals and their importance for industry. Railways, which first came to Glasgow at the beginning of the third decade of the century, were to prove very much more important, not only for industry but also for ending Glasgow's geographical isolation and speeding people as well as goods in and out of the city. Passenger travel by stage-coach had developed considerably in the second half of the eighteenth century. The first Glasgow–Greenock coach began to run in 1763, taking nine hours for the journey. The first Glasgow–Aberdeen wagon, taking six days, ran in 1780. The following year came the first Glasgow–Carlisle diligence, connecting there with the coach for London, and it was claimed that in good conditions the Glasgow–London journey could be made in four days. In 1789 the time taken by the mail coach from London to Glasgow was reduced to sixty-six hours. In 1819 eight public coaches with four horses, and seven with two horses, left and returned to Glasgow daily: one to London, five to Edinburgh, three to Paisley, two to Greenock, and one each to Perth, Ayr, Hamilton and Kilmarnock. It was the excitement over the Reform Bill of 1832 that produced the fastest coach journey between London and Glasgow, which at that date averaged forty-four hours, using 180 horses in all, four-in-hand. Newspapers carrying reports of the passing of the Bill by the House of Lords, at twenty-five minutes to seven in the morning of 14 April 1832, were brought by the editor of the *Sun* from London to Glasgow (he carried with him copies of his paper containing twenty-two-and-a-half columns of the debate) in thirty-five hours and fifty minutes, including all stoppages. He left the Strand at twenty minutes to eight on that historic morning, the paper having been printed in just over an hour, and arrived at Miller Street, Glasgow, at half past seven on the evening of Sunday 15 April.

The coming of the railway soon made even this record a mere historical curiosity. As early as 1803 Telford had surveyed and proposed a railway between Glasgow and Berwick, at a cost of £2,926 a mile, but nothing came of it. In 1825 the Glasgow–Garnkirk railway – eight miles from St Rollox station – was begun, with a capital of £169,195. It was opened for mineral traffic in 1827 and for passenger traffic, with steam locomotives going at seven miles an hour, in September 1831. In 1830 the Pollok and Govan Railway Company, with a capital of £66,000, and the Rutherglen Railway Company, with a capital of £20,000, were formed, and the three-and-a-quarter mile Paisley and Renfrew Railway, with a capital of £33,000, arrived in 1837. But these were small affairs. More important was the commencing of the Glasgow and Greenock line in 1837, opened for passenger traffic in July 1840, and, also in 1837, the authorizing of the line through the Ayrshire coalfields to Paisley, Kilmarnock and Ayr which cost £812,000. On 12 August 1840, amid ceremonial rejoicings from its citizens, Ayr received the first train from Glasgow, which had set out from the new Bridge Street Station (formerly the Methodist chapel of the Rev. Valentine Wood) on the south side of the Clyde.

The Edinburgh and Glasgow Railway Company was formed in 1838, and the forty-six-mile railway was completed at the beginning of 1842 at a cost of one-and-a-quarter million pounds. The tunnel between Queen Street and Cowlairs alone cost some £40,000 and was the greatest engineering feat of its kind so far attempted in Scotland. The formal opening of this railway took place, with great ceremonial rejoicing in both cities, on 18 February 1842. Parliamentary approval of a line from Edinburgh to Berwick with a branch line to Haddington enabled the North British Railway Company to be formed in July 1844. In 1865 the Edinburgh and Glasgow Railway Company amalgamated with the North British Railway Company to make the latter one of the two great Scottish railway companies, the other being the Caledonian Railway. The Caledonian was formed in 1845 after parliamentary authorization for a line from Carlisle to Edinburgh. Its nucleus goes back to the Glasgow and Garnkirk line of 1831. In 1855 the Glasgow, Dumbarton and Helensburgh Railway Company, with a capital of £240,000, was authorized to build a line from the junction of the Glasgow and Edinburgh line at Cowlairs to Bowling, with a branch to Helensburgh, which had by now become a favourite watering place for Glasgow citizens and a place for week-end residence or eventual retirement. Helensburgh was called after Helen, wife of Sir James Colquhoun of Luss, the ground landlord of the site.

At first, mail coaches and railways co-operated in speeding up journeys, as this advertisement of the Caledonian Railway in 1847 illustrates:

> On and after 10 September, 1847, until further notice, mail coaches will run from Glasgow and Edinburgh to Beattock, and connect there with trains for Lockerbie, Carlisle, Preston, Liverpool, Manchester, and London, the journey to the metropolis being performed in 21½ hours from Glasgow and 20 hours from Edinburgh. For hours of starting and fares see time-table. J. W. Coddington, Secretary.

It was not long before the whole journey from either Scottish city to London could be done by train. In February 1848 the Caledonian Railway, in association with other railways, ran, as a demonstration of what it could do, a train from Euston to Glasgow in nine hours thirty-six minutes, of which forty-six minutes were taken up by halts.

The Scottish railways had to beat off attacks by English railway interests and, in spite of, or even (as a recent historian has argued) in some degree because of, the fierce competition between the different companies, succeeded in building up a completely new network of communications in Scotland, with all kinds of social consequences.

Railways running in and out of Glasgow meant the development of railway stations in the city. Queen Street station, the original station of the Edinburgh and Glasgow Railway Company, was completely rebuilt by the North British Railway Company about 1880. Buchanan Street station was opened for passenger traffic by the Caledonian Railway in 1849. The Caledonian Railway later built Central Station, which was opened in July 1879. The Glasgow and South-Western Railway Company, formed in 1850 by the amalgamation of the Glasgow, Paisley, Kilmarnock and Ayr Railway Company with the Glasgow, Dumfries and Carlisle Railway Company, at first used Bridge Street station on the south side of the Clyde. Then, having in 1870 built a new line from Pollokshields through the Gorbals that bridged the Clyde to St Enoch Square and for ten years used a makeshift station in Dunlop Street, the Company built St Enoch's station and hotel, both opened in 1880. St Enoch's Hotel, the first large railway hotel in Scotland, was designed by Miles Gibson and Thomas Willson of Hampstead. Its massive Victorian presence dominated the square and completely changed its character (St Enoch Square had been begun in 1782). Only Queen Street and Central Station now survive as major Glasgow railway stations.

Development of the railways did not divert attention from the importance of Glasgow's other great means of communication, the

Clyde. The Clyde Trustees continued to seek and obtain Parliamentary Acts enabling them to develop facilities on the river. An Act of 1864 empowered them to lay down lines of rails or tramways in connection with the quays at the harbour. In 1867 Kingston Dock – the first authorized by an Act of 1840 – was opened on the south side of the river, with wharves all round its five-and-a-half acres of water space and 830 lineal yards of quayside. An Act of 1868 authorized the Clyde Trustees to construct what became known as 'No.1 Graving Dock' on the south side of the river and the Quay later known as Yorkhill Quay on the north side, together with river walls, streets and other works. The work thus authorized was completed in 1875. An Act of 1870 authorized the building of the tidal dock first known as Stobcross Dock and then as Queen's Dock, completed in 1880; Stobcross Quay, completed in 1882 and, on the opposite (south) side of the river, Plantation Quay, completed in 1874, were authorized by the same Act. Further developments took place in accordance with further Acts passed between 1872 and the end of the century.

Nineteenth-century Glasgow was immensely proud of its harbour. Tweed's Guide of 1872 included it among the principal sights of the city: 'The stranger who visits Glasgow for the purpose of seeing what is to be seen in and around it, will miss one of its greatest marvels if he neglects to spend a few hours strolling along the quays of the harbour. He may have seen much of shipping in his travels – may have roamed along the crowded docks of Liverpool, or sailed through the forest of masts which stretches for miles below London, but he has probably never witnessed a greater triumph of human industry, enterprise, and sagacity than Glasgow Harbour.' In 1899, John M'Dowall, in his *People's History of Glasgow*, proudly described the harbour:

> The present Harbour, nearly two miles in length, is formed by quays on each side of the river, the widths between averaging from 360 to 620 feet. The following table shows the progress made during the past 100 years:-

	1799
Length of quays and wharves	382 lin. yards
Area of water space	4 acres
Revenue	£3,319 16 1

	1898
Length of quays and wharves	14,568 lin. yards
Area of water space	206 acres
Revenue	£430,327 6 4

A large and increasing trade is carried on with all parts of the world. Regular steamship lines to Canada, United States, Mediterranean, India and China, and the Continent. Daily communication is kept up with Liverpool, Dublin, Belfast, etc.; and bi-weekly with the West Highlands, Southampton, Bristol, and the South. The Harbour is divided into two sections, called the Upper and Lower Harbours. The Upper Harbour, extending from Glasgow Bridge to Victoria Bridge, has a depth at low water of 10 feet, with the quayage all on the north side of the river, and is chiefly used by vessels in the mineral and coasting trades. Small lighters can also ascend the river for a further distance of two miles, to the numerous works on the banks. The Lower Harbour has a general depth of from 16 to 20 feet at low water, and extends from the mouth of the River Kelvin to Glasgow Bridge, the water area being 111 acres, with 5,116 lineal yards of quayage. From the River Kelvin outwards to Port-Glasgow, a distance of about 16 miles, a navigable channel, with a depth at low water of 20 feet, is maintained.

By the end of the century there were six bridges over the Clyde at Glasgow. The first was the Victoria or Stockwell Bridge, on the site of the original wooden bridge. Then there was Jamaica Bridge, or Glasgow Bridge, just south of Jamaica Street, first opened in 1772, rebuilt in 1833–6 (designed by Telford), and giving way in turn to a new eighty-feet-wide seven-arched bridge opened in May 1899. The Rutherglen Bridge was first built in 1776, replacing a ford: a new bridge on the same site was opened in August 1896. The Hutcheson-town or Albert Bridge, joining the Saltmarket on the north with Crown Street on the south, was begun in 1794, with Hutcheson's Hospital subscribing £2,000, but on 18 November 1795, while it was still unfinished, a great flood swept away two of the arches and destroyed much of what was left. In 1803 a wooden foot bridge was erected where the original bridge had been, and a new stone bridge was built in 1830. That bridge was closed as unsafe in June 1868 and a new bridge, called after the Prince Consort, was opened in June 1871. A suspension bridge running north from South Portland Street was built in 1853, and for some years passengers had to pay a toll of one halfpenny to cross. St Andrew's Suspension Bridge, running south from the middle of Glasgow Green, replaced a ferry at that point in 1855. In addition to these bridges, a harbour tunnel, begun in 1890, was opened in 1895: it had three separate tunnels for north-going vehicular traffic, south-going vehicular traffic, and pedestrians, with the approaches consisting of hydraulic lifts for vehicles and stairs for passengers.

One cannot leave the nineteenth-century Clyde without a mention of the famous 'Cluthas', the small screw-steamers that carried passengers from one pier to another in Glasgow Harbour for a charge of one penny. They were first introduced in 1884, and by the end of the century there were twelve, plying between Victoria Bridge and Whiteinch Ferry, a total distance of about three miles, with eleven landing stages (on alternate sides of the river) en route. In 1896 the Cluthas carried two-and-a-half million passengers. They were lost in 1903 to the Glasgow tramcar, which in turn disappeared from the Glasgow scene in a riot of nostalgia in September 1962.

There were of course more impressive steamers on the Clyde than the little Cluthas. Trips 'doon the watter' from the Broomielaw were the Glaswegians' favourite recreation. Tweed's Guide gives a vivid picture of Clyde traffic in 1872:

> From [the Broomielaw], when the summer trade is at its height, from 40 to 50 steamers frequently leave for the coast during a single day, carrying loads of passengers to every accessible nook between Bowling and Arran. Here is the Iona, crammed fore and aft, bound for Ardrishaig on Lochfyne, here the Vale of Doon, equally well laden, for Ardrossan and Ayr; there the Lancelot, bound for Millport; and next her, the plain little steamer, with a human freight for the lonely waters of Lochgoil, while close to the bridge are the steamers for the popular Dunoon and Rothesay route. It is a busy and exciting scene from 7 till 9 o'clock in the fine summer mornings.

What Alan Paterson, their historian, has called 'the golden years of the Clyde steamers' were the years 1898 to 1914. In the latter year, forty steamers were plying between Glasgow, Gourock or Greenock and the Clyde estuary, with eighty-five stopping places. Sailings stopped from the Broomielaw when Bridge Wharf was opened in 1927. But that was already an age away from the golden years when in crowded luxury Glaswegians and visitors savoured the beauties of the Clyde estuary from the decks of such as the *Iona*, the *Columba*, the *Isle of Arran* or the *Duchess of Rothesay*; to many older people in Glasgow today they appear as symbols of a lost mode of happiness.

146

CHAPTER 12

'The most aggressively efficient city in Great Britain'

In most of the major cities of Victorian Britain there had been much suburban development before the coming of the railways, with the result that one of the functions of the railways when they came was to provide transport for those who lived in dormitory suburbs and worked in the city centre. This in turn increased the move to the suburbs, but in spite of the expansion we have noted as taking place in Glasgow in the eighteenth and nineteenth centuries that city was slow to develop far-flung suburban life. The better-off middle classes settled in the Pollokshields–Langside area, south of the river, and in Kelvinside, to the north-west, neither more than two or three miles from the centre. 'Indeed,' John Kellett has observed in his study of the impact of railways on Victorian cities, 'Glasgow never developed symptoms of the suburban sprawl typical of many other cities until well into the twentieth century, and remains an extraordinarily compact and densely populated city.' In the nineteenth century, Kellett points out, 'Glasgow itself was the dormitory, the Singer works at Clydebank, or the various steel works at Newton and Coatbridge, were the work destinations.' This was the reverse of the usual situation, and late in the nineteenth century workmen's trains were introduced to deal with this. Robert Miller, General Manager of the Caledonian Railway, giving evidence to the Select Committee on Workmen's Trains of 1903–4, was questioned on this point:

It was the reverse of London? You took from your populous centre workmen to work away from the centre and you brought them back at night? – This is so; and that is the rule in Scotland. It is not absolutely the case, but it is the rule. A great many engineering works starting in Glasgow originally, the population settled down round about the engineering and shipbuilding works. As the city increased, the works were sent out into the country and the population remained.

The Cathcart District Railway, opened in 1886 and running from Central Station by East Pollokshields and Queen's Park to Crosshill and thence to Mount Florida, then extended to Cathcart, then in 1894 made circular, via Langside, Pollokshaws and Shawlands, was intended to encourage southern suburban traffic, but it came too late to make any significant change in the pattern of suburban building. In any case, the maximum distance of a journey on the Cathcart Circle was only three miles. Omnibuses and tramways were really more suited to Glasgow. The horse-drawn omnibus was first introduced in London in 1829 and reached Glasgow in 1845,* when Robert Frame started a service from Barrowfield Toll, Bridgeton, to the Gusset-House, Anderston. He was followed by others, notably Duncan MacGregor and Andrew Menzies, both Highlanders, whose fierce rivalry operated to the advantage of Glasgow businessmen, who were now able to move cheaply and easily about the city, twopence being the highest fare charged. MacGregor and Menzies, each of whom painted his buses in his own clan tartan, continued to run their rival buses for over twenty years, but Menzies came out on top in the end. By the time both firms were taken over by the new tramway company in 1872, Menzies owned fifty buses and five hundred horses.

The Tramways Act of August 1870 endorsed the right of Town Councils to decide whether they wanted tramways in their town and to own tram lines but not to run trams on them. The tramcars themselves had to be operated by a private company, though the Town Council could take the company over after twenty-one years. The Council had to maintain the lines, the roadway between them and the roadway for eighteen inches on either side. Glasgow Town Council laid two-and-a-half miles of tramlines from St George's Cross along New City Road, Cambridge Street, Sauchiehall Street, Renfield Street and Jamaica Bridge to Eglinton Toll in 1872, and leased them to the Glasgow Tramway and Omnibus Company Ltd. The first tramcar was ceremonially sent on its way along this route on 19 August 1872. Further routes soon followed, to a total of between thirty and forty miles.

When the Glasgow Tramway and Omnibus Company's lease expired in 1894, the Town Council had already decided to take over the running of the tramcars themselves. The city boundaries had been extended in 1891, with the annexation of the police burghs of

---

*Before this, from 1834, there were some horse-drawn public vehicles plying between the harbours on the Clyde and on the canals, and Broomielaw, Port Dundas and Port Eglinton and there were some unregulated one-horse public vehicles, both two-wheel and four-wheel, in the city in the early 1840s.

CIRCUMSTANCES ALTER CASES.

Quiz comments in 1895 on the newly-established Glasgow Corporation
Tramways

Crosshill, Govanhill and Pollokshields in the south and Maryhill and Hillhead in the north, and it seemed appropriate that Glasgow Town Council should be responsible for municipal transport as well as for the other services it now provided in these areas. Extensive preparations were made during the last year of the company's operation, with the building of new depots and stables, the provision of three hundred new and more comfortable cars and of 3,000 horses, the hiring and training of drivers and conductors, and the appointment of an imaginative and energetic tramways manager, John Young. The new corporation tramcars took over on 1 July 1894 and proved an immediate success, carrying 6,114,789 passengers in the first four weeks. (It was, incidentally, at this time that Glasgow Town Council was given the official title of 'The Corporation of Glasgow', hence 'Glasgow Corporation Tramways'.) In 1898 there were thirty-seven miles of tramway belonging to Glasgow Corporation, with an additional four miles leased from Govan. On 13 April of that year electric cars were introduced between Springburn and Mitchell Street. These proved an immediate success, with the result that John Young decided on the immense task of electrifying the whole system (which involved, apart from the erection of poles to carry the overhead electric wires, re-laying with heavier rails over forty miles of double track, making over eighty miles of track in all). Horse trams were finally phased out completely at the end of April, 1902. Two years later James Dalrymple was put in charge of Glasgow Corporation Tramways; his reign, which spanned the golden age of the Glasgow tramcar, lasted until 1926. Lines were pushed out into country districts, and by the outbreak of the First World War the corporation operated about a hundred miles of tramway and was carrying – at a profit – over 300,000,000 passengers annually.

Glasgow's tramcars lasted until 1962, when on the evening of 4 September a memorable and, to most observers, moving procession of cars old and new made their last journey through the streets of the city. The crowds who watched this last chapter in a remarkable story of city transport had reason to be moved. Writing on Glasgow transport a few years before the tramcars were finally abolished in favour of buses, John Sleeman noted the strong public feeling on the subject, 'for the Glaswegian has a strong attachment to his "caurs", with memories going back to the model service they gave in the days of the late Mr. Dalrymple before 1914'. It was indeed a model service: in efficiency, cheapness (the Corporation had reduced fares when they took over from the company), comfort and colour, Glasgow's tramcars in their heyday were the equal of any in the world and had a good claim to be the world's best. They were unique in having different colours on the panels round the top deck for different groups of routes (red, blue, green, yellow, white) so that they were easily identifiable from a distance. In 1900 Glasgow's trams carried one fifth of the number of all the passengers carried on all the tramways of England and Wales. In 1914 you could travel from Riddrie in the north to Rouken Glen in the south (an estate presented to the city for use as a public park by Cameron Corbett in 1906), a red route, for 4d., from Maryhill to Shawlands via Gorbals Cross (blue) for 2½d. and from the University to Dumbreck (a white car, familiar to generations of students) for 2½d. The cheapest adult fare for a complete route was a halfpenny (Finnieston to Stobcross Ferry: this route was served by one small single-deck car and had no distinguishing colour). For the maximum fare of seven-pence you could travel the fourteen miles from Uddingston to Paisley. It was Dalrymple who persuaded the Corporation to take over the private companies that ran tramcars in the Paisley area and between Coatbridge and Airdrie. The system was extended in 1923 to provide the cheapest journey on rails on Britain – the twenty-one miles from Airdrie to Paisley for twopence.

In 1905 Frederic Clemson Howe, an American professor research-ing on European cities, spent some time in Glasgow, which he described as 'in many ways the most aggressively efficient city in Great Britain'. He noted the 'enthusiasm, and interest, devotion and pride' of the people. They were especially proud of their tramways, and Professor Howe also noted the conviction of James Dalrymple, one of the Glasgow characters he made a point of meeting, that 'no other people in the world can do what Glasgow has done'. In the matter of tramcars he did not dissent.

Glasgow also acquired its own underground railway, the 'Subway', as it was popularly called. The Glasgow Subway Cable Bill was promoted in Parliament in 1887 but was not passed until 1890 in the teeth of fierce opposition. Work began in 1891 and the line was opened by the Glasgow Subway Railway Company on 14 December 1896. However, an enormous and unexpected rush of passengers, followed by an accident in which nineteen people were injured, caused it to be closed until 21 January 1897, when it was successfully re-opened. The line runs in a circle from St Enoch Square via Kinning Park, Govan, Partick, Hillhead and St George's Cross back to St Enoch and another line covers the same route in the reverse direction, but in a separate tunnel. The lines pass once under the Kelvin and twice under the Clyde; the circle is six-and-a-half miles in circumference with fifteen stations. At first the Subway was cable-operated, with a power station in West Scotland Street providing two engines each capable of developing 1,500 horsepower, which propelled two endless cables 36,300 feet long and one-and-a-half inches in diameter drawing the cars (fitted with grippers) at twelve miles an hour. But in 1923 it was taken over by the Corporation which converted it to electric traction in 1935. Its scale is small, with a narrow gauge of four feet and tunnels and stations of very restricted dimensions, so that only specially designed trains of two cars can be used. The original cost of laying the Subway was £1,500,000, the tunnelling under the Clyde proving unexpectedly difficult and expensive, and the Subway Company continued in financial difficulties until the Corporation's take-over and electrification of the system, after which it increased enormously in popularity. In the year ending 31 July 1898 it carried 5,779,119 passengers. In the middle 1950s it was carrying thirty-four million passengers annually. In 1977, it was closed for extensive modernization.

The early electrification of Glasgow's tramcars was not matched by any early introduction of electric lighting in the city. Most citizens were for long quite content with the gas lighting with which Glasgow had made an early and eager start (the Glasgow Gas Light Company was formed as early as 1817). Although St Enoch Station was lit by electricity in 1879, the first building in Glasgow to be so lit, and it was followed by the head post office and a few other buildings such as Lord Kelvin's house at the University, there was no rush to adopt the new method. In 1890 the Town Council obtained the right to provide electric energy and in February 1893, after the building of a new power station in Waterloo Street, current was switched on. During the first year there were only 108 consumers. Even in 1901 there were fewer than 3,000 domestic consumers of electricity in the city. The first electric street lighting appeared in 1893, but gas was to remain the accepted method long after this, as the fitting of incandescent gas lamps in all the principal streets in July 1894 clearly indicated.

Meanwhile Glasgow continued to absorb its suburbs and many adjacent burghs. In 1846 after considerable controversy the city had incorporated the burghs of Anderston to the west and Calton to the east as well as the Barony of Gorbals,* at that time a fashionable suburb. In 1891 a more far-reaching development occurred, when suburban offshoots were absorbed and the six adjacent, independent

---

*Glasgow had acquired the feudal superiority of the ancient burgh of the Gorbals in 1647, by purchase from the successors of Sir George Elphinstone, who had been Provost of Glasgow in 1605. This superiority produced the anomalous position that for two hundred years the Gorbals magistrates were appointed by the magistrates and Town Council of Glasgow.

burghs of Govanhill, Crosshill, Pollokshields East and West, Hillhead and Maryhill were annexed. These police burghs (so-called because they had acquired their burgh status under the Police Act of 1850), had, by clinging to their independent burgh status, obstructed the growth of Glasgow to the north, west and south. Their incorporation now added some 6,000 acres to the city and raised its population from 565,714 to 656,946. Alteration of the representation of Glasgow Corporation followed and in November 1896 the city was divided into twenty-five wards, each having three representatives. A third major boundary extension took place in 1912, with the annexation of Govan, Partick and Pollokshaws, increasing the city's acreage by a further 6,000 and its population by some 226,300.

By the end of the century Glasgow's public transport included tramcars, trains (both underground and overground, although the tramcars soon began to take traffic away from the surface railways, with the resulting closure of Govan and Gorbals stations) and the Cluthas which plied on the river between Victoria Bridge and Whiteinch Ferry. There were also cross-river ferries at different points on the Clyde. These at first were small and often overcrowded rowing boats and the overturning of the Govan ferryboat at Partick on 6 April 1861 with the loss of seven lives was caused by overcrowding; one consequence of this disaster was the building of a pier at Partick. A more serious disaster occurred on 30 November 1864 when twenty-seven workmen packed themselves into the Clyde Street ferryboat at a time when the water was rough: the swell from the *Inverary Castle* which was passing at the time sent water over the broadside of the boat with the result that the passengers rushed to the lee side and the boat overturned, and nineteen people were drowned. The Clyde Trust then introduced larger, steam-powered ferries. By the end of the century there were seven passenger ferries and three for vehicular and passenger traffic combined: the former used eleven ferry-boats with screws at each end to obviate the necessity for turning, and they were licensed to carry from 93 to 148 passengers. The vehicular ferries were at Stobcross, Whiteinch and Govan. Stobcross ferry was the first to introduce a large four-screw boat with an elevated deck capable of being raised or lowered in accordance with the state of the tide: these boats were designed to take 258 passengers and ten carts with horses or 700 passengers without vehicles. Whiteinch ferry introduced such a boat in 1905, but Govan continued well into the present century to use an older type of boat worked by steam on two chains laid across the river. The opening of the Clyde Tunnel in the 1960s, with its two-lane carriageways linking Shieldhall Road on the south side of the river with Dumbarton Road on the north, severely reduced the use of the ferries and eventually replaced Whiteinch ferry altogether.

One disadvantage of travelling by river was the smell. As the nineteenth century progressed the Clyde became more and more polluted. Until the Corporation built its sewage works at Dalmarnock and then at Dalmuir at the very end of the century (followed by a third on the south side of the river, at Shieldhall, in 1910), the Clyde was something of an open drain, and, especially at low tide in warm weather, it stank frightfully. 'The volume of filth thrown into it', remarked a Glasgow writer at the end of the century, 'renders the river little better than an open sewer, the contents of which exhale an evil odour perceived a long way from its banks, and which, churned up by propellers and paddles of steam vessels, yield in summer an almost intolerable stench. Truly the price we pay for our highly organised condition of city life is very heavy!'

The pollution of the Clyde by sewage also represented a hazard to health, but this was mitigated by the spectacular improvement of the water supply after the opening of the Loch Katrine scheme in 1859. The figures for deaths by cholera graphically illustrate this. In an outbreak of cholera which lasted from November 1848 until March 1849, 3,777 people died. An outbreak in 1854 produced 3,885 deaths, with 1,023 occurring in the month of August alone. But a third outbreak in 1866 produced only fifty-three deaths.

We have already referred to the appointment of Glasgow's first Medical Officer of Health in 1863. He was Dr W. T. Gairdner, who was succeeded in 1872 by Dr J. B. Russell. Dr Russell's speeches during the next two decades on such subjects as 'Life in One Room' and 'The Children of the City' eloquently portray the condition in which so many of Glasgow's citizens lived: in 1880 a quarter of the city's families lived in one-room houses and in fourteen per cent of these there were also lodgers, while twenty-seven per cent of those living in two-room houses took in lodgers. In 1888 Dr Russell reported:

> Of all the children who die in Glasgow before they complete their fifth year, 32 per cent die in houses of one apartment; and not 2 per cent in houses of five apartments and upwards. There they die, and their little bodies are laid on a table or on the dresser, so as to be somewhat out of the way of their brothers and sisters who play and sleep and eat in their ghastly company. One in every five of all who are born there never see the end of their first year.

In 1894 Dr A. K. Chalmers calculated that out of every 200,000 children born in Old Glasgow* between 1881 and 1890 the number surviving at the age of five was 136,862 compared with 139,688 in Manchester, 153,671 in Brighton and 149,669 in England and Wales.

In 1866 Parliament passed the City of Glasgow Improvement Act, under which the City Improvement Trust was set up, with power to levy 6d. in the £ for five years and 3d. in the £ for the next ten years and also power of compulsory purchase of property in defined areas. In spite of the very limited finance this provided the Trust was able to clear over 15,000 houses from the centre of the old city, helped by the activities of the railways in acquiring land and property in order to erect stations and sidings. It was the railways that were largely responsible for the removal of the University of Glasgow from its old site in the High Street to its new site at Gilmorehill: the College Goods station was built on the High Street site. In some respects the activity of the railways exacerbated the social problem, for they provided no new homes for those they displaced. Yet the clearance of the area around the Old College was long overdue. Dilapidated and overcrowded, it included the notorious Vennel and Havannah slums, inhabited by rag dealers, thieves, prostitutes and receivers of stolen goods. The College had been forced to abandon its evening law classes because each evening the air was thick with the sound of human screams and policemen's rattles, while it was felt improper that students should have to walk to the College past a parade of prostitutes. In some cases railway development hastened the social degeneration of the area acquired. A notable example of this is the area south of the river, between the two bridges, laid out as an elegant residential estate by David and James Laurie early in the century. First industrial encroachment then the acquisitions of the Caledonian and the Glasgow and South Western Railway Companies destroyed its character, until Laurieston degenerated between 1840 and 1900 into what John Kellett has described as 'a slum annexe to the Gorbals; a useful overflow district (for some of the thousands displaced by more central railway demolition) with large homes capable of subdivision into warrens housing a hundred and fifty people under one roof'. Abbotsford Place had been designed as a street of elegance and distinction, but the railways changed all that. Further west, still south of the Clyde, at Heatheryhall, Clydeville, Cessnock Bank, Mavis Bank, Green Bank and Plantation, railway yards and new docks combined to change the character of the area. To quote Kellett again: 'In the 1820s the area had been described as "snug" by contemporaries: "Mavisbank, Greenbank,

*The area of Glasgow before the extension of boundaries in 1891; this area was 6,111 acres and had in 1891 a density of population of 93 persons per acre.

Plantation, the very names seem to breathe a spirit of retired quiet''. Such a spirit proved very fragile in the railway age, and the only remedy for these smaller proprietors was, like Laurie's successors, to make the most they could out of the financial compensation.' Hutcheson's Hospital owned a great deal of land south of the Clyde, and sold 27,715 square yards immediately south-west of the Gorbals to the Glasgow and South-Western Railway Company in 1865. The Caledonian Railway Company bought a further 40,000 square yards from Hutcheson's Hospital south of the river in 1873.

In 1871 the City Improvement Trust received a further extension of time for the compulsory purchase of land and property and in 1880 the City of Glasgow Improvement Act was amended, giving the Corporation power to levy 2d. in the £ for city improvement. £1,616,000 was spent on compulsory purchase and a further £125,000 outside the areas of compulsory purchase. A variety of improvements were carried out by the Trust, which spent £103,000 in laying out streets and squares and building sewers, covering the Molendinar Burn and the purchase of Alexandra Park as a recreation area for the citizens. The Trust also built model lodging houses, one in the Drygate for men and one in East Russell Street for women. These were the first of a number of lodging houses set up to provide decent accommodation for single working men and women. For sixpence a night the lodger had a comfortable bed in a decent small room, facilities for washing clothes and cooking, a dining hall where he could eat, and a special shop where he could buy necessities at reasonable prices. These model lodging houses replaced the old common lodging houses, notorious for their overcrowded and insanitary conditions. In 1888 the Trust began to build tenement blocks in the Saltmarket and elsewhere, in some cases buying agricultural land for the purpose.

In 1897, under the new Glasgow Corporation Improvements and General Powers Act, six acres of congested slum area in the centre of the city were cleared and warehouses, shops and tenements were built on the cleared sites. By 1909, Glasgow Corporation had built over 2,000 houses, of which something over a quarter were designed for poorer tenants. There was also a considerable amount of privately built housing for rent. But the provision of rented housing for the poorer classes was not now an economic proposition. Rents were often difficult to collect, and the cost of maintenance kept rising. Private property companies, such as the Glasgow Building Company, which dated back to the 1780s, the Gilmorehill Land Company and the Stobcross Proprietors, had at one time looked on tenement buildings as a good source of investment. But soon after the beginning of the twentieth century private enterprise ceased to build dwelling houses for rent and the large tenement houses of Victorian Glasgow grew more and more crowded and dilapidated. The cessation of building has been laid at the door of Lloyd George's budget of 1909–10, which put a twenty per cent tax on the increment value of all heritable property, as well as the special features of the Scottish rating system. One cause, however, seems to have been simply the reluctance and sometimes the inability of many tenants to pay rent – so much so that, in spite of gross overcrowding, many houses remained empty, tenants finding it cheaper to take lodgings than to pay rent for a house or flat of their own. From 1919, when Parliamentary legislation provided subsidies to local governments for building houses for working people, Glasgow Corporation's programme of building houses proceeded vigorously, only to present the city eventually, as we shall see, with new social problems.

In spite of the activities of the Glasgow Improvement Trust in the last decades of the nineteenth century and the early years of the twentieth, the problem of overcrowding was not solved. In 1912 a Royal Commission examining the problem found that Scottish cities contained six times as many families living in one or two rooms as were found in cities in England and Wales; most of the examples came from Glasgow. And the Glasgow fondness for four-storey tenements meant people living on top of each other with a limited number of shared water taps and lavatories, creating a characteristic pattern of living which, while possessing its disadvantages, also produced kinds of inter-dependence and community living. For all the squalor and the delinquency associated with Glasgow's slums, they were looked back on with fond regret by many of those who were eventually removed to more hygienic and less community-oriented modern buildings.

CHAPTER 13

The Face of Victorian Glasgow

IF we are to get a balanced picture of Glasgow in the nineteenth century we must not deny the realities represented by slums, overcrowding, public health problems and drunkenness. But neither on the other hand must we ignore the city's splendours. Victorian Glasgow was a great city, full of extraordinary vitality and self-confidence, with a colour and a character all its own. It was also a remarkably handsome city.

We have seen how in the latter part of the eighteenth century the flat area between the Trongate and Ingram Street was laid out in a series of streets running north and south, with George Square at the north-west corner containing elegant terraced houses built in the 1780s. This was followed at the beginning of the nineteenth century by further development westward and north-westward up Blyths-wood Hill, an area built up by a variety of speculative builders, many of whom got into financial difficulties. In spite of the unorgan-ized, piecemeal method of building, the result was a not unattractive scene – 'pure Glasgow' Gomme and Walker call it in their definitive work on Glasgow architecture – consisting mostly of fairly short terraces two or three storeys high of pleasing classical design with ashlar facing. Bath Street, West Regent Street, West George Street and St Vincent Street, running east and west, north of and parallel to Argyle Street, are all part of this area, which still has a number of early nineteenth-century buildings, notably a terrace of houses at 232–242 St Vincent Street which now contains the hall of the Royal Faculty of Physicians and Surgeons and a most elegant house, probably by John Brash, at 198 West George Street. Blythswood Square itself, designed by Brash and built in 1823 by William Hamilton Garden (whose speculative building on Blythswood Hill resulted in his eventual financial ruin and flight to America) and first called Garden Square in his honour, is still not greatly changed from its original impressive appearance.

A westward continuation of Sauchiehall Street, beyond Charing

Cross, which was first known as Sauchiehall Road, extended the city still further to the west. Pagan's map of 1847 shows Sauchiehall Street becoming Albany Place before it turns south-west as Sauchiehall Road to join the 'road from Dumbarton to Glasgow' (now the western part of Argyle Street, east of the present Dumbarton Road). Pagan's map shows Newton Place as a short terrace running alongside Sauchiehall Road just where the new extension south-westward begins. This terrace, begun in 1840 by George Smith, architect and builder (and father of the notorious Madeleine Smith), was the first of a number of attractive terraces flanking Sauchiehall Street between Charing Cross and Kelvingrove. Pagan's map also shows Royal Crescent, conspicuous at the end of Sauchiehall Road, built in the 1840s and certainly the oldest of the Sauchiehall Street terraces with its total abandonment of classical restraint and curious mixture of styles.

A more striking westward extension was provided by Great Western Road, laid down in the 1830s to run north-west virtually from the Cowcaddens for four miles towards Dumbarton and Loch Lomond. This broad street runs out across the River Kelvin, past the Royal Botanic Gardens (originally the physic garden of the old College, and laid out in 1841 by Joseph Paxton on its present site, open to the public), in the vicinity of which we find a series of splendid Victorian terraces, more spacious and grander than those in Sauchiehall Street. Kirklee Terrace, originally called High Windsor, just beyond the gardens, was begun in 1845 to the design of the Glasgow architect Charles Wilson, and has impressive, even grandiose, Italianate features. Buckingham Terrace, designed by the Edinburgh-born architect J. T. Rochead, on the other side of the Botanic Gardens, is in two groups of houses, one of three storeys and one of four storeys. On the other side of Great Western Road, opposite the Botanic Gardens and facing north-east, is Rochead's Grosvenor Terrace of 1855, with its beautiful and striking façade reminiscent of a Venetian palazzo. The most famous of the Great Western Road terraces is that called simply Great Western Terrace, beyond the Botanic Gardens on the south side of Great Western Road. This dates from 1869 and is by the most famous of all Glasgow architects, Alexander Thomson, known as 'Greek' Thomson because of his association with the Greek revival in Glasgow. Its regularly spaced Greek porches, plain windows, and intermittent three-storey pavilions punctuating the long main line of the two-storey terrace produce a unique dignity and balance.

Pagan's map shows Woodside Place running parallel to Newton Place just to the north of it, with Woodside Crescent (now Woodside

Terrace) behind it. To the west still lay open fields and woodlands, but plans were already made for building on much of this space: the architect John Baird built a mansion to the west of Woodside Terrace as early as 1842 and in 1847 extended it to make Claremont Terrace, which though not shown on Pagan's map was in existence when it was published. North-west of this, in the valley of the Kelvin, Joseph Paxton and Charles Wilson were commissioned in 1854 to lay out the West End Park (now called Kelvingrove Park) for the recreation of the citizens living in the flourishing residential areas of the west end. The development of the Woodlands Hill area began early in the 1830s with Woodside Crescent. This development was the work of George Smith, who also designed the sweep of Lynedoch Crescent north of Woodside Terrace in the mid 1840s, but it was Charles Wilson's imaginative Park Circus in the late 1850s that provided a centre to the Woodlands Hill townscape and so helped to make Woodlands Hill what Gomme and Walker have called 'the most striking piece of town design in Glasgow'. Varieties of classic and Victorian design co-exist happily in this group of streets, where, to quote Gomme and Walker again, 'three things stand out . . . – the imaginative use of the site to make possible a fresh kind of urban experience, the amount of variety in layout and street-shape in a small area, and, this notwithstanding, the unity of place which links so many designs together into one composite design.' One should add that Wilson's Free Church College (now Trinity College) of 1854 in Lynedoch Street, with its strikingly original, classical design and three remarkable towers and Rochead's very different Victorian Gothic Park Church of 1858 in Park Circus Place provide interest to the rhythm of the domestic buildings and of the skyline.

In an attractive group of streets north of Woodlands Hill and just south-west of St George's Cross is John Bryce's semi-circular Queen's Crescent of 1840, with its neat porticoes and quiet classical elegance, that can still be appreciated despite its present shabbiness. Other and later streets and crescents on the north side of Great Western Road have the typical flavour of residential Victorian Glasgow.

The massive sweep of St Vincent Crescent, built in the mid 1850s by the eclectic Alexander Kirkland, shows Glasgow Victorian domestic architecture on a quite different scale. It lies south of Argyle Street, facing the lower harbour, and extends for almost half a mile roughly in the shape of a boomerang, a determinedly classical three-storey terrace dominating the street and the gardens below. Kirkland was also responsible for the four-storey tenement blocks in Minerva Street, which runs into Argyle Street. Where it bends there is an arcaded ground floor with Ionic pilasters on the first and second floors supporting a finely moulded cornice below the third floor: it creates one of the most distinctive corner buildings in Glasgow.

Glasgow has been called a city of tenements, and this phrase could certainly be applied to Victorian Glasgow, where, in addition to the terraced houses in the west, an increasing number of blocks were built with separate flats on each floor. In the earlier part of the century the occupation of a flat in a tenement was a clear sign of inferior social and economic position, but as the century advanced it became more and more respectable, although the middle classes tended to live in three-storey and the working classes in four-storey tenements. The basic design of the tenement was not unlike the simpler forms of Georgian classical architecture: indeed, anyone in Glasgow or Edinburgh who walks from a genteel three-storey terrace to a four-storey tenement block will frequently be struck by the similarity of design, even though the tenement block will be plainer and less varied. The tenement is often more subtly designed than is apparent to the casual observer: the careful grading of window size from floor to floor, and the imaginative grouping of them (each of the same basic shape, but in different clusters alternating in a specific order), the variety of stonework both horizontally and vertically, all help to break the monotony. Towards the end of the century bay windows (set in an outward projection from the wall) and later still bow windows (curved bay windows) became increasingly common, sometimes – when bays are imaginatively alternated with single windows – to pleasing effect, but at other times, particularly when bows and bays are used together, appearing both massive and fussy.

On the whole, the tenement blocks of Glasgow are not associated with the names of individual architects of distinction, the city developing its own tenement style that became common property. But 'Greek' Thomson designed some fine tenements, mostly on the south side of the river where the larger part of his work is to be seen. Queen's Park Terrace, 355–429 Eglinton Street, which dates from the late 1850s, is one of his most striking tenement buildings (now with shops on the ground floor). At about the same date Thomson built the tenement at 37–9 Cathcart Road, Govanhill, notable for the way in which it is integrated with his impressive and highly individual Caledonia Road Church of 1856–7. Among other tenements probably by Thomson are 12–24 Norfolk Street, Gorbals, about 1860, and the adjacent 32–68 Gorbals Street, about 1875; the block at 485–503 Govan Road, Govan, dating from 1872; and 36–40 Pollok Street, Kingston, of about the same date. Many other Glasgow tenement buildings are either possibly by Thomson or show his influence. The modern decline into shabbiness all too characteristic of so many tenement blocks on the south side cannot submerge the essential dignity of their architecture.

To return north of the river, we find an early four-storey range of tenements at Franklin Terrace, 1175–1263 Argyle Street, sober and dignified; William Clarke's Granby Terrace (2–28 Hillhead Street, which runs from University Avenue north to Great Western Road), a three-storey tenement block of more delicate and more varied treatment and an interesting grouping of windows, dating from 1856; and the lively four-storey tenement block at Walworth Terrace, 48–88 Kent Road (running south of and parallel to Sauchiehall Street), 1858–60, notable for its well-balanced alternation of bay and single windows. Finally, we might pick out the four-storey terrace at 268–318 Bath Street dating from the early 1850s, now three-quarters demolished; its slight curve carried the quietly diversified storeys with a simple dignity that flowed into the general townscape of the area. Nineteenth-century Glasgow tenements have become associated with dull buildings and slums, and it is indeed true that the tenements erected in that century by the City Improvement Trust are dull and uninteresting and also that many were allowed to degenerate into slums or semi-slums. But it is important to remember both that the nineteenth-century Glasgow tenement at its best represents a distinctive and impressive style of architecture and that this style – or more accurately this range of styles – produced streets of real character and dignity.

The domestic architecture of Victorian Glasgow also includes villas, used here in the Complete Oxford English Dictionary's definition of 'any residence of a superior type, in the suburbs of a town or in a residential district, such as is occupied by a person of the middle class; also, any small better-class dwelling house, usually one which is detached or semi-detached'. Villas of a great variety of kinds grew up west of the area we have so far considered, notably in Partickhill, and in the south-western suburb of Pollokshields across the river. The majority of these are of little architectural interest, but some of 'Greek' Thomson's houses and villas on the south side – only a few of those associated with his name are known certainly to be his – show him experimenting interestingly in a number of different styles. The most remarkable of Thomson's villas is Holmwood House, Netherlee Road, Cathcart, built in 1856–8 and now the Convent of Our Lady of the Missions, a complex building of varied shapes and changing planes. Thomson's earlier villa 'The Knowe', 301 Albert Drive, Pollokshields (1852–3), is a less integrated effort in a similar variety of styles. His double villa at 25 Mansionhouse Road,

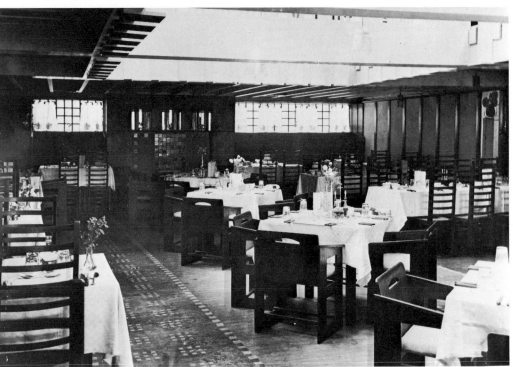

The 'Room de luxe' (*top*) and the 'Oak Room' (*bottom*) in the Willow Tea Rooms at 217 Sauchiehall Street: Charles Rennie Mackintosh's finest achievement in interior decoration.

The *Queen Empress* at Bridge Wharf in 1929.

A working day at the John Brown shipyards in the 1930s which were, nevertheless, years of high unemployment in the shipbuilding industry.

Langside (Mansionhouse Road runs south of what is now Queen's Park, which was laid out by Sir Joseph Paxton in 1862) dating from 1856, is a curiously un-Victorian building, which has seemed to some observers to look forward to the early work of Frank Lloyd Wright. The most curious and in many ways the most pleasing of Thomson's villas is at 200 Nithsdale Road, Pollokshields, and was built in 1871. Its style is quite *sui generis*, 'irrepressibly gay, happy, and light-hearted without being frivolous' as Gomme and Walker express it. It has none of the confident middle-class respectability shown by the majority of unadventurous villas of late nineteenth-century Glasgow. Not that Victorian Glasgow architects and builders did not experiment in a great variety of styles, from Gothic to Egyptian, but this is best illustrated in the city's public and commercial buildings.

Victorian public buildings in Glasgow might be said to begin in 1842 with the erection of the City and County Buildings in Wilson Street, a large and pretentious neo-classic edifice that occupied the whole block between Ingram Street and Wilson Street. Its massive Ionic portico belongs to its first stage; other sections were added in 1871 and 1892. It speaks grandiosely of self-conscious civic pride. The architects of the original section were William Clarke and George Bell. The attractive Georgian-styled warehouse by James Salmon at 81 Miller Street, built in 1849–50, speaks with considerably more charm of business pride. Just south of this, at 37–51 Miller Street, Alexander Kirkland's elaborate Venetian-styled warehouse has been demolished; it had the appearance of a sumptuous princely residence. Also by Kirkland are the less pretentious Eagle Buildings at 205–229 Bothwell Street, with their delicately wrought façade. (Bothwell Street runs east and west south of Blythswood Square, between Argyle Street and St Vincent Street.)

The use of a classical style in warehouses and other commercial buildings survived until the end of the century. But Victorian Glasgow also pioneered in iron-framed warehouses, one of the first being that built in mid-century for Wylie and Lochhead at 28 Argyle Street (no longer in existence). Many such cast-iron buildings with glass façades followed, especially in the 1850s, and of those that survive, Gardner's warehouse by John Baird of 1855–6 at 36 Jamaica Street (now known as the Jamaica Street warehouse) is the most striking, with its beautifully delicate treatment of windows and subtle variations between storeys. Next door to it at 24–30 Jamaica Street, is the very different, stone warehouse by John Honeyman, built in 1864 in the Venetian style that appealed to so many Glasgow architects.

M

Detail of South tower of
Alexander 'Greek' Thomson's
St Vincent Street Church
(1860)

Banks represent an important section of the buildings of Victorian Glasgow. There had been rapid developments in Scottish banking since the foundation of Glasgow's Ship Bank in 1750 and these are reflected in their nineteenth-century buildings. The first bank built in Victorian Glasgow was Robert Black's City of Glasgow Bank of 1838, long since demolished. Charles Wilson's Royal Bank of Scotland in Buchanan Street, a dignified square building that combines stylishness with utility, dates from 1850-1, while David Rhind's head office of the Commercial Bank of Scotland (1857) is an altogether more elaborate Italianate building with some features reminiscent of the Farnesine in Rome. James Sellars' City of Glasgow Bank in Queen Street, an elaborate Renaissance-styled building with six immense Corinthian columns in front of the recessed second and third storeys, was built in 1878 and demolished in 1959. John Burnet's Clydesdale Bank at 30–40 St Vincent Place is a striking baroque building, erected in 1870–3 and it still stands although never completed on the eastern side.

And then of course there were churches. We have already referred to Alexander Thomson's Caledonia Road Church of 1856. Its impressive tower and strange, but wholly effective, mixture of styles make it one of the most remarkable churches in the city. Thomson's Queen's Park United Presbyterian Church of 1867 was burnt down as a result of bombing in 1943, a grave loss to the city's architecture. Like so many of Thomson's buildings, it combined a number of styles and influences in a highly original and striking manner with an Egyptian-looking portico and a high, narrow dome. His St Vincent Street Church of 1860, with its combination of Greek temple and Italian tower is still standing.

Among other Glasgow Victorian churches are Elgin Place Con-gregational Church (by John Burnet, 1856) at 240 Bath Street and Hugh Barclay's St George's-in-the-Fields, St George's Road, Woodside, both in Greek temple style; John Honeyman's Barony North Church in Cathedral Square of 1878 and James Sellars' Finnieston (now Kelvingrove) Parish Church at 41 Derby Street, Kelvingrove, of the same date, both classical though in very different ways.

In due course the Gothic revival reached Glasgow, and though only one Glasgow architect, William Leiper, went in consistently for Gothic, others, like Honeyman and Sellars, could work in either the classical or the Gothic idiom. Sir George Gilbert Scott used elements of what might be called Victorian Gothic in Glasgow University, re-built at Gilmorehill in 1866–70, a mixed affair with features from sixteenth-century Scottish baronial architecture combined with others from French and Flemish Gothic. He followed this in 1870 with St Mary's Episcopal Cathedral in Great Western Road. As early as 1849 the English architect J. T. Emmett had built a Gothic church for an Independent congregation at the west end of Bath Street (it is now known as St Matthew Blythswood), an accurate copy of fourteenth-century English Gothic with a parti-cularly successful spire. Honeyman's Lansdowne Church at 416–20 Great Western Road is a successful adaptation of Early English Gothic. William Leiper's first Gothic church was Dowanhill Church of Scotland at 98 Hyndland Road, built in 1865, also in the Early English style. He followed this in 1878 with the Camphill Church of Scotland, Balvicar Drive, Queen's Park, which happily borrows some features from Normandy Gothic. James Sellars' Belmond and Hillhead Parish Church, Saltoun Street, Dowanhill, of 1875, which some claim was based on a design by Leiper, adapts the design of the Sainte Chapelle. Sellars' Belhaven Church, 29 Dundonald Road, Dowanhill, dates from 1877: it is now St Luke's Greek Orthodox church, and is one of Sellars' more successful adaptations of Gothic features. But the finest of all Victorian Glasgow's Gothic churches is generally held to be the Barony Church at 1 Castle Street by John James Burnet (son of John Burnet) and J. L. Pearson, built in 1886–90. This is the most impressive of a fine group of four churches that face Cathedral Square. In 1898 the London architect J. J. Stevenson designed the Stevenson Memorial Church at Belmont Bridge, Belmont Street (over the Kelvin, north-east of Great Western Road) in a rather odd mixture of different Gothic styles. This was the last Gothic church built in Victorian Glasgow. But Gothic churches continued to be built in Glasgow in the early years of the twentieth century.

Terraces, tenements, warehouses, banks, churches – there was much in Victorian Glasgow to afford the strolling Glaswegian both pride and pleasure, even though, as we saw in an earlier chapter, there was also much to shock the inquirer into standards of health and housing. There was a temporary break in the city's optimism after the financial crisis of 1878, which hit Glasgow hard. The City of Glasgow Bank failed, with a final deficit of over £5 million, and since it was an unlimited company its directors were ruined and shareholders impoverished. Some of the directors were tried and imprisoned for fraud. James Sellars' magnificent new bank building, only recently occupied, had to be vacated and turned into a warehouse. But in spite of closed factories, uncompleted buildings, ruined investors and general financial depression, Glasgow survived to move with surprising speed into a new area of prosperity. One result of the crisis was an Act of 1879 compelling the Scottish banks to register as limited-liability companies. These measures, along with other financial reforms and abetted by the recovery of the shipbuilding industry which began to expand to new dimensions, soon put the city back on its feet. No city that lacked confidence in itself could have planned the lushly exhibitionist City Chambers as Glasgow's city fathers began to do at the beginning of the 1880s. A competition for the best design was won by a London Scot, William Young. The building was on the site of Alexander of Ballochmyle's town house, and its luxurious profusion of styles, speaking so clearly of wealth and display, changed the whole appearance of George Square. It was completed in 1888, when it was opened by the Queen.

Victorian Glasgow was also proud of its schools. We have already referred in Chapter Three to the seventeenth-century endowment of Hutcheson's Hospital and School and to the building (by David Hamilton) in Ingram Street opened in 1805, still an important feature of Glasgow's townscape. A new and rather fancy Hutcheson's School, by David and James Hamilton, in Crown Street, south of the river, was opened in 1841. In 1869, with the opening of the unpretentiously classical Hutcheson's Girls' School in Elgin Street (just south of the Gallowgate), the Crown Street school became the Hutcheson's Grammar School for Boys. (It had originally been intended that boys and girls should be educated in different wings of the Crown Street school.) James Sellars' Kelvinside Academy of 1877, in Bellshaugh Road, Kelvinside, has an air of academic severity on its classical features. Hugh and David Barclay's Govanhill Public School of 1887, in Annette Street, Govanhill, is an original and sturdy version of the Renaissance palazzo which still stands in quiet dignity.

Enough has been said to indicate the variety and splendour of Victorian Glasgow. A few more buildings might be mentioned, not to complete the picture – that would require almost a street-by-street coverage of the city – but to add to that impression of grandeur and diversity. The Custom House in Clyde Street, dating from 1840 and probably by George Ledwell Taylor, is a notably handsome classical building. There are several further buildings by Alexander Thomson that deserve singling out, such as the imaginative iron-frame Buck's Head in Argyle Street (1863); the so-called Grecian Building at 336–56 Sauchiehall Street, with its Egyptian columns (1865); and the Egyptian Halls at 84–100 Union Street (1871–3). John Burnet's ornate Italian Gothic Stock Exchange of 1875 speaks flamboyantly of money. And Robert Rowland Anderson's Central Station Hotel of 1884, towering over the corner of Gordon and Hope Streets, combines with remarkable assurance features from a great variety of styles to stand an unmistakable part of the Glasgow townscape.

Victorian Glasgow was not all streets and buildings. Glasgow Green, the first and for a long time the only one of Glasgow's parks, remained as a great open space for recreation. Then came the Botanic Gardens in 1841. Sir Joseph Paxton, the architect of Crystal Palace, was invited to plan three parks – the West End Park, which, as I have already noted, was opened in 1853; Queen's Park, on the south side, opened in 1862, with its marvellous view from what Tweed's Guide of 1872 called 'the eminence from which the flagstaff rises'; and Alexandra Park to the east of the city, completed in 1870. But Glasgow Green remained the centre of open-air recreation for ordinary Glaswegians. It is appropriate to conclude this chapter with Tweed's 1872 salute to it:

> This noble park, which we enter at its east end below Rutherglen Bridge, is the largest and, in spite of the attention lavished on its new-born rivals, is in some respects perhaps the finest of which Glasgow can boast. It lacks the undulating and wooded beauty of the West-end Park, and the blooming parterres of the Queen's; but it can boast of its noble elms, its well-kept footpaths, its three-mile drive, and its incomparable fields for many sports, and then, gentle reader, it serves also the purposes of a bleaching green! But that is not all; the Clyde washes its banks from Rutherglen Bridge to Jail Square; and here on summer evenings, skimming over the broad river's bosom, are crowds of skiffs, punts, and jolly-boats, pulled by the rising aquatics of the east end. No part of Glasgow can boast of one-tenth of the interest of the Green on a Saturday afternoon, when its fields are dotted with cricketers, when the footballs describe their parabolic curves in the air, and when the flashing oars gleam in the sunlight as a hundred boats dart hither and thither on the river.

This sunlit scene is hardly the dear, dirty, rainy city beloved of so many nostalgic Glasgow writers; but it is an equally real part of nineteenth-century Glasgow.

CHAPTER 14

Victorian Pomp and Circumstance

THE Burgh Reform Act of 1833 marked the end of one phase of Glasgow's civic government and the beginning of another. As we have seen, it gave the municipal franchise to those who had been granted the parliamentary franchise under the Scottish Reform Act (about 9,000 out of a total population of 202,400). The five wards into which Glasgow was now divided elected six councillors each, with the Dean of Guild and the Deacon Convener as *ex officio* members bringing the total number up to thirty-two.

Agitation for municipal reform had begun at least as early as 1605, when only internal quarrelling prevented the Town Council from being authorized to elect its own bailies. In 1641 Parliament granted the right to the Council, although the Provost was to be chosen by the Duke of Lennox from a list of three Council nominees. When episcopacy was restored in 1661 the Provost was again chosen by the Archbishop, and only the final abolition of episcopacy in Scotland in 1690 brought the right of the election of the Provost first to the Crown and then in the same year to the Council.

The pattern of municipal government set up in 1690 functioned well enough during the eighteenth century, but proved incapable of handling the proliferating social problems which accompanied the Industrial Revolution. The tackling of these problems required both power and cash, and the latter was not easily wrung from a city population that had no say in the election of its Town Council (which until 1833 was self-perpetuating). Only a representative body would have the power to levy rates for such services as police, sanitation and poor relief. The process of democratizing local government had in fact begun before the Burgh Reform Act of 1833, with the replacement in 1800 of the old 'watch and ward' method of policing by a police system financed by rating administered by a specific body of 'commissioners' elected by the rate-payers. Each of the twenty-four wards of the city elected a commissioner, and the commissioners, together with the bailies, the Dean of Guild and the

Deacon Convener, constituted the Police Board. The immediate consequence of this new system was the emigration of crime to the suburbs, and it was only the acquiring of similar police powers by the suburban districts by separate Acts of Parliament (Gorbals in 1808, Calton in 1819, Anderston in 1824) that reversed this trend. In 1846, when these burghs were annexed to Glasgow, their police systems were integrated with that of the city. The commissioners were replaced by a 'police and statute labour committee' elected by the Town Council. This functioned until 1877, when the magistrates and Council took over the management of police affairs. Finally, under the Glasgow Corporation and Police Act of 1895, the Corporation took over the responsibility for all municipal affairs, including police.

At the first meeting of Glasgow's reformed Town Council on 8 November 1833 the spirit of change was in the air. One of the bailies, Mr M'Gavin, pointed out 'the ridiculous nature and buffoon-like appearance of the dress which had hitherto been worn by the Bailies; and thought that the time had now arrived when they should be allowed to apparel themselves as they chose – whether in black or in white.' He proceeded to move two motions. His first was 'that in future the three-cornered hats should be dispensed with' and the second 'that the gold chains, and other Magisterial toys, should be immediately sold, and the proceeds put into the City Treasury'. After considerable discussion, the cocked hats were eventually discarded, but the chains remained.

The new system did not at first run smoothly. Doubt about whether under the Act of 1833 the retiring Provost (or Lord Provost, as they now preferred to call themselves) should continue in office until the actual election of his successor or should retire immediately before, led to the extraordinary comedy in 1837 of two men, Fleming and Dunlop, each claiming to be the legally elected Provost. The retiring Provost construed the law to mean that he should preside over the election of his successor (which meant he had a casting vote in case of a tie), while an opposition faction argued that he should retire previous to this and was no longer legally Provost on the day of the election, so that he could not preside at that election and would therefore have no casting vote. In the event the retiring Provost and one of the bailies simultaneously took the chair at the election, each refusing to give way to the other, and when the rival candidates for election to the provostship both received fifteen votes, the two chairmen gave their casting votes, one on each side, so that, with each candidate recognizing a different chairman as valid and only his vote as legal, both insisted that they were the Provost. At a meeting of the River Trust on 28 December 1837 both Fleming and Dunlop took the chair, each claiming to be the legal Provost, and, as a later nineteenth-century transcriber of the minutes observed, 'it may be safely said there has not been such a boisterous scene'. Dunlop eventually obtained a High Court injunction to restrain Fleming from claiming the provostship and sat out the remainder of his term undisputed.

The Glasgow magistracy of the Victorian age were greatly given to lavish civic banquets (at the rate-payers' expense), and used every opportunity for such a celebration. Business men also gave public banquets. When the Edinburgh and Glasgow railway was opened for public traffic on 18 February 1842 and the first train arrived from Edinburgh 'a grand banquet was given by the Directors in the station, Queen Street'. Civic banquets followed the installation of 'the Hon. T. B. Macaulay' as Lord Rector (a courtesy title now increasingly used instead of the strictly proper Rector) of Glasgow University on 22 March 1849 and his receipt of the freedom of the city the following day, David Livingstone's receipt of the freedom of the city on 16 September 1852 and the laying of the foundation stone of the Albert Bridge on 3 June 1870, while on the opening of the new University buildings at Gilmorehill on 7 November 1870 'a sumptuous banquet' for two hundred gentlemen was provided in honour of the Principal and Professors of the University by the subscribers of £100 and upwards to the building funds.

When Queen Victoria and Prince Albert sailed into Dumbarton on 16 August 1847, 'the Lord Provost, Magistrates and Councillors, the Clyde Trustees and a large number of ladies and gentlemen' sailed down the Clyde in the steamboat *Thetis* to meet the Royal Squadron. John Tweed described in 1883 what happened, from official reports of the time:

Owing to foggy weather the squadron was delayed and the party on the *Thetis* went on to Lochryan where they met the squadron late in the afternoon. The squadron cast anchor; the Lord Provost with several of the Magistrates in a small boat then went along side the Royal Yacht, when the Lord Provost asked to come on board. He then received instructions to meet Her Majesty at Dumbarton the following day at one o'clock . . . On proceeding to Dumbarton the Lord Provost, Bailie M'Kinlay, Bailie Stewart, and Mr Forbes, Town Clerk, went out in a small boat, when the authorities at Dumbarton refused to allow them to land at the quay, on the grounds that the Magistrates of Glasgow had no jurisdiction there. The Lord Provost said he was there by command of Her Majesty, and that he would land somewhere. His party got ashore at an old pier, and went forward to the enclosure where Her Majesty was to land, but were refused admission. Captain Mullen, who was in command of the enrolled pensioners who were to act as Her Majesty's body guard, came forward and demanded admission for the Glasgow authorities, as they were there by command of Her Majesty; – consequently the command was at once obeyed. On the arrival of Her Majesty and the Prince they proceeded to the castle, where the Lord Provost was presented to Her Majesty. His Lordship presented a loyal address to Her Majesty in the name of the citizens of Glasgow.

When the Queen visited Glasgow itself on 14 August 1849 – the first visit of a reigning British monarch to Glasgow since the days of James VI – in the royal yacht *Victoria and Albert*, she was received with all the panoply the city could put forth. After sailing to Arrochar, for a visit to Loch Lomond, the Queen landed at Glasgow at noon on the 14th to receive a ceremonial welcome by the Provost and Magistrates in court dress and the Town Clerk and City Chamberlain in their gowns of office. A large contingent of the Celtic Society of Scotland, in full highland dress, was also in attendance. On disembarking Her Majesty called for a sword and knighted the Lord Provost, James Anderson. Addresses were then presented to the Queen, before the procession started, with troops of the Glasgow Yeomanry, city officers, police, escort of cavalry, detachments of the Celtic Society of Scotland, and fourteen carriages moving along Clyde Street to the Jamaica Street bridge, across the bridge to Jamaica Street, then to Argyle Street, up Buchanan Street, and along West George Street to the High Street, and so on to the Cathedral. After a ceremony there the procession went on to the University, where they were received by the Principal and the Professors in their gowns. Then they went down the High Street to Trongate and turned up Queen Street to reach the terminus of the Edinburgh and Glasgow Railway. There the royal party were received by Mr Blackburn, the Chairman, and other officials, before entering a specially prepared train and setting off in it for Perth. A triumphal arch had been erected at the station. On 6 September 1854 a statue of Queen Victoria was unveiled in George Square, with high ceremonial, to commemorate this visit.

There were many other occasions for civic pomp in Victorian Glasgow. On 18 January 1843 the new Corn Exchange was opened in Hope Street. On the evening of 26 November 1860 the Empress Eugénie (wife of Napoleon III) arrived at the Dundas Street station of the North British Railway on her way back from the Highlands, where she had been staying for her health. She received an ovation from the crowd, and a formal address of welcome from the city, to which she replied warmly before disappearing into the Queen's Hotel where she stayed the night. On 1 November 1865 Gladstone was given the freedom of the city in the City Hall. (This was part of a building completed in 1812 at the north-west end of Glasgow Green to accommodate the Municipal Offices,* the Courts of Justiciary and a new jail: it was on the site of the old slaughter house and the Skinners' Green, and replaced the old Tolbooth that had been rebuilt in 1626 and of which only the steeple now survives.) On 8 October the Prince and Princess of Wales arrived in Glasgow by the North British Railway and the Prince of Wales laid the foundation stone of the new university buildings at Gilmorehill. On 19 November 1873 Disraeli was installed as Lord Rector of the University, and gave his rectorial address on 'Self-Knowledge'. Gladstone was installed as Lord Rector on 5 December 1879, and gave his rectorial address in the Kibble Palace, Botanic Gardens. (The Kibble Palace was the popular name of a Winter Garden originally built by Mr John Kibble at his residence at Coulport on Loch Long and in 1871 removed from there to the Botanic Gardens, where it was re-erected on an enlarged scale.) On 22 August 1888 Queen Victoria formally opened the new City Chambers in George Square.

Less of an occasion for civic pride, but of considerable historical importance, was the last public hanging in Glasgow, which took place before a huge crowd on 28 July 1865 outside the South Prison on Glasgow Green. The hanged man was Dr Edward William Pritchard, a medical practitioner in the city, who had been convicted at the High Court of Justiciary in Edinburgh of having murdered his wife and mother-in-law. He had murdered his wife by slow poisoning, and then rapidly dispatched her mother when she suspected what was happening, his object being to be free to make love to their young Highland maid. Pritchard was a dapper ladies' man who dressed in the height of fashion and made love to his female patients: his execution relieved many outraged husbands in Glasgow and neighbourhood.

Meanwhile the city was growing steadily: in the nineteenth century its area grew from 1,768 acres to 12,688 acres, the larger part

*In 1870 the Town Council and the municipal offices moved to new quarters built on to the north end of the City and County Buildings, Wilson Street, (by William Clarke and George Bell, 1842–4) so as to face Ingram Street. These buildings were reconstructed five times between 1844 and 1900. In 1895 the Town Council and municipal offices moved to the splendid new City Chambers in George Square and the County Buildings expanded to include the whole block between Wilson Street and Ingram Street.

of the increase arising from the extension of boundaries in the latter half of the century. The population grew from 77,000 in 1801 to 762,000 in 1901. In 1871 the population was 478,000, a six-fold increase over the population of 1801 compared with a two-fold increase in the population of Scotland as a whole during those seventy years. The extension of the city's boundaries in 1846 increased the number of wards in the city to sixteen and membership of the Town Council to fifty (the Dean of Guild and Deacon Convener still included *ex officio*). The expansion also led to a re-definition of its geographical status. Historically Glasgow was situated in Lanarkshire and in the nineteenth century extended to a small extent into Renfrewshire. In 1892 an order of the Boundary Commission for Scotland placed Glasgow wholly within Lanarkshire, at the same time giving it independent status as a 'county of a city', and, in spite of subsequent expansions involving territorial losses to Glasgow from Lanarkshire, Renfrewshire and Dunbartonshire, this remained an administratively independent county of a city until the far-reaching re-structuring of the Local Government (Scotland) Act of 1973 came into effect in May 1975.

After the second major expansion of Glasgow's boundaries in 1891 the number of wards was increased from sixteen to twenty-five and the number of the Town Council to seventy-seven. But though the Council was an active and powerful body, making genuine attempts to tackle the city's many problems and to provide the necessary municipal services, there was little enthusiasm in municipal elections, even after the introduction of election by ballot in 1872. In most of the elections candidates were returned unopposed. It was not until 1920 when a reorganization of wards involved the retiral of all elected members of the Council (now one hundred and eleven) to give the electorate the opportunity to put in new members if they so wished, and the simultaneous emergence of party politics at the municipal level, that a dramatic change took place and the new Labour Party first showed its power in Glasgow's government.

As the nineteenth century advanced, various independent local boards were created to tackle problems of health, education, poverty and other social needs; eventually their separate functions merged into the Corporation. In 1855 the Corporation assumed responsibility for water (with the resulting opening of the Loch Katrine supply in 1855); in 1869 it acquired the Partick Gas Works and bought out two private companies to take responsibility for the gas supply. In 1890 it obtained power to supply the city with electricity and in 1891 with public transport. (There was even a Corporation telephone service from 1900 to 1907, when the Corporation sold its system to the Post Office.)

The Education (Scotland) Act of 1872 provided for the setting up of local School Boards under the general supervision of the Scotch (it is interesting that they used this form of the word, not 'Scottish') Education Department. Before this, control of education in Glasgow as elsewhere in Scotland was in the hands of the Church, with which the Town Council co-operated in all educational matters under its jurisdiction (it also frequently sought the advice of the University). It was the joint efforts of Church of Scotland ministers and professors from the College that produced the curriculum of Glasgow's Grammar School in the late seventeenth century. In 1834 the Grammar School became the High School and the curriculum was modernized with the introduction of English, modern languages, geography and mathematics. But the establishment of the Glasgow School Board after the 1872 Act gave the School a new lease of life while at the same time severing at last its links with the Church. In 1878 it moved into Charles Wilson's handsome Elmbank Street building that had been occupied by Glasgow Academy from its foundation in 1846, while the Academy moved to new premises at Kelvin Bridge. Kelvin-side Academy was founded in 1877, because, as John M'Dowall wrote in 1899, 'owing to the growth of the city it became desirable to have another first-class educational establishment in the West End, and the gentlemen of the district are to be congratulated on adding such a high-class beautiful school to meet the wants of the locality'. There were of course still schools provided by the Church – not only Sunday schools (in the provision of which the socially-conscious ecclesiastical politician Dr Thomas Chalmers was active in the first half of the century) and infant schools, but also 'sessional schools' supervised by the Kirk Sessions, and colleges for the training of teachers, of which the Normal School for the Training of Teachers, founded by David Stow in 1836, was the pioneer. After the Disruption of 1843, the seceding Free Church set up its own schools.

The School Board of Glasgow tackled its tasks energetically. On coming to office it found that the city's 228 schools could accommodate only 57,290 of the 87,294 children calculated to be of school age in the city. And only 52,644 actually attended. By 1895 the Board had made available accommodation for over 66,000 children, mostly in its 67 Board Schools. The Board's policy was to reduce the number and improve the quality and capacity of the schools, so that between 1873 and 1895 the number of schools was halved (from 228 to 114) while the accommodation increased by 65 per cent (from 57,290 to over 94,000). The number of those actually attending rose from 52,644 to 90,629. The Board was especially active in extending the curriculum beyond the elementary level, in 'grant-aided primary schools with higher departments' and 'higher grade board schools', while the former burgh schools, now teaching classics, mathematics, modern languages and science, were managed by the Board as Secondary or High Schools. There were also proprietary secondary schools, including both Glasgow Academy and Kelvinside Academy and the Park School for Girls (founded in 1880), and endowed secondary schools, including four run by the Roman Catholic Church (two for boys and two for girls), the two Hutcheson's Grammar Schools referred to in the preceding chapter, and Allan Glen's Institution, a school founded by Glen, a Glasgow wright, to provide 'a good practical education' free for about fifty sons of tradesmen or artisans. Under an Act of 1876 it became a fee-paying secondary and technical school for boys intending to embark on industrial and mercantile careers and eventually became part of Glasgow and West of Scotland Technical College. (As a result of the provision of free elementary education under the Education [Scotland] Act of 1872 many endowed charitable schools were able to transform themselves into fee-paying secondary schools.)

On the whole, the development of primary and secondary education in Victorian Glasgow was something the city could be proud of. In the middle 1830s it was estimated that only one-fourteenth of the population of Glasgow were attending school. Thirty years later, at the time of the passing of the Education Act, the situation had much improved, in spite of the fact that less than half the children of school age in Glasgow were on school rolls and more than one-fifth of these were in sub-standard schools. (It is worth remembering that in Scotland in the years just before the passing of the Education Act one out of 250 pupils was receiving education, while the figure for England was one out of 1,300. And Scotland's ratio of university students to population was six times that of England.) Right through the century the proportion of those receiving secondary education rose. By the end of the century a total of 4,738 Glasgow children were receiving secondary education, representing over six per thousand of the population.

The University also flourished in Victorian Glasgow. The opening of the Royal Infirmary in 1784 had given an impetus to medical studies, and of the twelve new Chairs founded in the first sixty years of the twentieth century the great majority were in one branch or another of medicine. But it was not until after the implementation of reforms under the Act of 1858 (described in Chapter Seven) that really significant advances in both medicine and law took place, both these subjects having been inhibited by the old privileged incorporations in Glasgow: the Faculty of Physicians and Surgeons, founded in 1599, and the Faculty of Procurators, founded in 1796. Science flourished under the influence of the great scientist and inventor William Thomson (created Lord Kelvin in 1902), who was Professor of Natural Philosophy (physics) at the University from 1846 to 1899, even though a separate Faculty of Science was not established until 1893. Of the thirty-one Chairs held at the University of Glasgow at the end of the century, in the five faculties of Arts, Science, Medicine, Law and Theology, eighteen were founded in the nineteenth century. (There were sixty-five Chairs by the middle of the twentieth century.) Women students were first admitted to the University in 1892.

In 1874 the tobacco merchant Stephen Mitchell left a bequest to the Town Council to be used for founding a library. The Mitchell Library was opened first in Ingram Street, then moved to Miller Street, and in 1911 moved to the domed building by W. B. White in North Street, Charing Cross. It has developed into the largest public reference library in Scotland, especially rich in Scottish literature and history.

Glasgow's pride in its intellectual activities was grandiosely symbolized by the International Exhibition of Science and Art in 1888. Buildings were erected at Overnewton, by the Kelvin, and a bridge was built across the Kelvin so that a large part of the West End Park and the University grounds could also be used for the exhibition. Kelvingrove Museum (originally the old Kelvingrove Mansion, in the West End Park, on the banks of the Kelvin, turned into a museum by the Corporation in 1870 with an addition to the building in 1874) was used to display the presents the Queen had received on celebrating her Jubilee the year before: she placed them at the disposal of the organizers of the exhibition. The exhibition was opened by the Prince and Princess of Wales on 8 May 1888 when – as M'Dowall proudly recorded – 'in addition to the police, there were 10,452 persons under arms from the Regular Army, the Volunteers, and the Boys' Brigade'. The Queen visited the exhibition twice in August. In the six months during which it was open 5,746,000 persons went through the entrance, paying a total entry money of £225,928 15s. 2d., of which £54,000 was profit. The exhibition gave Glasgow a new prestige as an intellectual centre: while it was running, the annual meetings of the British Medical Association, the British Archaeological Association, the Library Association and the Institute of Naval Architects all took place in the city.

The pioneering interest in the fine arts shown by the Foulis brothers in eighteenth-century Glasgow did not altogether disappear.

Various bodies organized periodical art exhibitions, among them Glasgow's first Institute of Fine Arts, founded in 1821, the Dilettanti Society founded in 1823, and the West of Scotland Academy (which later gave birth to the Glasgow School of Art) founded in 1840. Wealthy business men acquired prestige by collecting paintings. One of them, John Bell, built North Park House by the banks of the Kelvin to house his collection: many years later it became Queen Margaret College for women students and later still the headquarters of the British Broadcasting Corporation in Scotland. Bailie Archibald McLellan, Glasgow coachbuilder, exhibited his collection of pictures and sculpture in a block of buildings with galleries behind known as the McLellan Galleries, in Sauchiehall Street. When he died insolvent in 1854 his collection went to the city, which sold many of the works to pay his debts and kept the remainder to form the nucleus of the city's permanent collection later housed in the Municipal Art Gallery in Kelvingrove. This gallery was partly financed from the proceeds of the 1888 exhibition, partly by cash gifts from prominent citizens, and partly by the Corporation, which provided, together with a free site in Kelvingrove Park, a sum equal to the profits of the exhibition. The Duke of York laid the foundation stone on 10 September 1897. Glasgow's second Institute of Fine Arts (later to become the Royal Glasgow Institute of Fine Arts) opened in Sauchiehall Street in 1880 in a building designed by J. J. Burnet (it was burned down in 1967).

Glasgow collectors of the latter part of the nineteenth century were, perhaps surprisingly, free of stolid conservative prejudices and open to experimental work. The art dealers John Forbes White and Alexander Reid brought to Glasgow the work of the Barbizan group. Whistler was much admired. As a result of the sense of excitement and experiment the Glasgow Group of painters emerged about 1880 under the leadership of W. Y. Macgregor. This surge of artistic creativity in Glasgow has been linked to the city's pride in craftsmanship. Glasgow's citizens, Ian Finlay has argued, 'were alert not merely to make money, but to make things; and the things they made were not mere counters to obtain profits, but things which they took joy in making supremely well. The atmosphere was still of craftsmanship, rather than of finance – Edinburgh, not Glasgow, was and is the centre of banking and insurance.' Further, 'Glasgow was no capital and therefore she had no academic fortress to be stormed.' But whatever the explanation, the fact remains that 'The Boys' of the Glasgow School of Painters, with their *pleinairiste* approach and bold use of colour made a valuable contribution to Scottish art.

The remarkable pioneering achievement of Charles Rennie Mackintosh, Glasgow architect, designer and water-colourist,

A scramble at a wedding in Gemmal Street in 1955: traditionally the groom would throw a handful of coins for the children to catch. The slums were rich in children's games, many of which have disappeared with the move to high-rise flats.

The Red Road flats in N E Glasgow (1966–8).

George Square today, from the west. The statue, on top of the 80 foot column, is of Sir Walter Scott, by John Greenshields (1837). Behind it stand the City Chambers; *left* the tower block of the new Strathclyde University; *right* the GPO.

The changed face of Glasgow: Charing Cross in 1974, looking north.

belongs partly to the end of the nineteenth century (his Glasgow Herald Building in Mitchell Street dates from 1893 and the first, eastern, section of his famous Glasgow School of Art in Renfrew Street from 1897) and partly to the first two decades of the twentieth. His achievement is perhaps best seen in the context of the artistic and intellectual activity in early twentieth-century Glasgow, and this will be discussed in a later chapter, as will the works of those Glasgow writers whose life spanned the turn of the century, some of whom gave renderings of Glasgow life that the Glaswegians took to their hearts.

Politically, Victorian Glasgow was essentially a Liberal city, which regularly sent to Parliament middle-class Protestant radical free-traders who were themselves Glasgow merchants or manufacturers. The occasional Conservative slipped in during the latter part of the period, and by the end of Victoria's reign those with vision could see that the great threat to the middle-class Liberals was going to come in future not from Conservatives but from working-class supporters of Labour. But that is essentially a twentieth-century development.

CHAPTER 15

Entertainment High and Low

GLASGOW's International Exhibition of 1888 was a great source of civic pride to the respectable but, like so many other things in the city that gave satisfaction to its genteel middle-class citizens, it was liable to provoke satirical mirth in other quarters. The theatres and music halls of Victorian Glasgow attracted and reflected an altogether more rambunctious element in the population than the occupants of genteel terraces by Great Western Road or in Pollokshields. There was a Glasgow music-hall song of late 1888 with the following chorus:

> Oh, my, I'm thankfu' that it's by –
> That dreidfu' Exhibition, ma temper it did try;
> For every nicht our Jock gaed there
> He cam' hame roarin' foo,
> And he always blamed it on the tea
> He got at the Bungaloo.

A tea-room in an Anglo-Indian bungalow specially erected for the Exhibition did not impress the city's working classes. The kind of humour in this song appealed to a variety of elements in society that were out of the mainstream of middle-class gentility: young men fancying themselves as gay dogs or men about town, adventurous students and certain sections (but only certain sections) of the working classes frequented the theatres. Even as late as the 1880s, according to the writer J. J. Bell (born in 1871) reminiscing about Glasgow in his childhood, the theatre was suspect:

> The comparatively few must have gone to the theatre fairly often, for the great majority did not go at all. Apart from the very considerable number who still regarded the theatre and all pertaining to it as being under the auspices of the Evil One, was a multitude who, like my father, never gave it a thought . . . Most business men kept later hours at the office than is usual today, and by the time

they sat down to the evening meal, the curtain was up. On Saturdays they found all they wanted in their homes. If such men went to the theatre, it was when they were on holiday elsewhere, or in another city on business, with an empty evening before them. In those days there was no talk of the theatre as an educative institution; it represented entertainment or frivolity – nothing more.

We have already referred, in Chapter Seven, to the opening of the Dunlop Street Theatre in 1782 and of the Queen Street Theatre in 1805 and to the popularity of the theatre in Glasgow after the opening of the latter. But, as Bell's account makes clear, it was popularity only in certain quarters. Indeed, it is an interesting aspect of the relation between culture, entertainment and class in nineteenth-century Britain that in Victorian London the music halls were largely frequented by those above and below the middle classes: by aristocratic rakes, young bloods on a spree, and working men packing the gallery, and that the theatres and music halls of Victorian Glasgow attracted the same audience.

The limited appeal of the theatre to the respectable was not the result of the actual buildings. The Queen Street Theatre was an imposing classical building with Ionic columns in front and Corinthian columns inside. The scenery was by the famous Edinburgh scene-painter Naismith, and included a drop for lowering between the acts showing a picturesque view of the Firth of Clyde, said to be one of the finest examples of scenic illustration in the kingdom. It had a capacity of nearly 1,500. Some of the greatest names in nineteenth-century acting are to be found in the programmes of this and other Glasgow theatres. Everything was splendid except the plays themselves, which all too often were fatuous, acted with friendly abandon before an audience of unsophisticates out for a good time. The announcement of the opening play of the Queen Street Theatre tells its own story:

The Public is respectfully informed that the New
Theatre will be opened Wednesday,
April 24, 1805
A NEW OCCASIONAL ADDRESS,
After which the new and favourite Comedy, now acting in
London with universal applause, called
'THE HONEYMOON,'
With entire new Dresses, Scenery, and Decorations,
and the farce of
'RAISING THE WIND.'

181

The Dunlop Street Theatre fell on bad times in the first decade of the century, and in 1807 part of it was converted into a warehouse for the sale of West Indian produce while the rest was let for a wide variety of public entertainments. A certain Mr Knowles lectured on astronomy, and a former jeweller by the name of Bauldy Cochrane sang popular songs while riding a pasteboard horse. Itinerant managers would put on pantomimes – 'Blue Beard', 'Cinderella', 'Robinson Crusoe', 'Beauty and the Beast' and others – and an Italian dancing master called Montignani served refreshments in a side room. The English champion boxer Tom Cribb was one of the many pugilists who appeared. And – to quote the expressive words of the Glasgow actor Walter Baynham, writing of the Glasgow stage from 1805 to 1862 – 'with hair as white as snow, blue coat, gilt buttons, white vest, long drab gaiters and inexpressibles, [William] Cobbett lectured in the same boxing arena on Parliamentary Reform, Repeal of the Corn Laws, abolition of the East India Company's Charter, and other favourite topics of that erratic pamphleteer'. After one of Cobbett's lectures a member of the audience rose to express the hope that 'the time may come when the poor man after the labour of the day would be able to refresh himself by reading Bacon'. 'Much more to the purpose, my dear sir,' Cobbett replied, 'if the time could come when the poor man, after the labour of the day, might refresh himself by *eating* Bacon.'

Meanwhile, Queen Street Theatre was enlivened by the activities of George Frederick Cooke, who had first made his name in Shakespeare's *Richard III* and who played with great acclaim a variety of Shakespearean and other parts. He was already addicted to drink by the time he came to Glasgow in June 1807, and though he often appeared drunk on stage he never lost the affection of the audience. Sometimes for several nights on end an announcement had to be made that Mr Cooke could not appear because of 'a sudden and serious indisposition'. He would apologize with dignity to the audience on re-appearing after a series of drunken bouts, explaining that he had had an attack of 'my old complaint'. But his Glasgow audiences loved him, and accepted his apologies with affectionate good humour.

In 1813 the young William Macready, whose father was then managing the Queen Street Theatre, made his début in Glasgow, as Hamlet. His father was more successful, however, in the production of a spectacular melodrama, *Aladin*, in which his son also acted. In 1814 Queen Street was taken over by Harry Johnstone, who scored a great success in bringing Edmund Kean to Glasgow in March of the following year: Kean's reputation brought a new kind of audience to the Glasgow theatre, and university professors as well as literary men from Edinburgh (including Francis Jeffrey) attended his performances, for which higher than usual prices were charged. Johnstone was less successful in trying to impose higher prices for the appearance of Miss O'Neil in August 1818 as Belvidera in *Venice Preserved*. There were shouts of 'O. P.' (old prices) from the audience when the curtain rose, and when Johnstone came on stage to quell the tumult he was hissed. But Miss O'Neil eventually soothed them, and remained popular in Glasgow until she retired from the stage on her marriage in 1819.

On 18 September 1818 it was announced that the 'Grand Crystal Lustre of the front roof of the Theatre, the largest of that time in Scotland, will, in place of the Wicks and the Candles and the Oil Lamps, be Illuminated with Sparkling Gas'. This was an attraction that drew even respectable citizens from their homes; the theatre was crowded, and many well-known citizens attended with their families (almost unheard of, for women did not go to the theatre). The performance was Mozart's *Don Giovanni* by an Italian opera company.

Among the most continuously popular plays at Queen Street as at other theatres in Glasgow and Edinburgh were the dramatizations of Scott's novels, especially *Rob Roy*, which opened at Queen Street on 10 June 1818 nine months before it was played in Edinburgh. The great Glasgow character-actor Charles Mackay gave the first of his enormously successful performances as Bailie Nicol Jarvie. Other Scott novels successfully staged in nineteenth-century Glasgow were *Guy Mannering*, *The Heart of Midlothian*, and *Ivanhoe*, while a version of his narrative poem *The Lady of the Lake* – more of a spectacle than a play – was also popular, especially in mid-century when Edmund Glover took the part of the outlawed Highland chief Roderick Dhu.

A particular brand of outrageously sensational melodrama was popular in the first half of the century, but after mid-century they tended to be relegated to temporary booths set up during Glasgow Fair week. Looking back at the end of the century, Baynham bemoaned their loss. 'The bold bad Baron, with his basket-hilted sword, the sentimental "Crichton" hero, the white-muslined heroine, the pallid ghost, find no moated dungeon in the modern sensational drama. Instead of these dear old friends of our boyhood, the thrilling music, and the soul-harrowing scenes, we have some insipid masher in evening dress, who consigns his hapless victim either to the colonies or a lunatic asylum.'

In the early 1820s there were some odd goings-on in the Dunlop

Street theatre, part of which was now a Circus, as the following announcement illustrates:

CIRCUS, DUNLOP STREET.

On Friday and Saturday, 28th and 29th December, 1821, the performances will commence with the admired ballet dance, called 'Hurry-Scurry', after which the very favourite Melodrama, called 'Frederick the Great', and Horsemanship. The whole to conclude with the admired Melodramatic Burlette, called the 'Mill of Glamis'. Splendid New-Year's Harlequinade Pantomime will be produced at the Circus. Mr. Simpson (from Manchester) with his wonderful performing dogs and sagacious bear are engaged, and will shortly appear in a new grand historical bruno-canine quadripedical melodrama.

Dunlop Street Theatre was soon afterwards taken over by the energetic J. H. Alexander in unusual circumstances. Part of the Dunlop Street building, now known as the Caledonian Theatre, was taken by the manager Frank Seymour just when Alexander was planning to take it himself. Alexander found that there was a large cellar with a lofty ceiling below the stage, and he moved in there and fitted it up as a stage and auditorium. Then, when Seymour was producing one play up above, Alexander would produce another simultaneously down below. Both plays were audible in both places – particularly a very noisy *Macbeth* which went on with 'the clanging of dishcovers, the clashing of swords, the braying of drums' up above while the equally noisy *Battle of the Inch* was going on below. The rival managers grew ever more furious, but the audience were delighted with the quite unexpected new species of entertainment.

Both sides appealed to the Court of Session, which simply ordered that neither side should annoy the other. But that is just what they continued to do. Seymour's people lifted the planks and poured water on those below and found various ways of spoiling some of Alexander's most spectacular scenic effects. At length Seymour took over the management of Queen Street Theatre, and after it burned down on 10 January 1829 he had a new theatre built in York Street (opening on 2 October 1829 with Edmund Kean as Shylock in *The Merchant of Venice*). Alexander took over the whole Dunlop Street Theatre, to which he made many alterations. On 5 December 1829 the press announced: 'Mr. Alexander hails with delight the moment which gives him an opportunity of presenting to the citizens of Glasgow a theatre which, he flatters himself, will be deemed worthy of their notice and support.'

In 1838 the equestrian performer Andrew Ducrow, who had already made a reputation in England, France and Flanders and produced much-admired spectacles in Drury Lane, opened an arena in Hope Street which for a while proved a dangerous rival to the theatre. But although he purchased an estate near Glasgow, intending to settle there, his marriage to one of his equestriennes, Miss Woolford, proved the beginning of the end; she had him locked up in a lunatic asylum and he did not long survive his release in 1842.

On 21 December 1842 D. P. Miller opened the Adelphi Theatre near Glasgow Green and its initial success caused Alexander some anxiety, for his own fortunes at the Dunlop were erratic. Alexander, himself an actor, played many parts and was in the habit of interrupting his performance and addressing the audience when their response was not to his liking. Many farcical scenes are recorded, including an especially ridiculous one when Alexander was playing Cassius in *Julius Caesar* and, objecting to a member of the audience who was tittering, abused him from the stage. Another rival to the Dunlop Street Theatre, the City Theatre on Glasgow Green, was opened by J. H. Anderson on 7 May 1845, but it burned down in November of the same year. The Adelphi burned down on 22 November 1848.

Charles Dickens was in Glasgow in December 1847, to take the chair at a grand 'soirée' to mark the opening of the Glasgow Athenaeum, a society founded the previous year and meeting in the Assembly Rooms in Ingram Street. He was back in the summer of 1848, this time as an actor: he appeared as Master Shallow at Dunlop Street in a production of *The Merry Wives of Windsor* in aid of a fund to establish a permanent curator of Shakespeare's house at Stratford. Thackeray also paid two visits to Glasgow, in 1851 and 1856, on the latter occasion lecturing at the Athenaeum on 'English Humorists' and 'The Four Georges'.

Jenny Lind came to Glasgow in October 1848 to sing in *The Daughter of the Regiment* at Dunlop Street. She was brought by the actor Edmund Glover, who in January 1849 converted an old hall in West Nile Street into the Prince's Theatre, where he offered ballet, opera, 'spectacles' (such as *A Court Ball in 1740*) and plays. He made a great bid for the respectable classes, and according to a report in the *North British Daily Mail* (a Glasgow newspaper founded in 1847) he had some success in this fifteen years later: 'After a tolerably extensive experience of the theatres in England and Scotland, we can conscientiously say we know of no theatre which ladies can visit with such comfort, propriety, and freedom from annoyances as the Prince's, Glasgow. The house is comfortably and prettily fitted up, the performances are conducted with the utmost propriety, the audience is highly respectable, and nothing calculated to offend the eye or ear is permitted on the stage or amongst the audience.' Paradoxically, such an endorsement only emphasizes the fact that theatres in Victorian Glasgow were not normally expected to be haunts of feminine respectability.

The threat of fire always hung over Glasgow's theatres. The worst loss of life, however, was at a false alarm of fire given at the Dunlop Street Theatre on Saturday 17 February 1849. The house was packed, and the gallery was full of working-class youngsters, some with their girls, who had come to see the spectacular melo-drama, *The Surrender of Calais*, with the main characters strikingly clad in suits of medieval armour. For some reason, someone in the gallery shouted 'Fire!', but at first a stampede was prevented by prompt reassurance from the manager and the continued playing of the orchestra. Then some sparks were seen coming from a gas pipe, but a couple of workmen immediately attended to this, the house was reassured, and the performance re-commenced. But then somebody spotted a uniformed and helmeted fireman, who had come to see what was going on, and the sight produced renewed shouts of 'Fire!!' accompanied by screams and a panic rush from the gallery down the main stairs. Sixty-five people were trampled to death or suffocated in the headlong flight downstairs, most of them young men, but also six girls and one three-year-old child. Alexander never really got over the shock of this disaster; he gave up the management of the theatre to Mercer Simpson of Birmingham in 1851 and died later the same year. The Dunlop Street Theatre finally did burn down on the night of 31 January 1863 on the last night of the pantomime *Blue Beard* – fortunately after the performance had ended and the theatre had emptied. It was repaired after the fire, and carried on for another five years before it was pulled down to make way for the approaches to St Enoch Station.

Edmund Glover took over the management of the Dunlop Street Theatre in 1852 and with a variety of lavish productions endeavoured, as he had done with the Prince's, to extend the social range of its habitués. He brought to the Dunlop Street stage Italian opera, Shakespeare, Sheridan, now-forgotten Victorian comedies, an immensely popular, dramatic version of *Uncle Tom's Cabin*, panto-mime, spectacular pieces such as *The Battle of Alma* and *The Indian Revolt, or the Relief of Lucknow* (in 1860), in which the young Henry Irving made his début in Glasgow, and a number of Irish plays of which the most popular was Dion Boucicault's *The Colleen Bawn*. When the Prince's Theatre closed in 1862 the company playing there

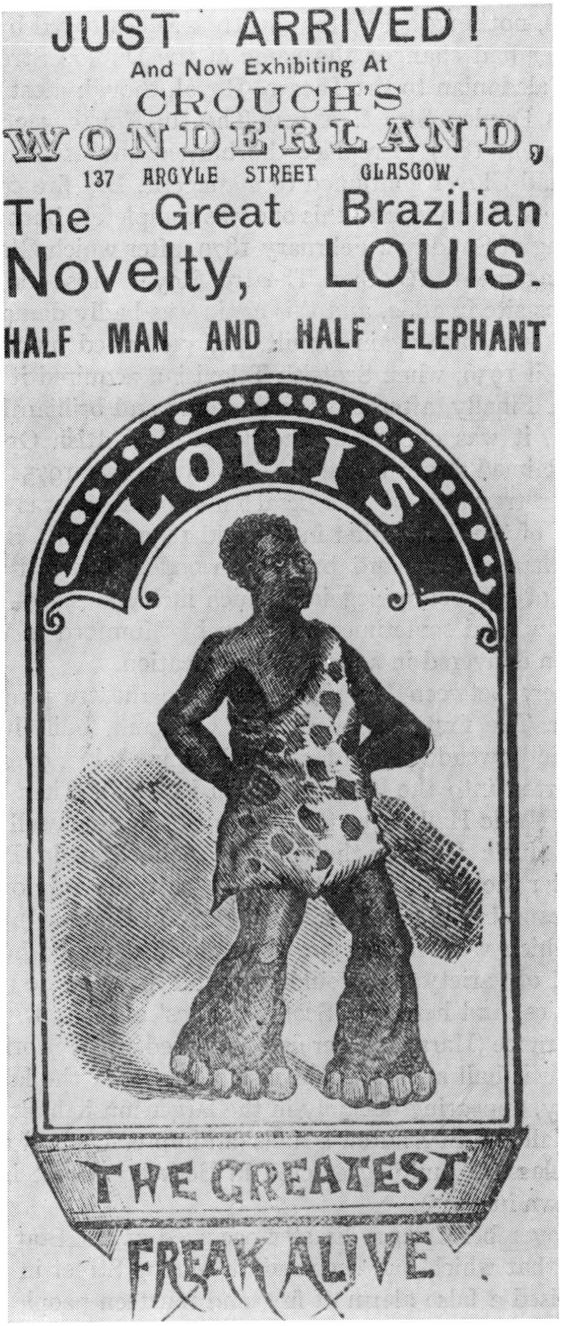
JUST ARRIVED!
And Now Exhibiting At
CROUCH'S
WONDERLAND,
137 ARGYLE STREET GLASGOW
The Great Brazilian
Novelty, LOUIS.
HALF MAN AND HALF ELEPHANT
LOUIS
THE GREATEST
FREAK ALIVE

moved to Dunlop Street, to play in short pieces preceding the pantomime, not long before the theatre was destroyed by fire.

Alexander had changed the name of the Dunlop Street Theatre from the Caledonian to the Theatre Royal, though most people still knew it as Dunlop Street. A new Theatre Royal went up in the Cowcaddens in 1869 to replace the burned one at Dunlop Street, and Edmund Glover continued to manage it. But fire continued to dog the Theatre Royal, and this one was completely burned down on the morning of Sunday 2 February 1879, after which Glover retired from management. Another Theatre Royal arose on the same Cowcaddens site in 1882, and this again was badly damaged by fire in 1895. It was once again rebuilt, and continued functioning as a theatre until 1956, when Scottish Television acquired it for studios and offices. Finally, after a thorough-going and brilliantly executed renovation, it was opened as the home of Scottish Opera with a widely acclaimed performance of *Otello* in October 1975.

A lowlier tradition of theatrical entertainment was established at the foot of the Saltmarket in the mid-1830s when a Bedfordshire puppeteer named Mumford built his wooden theatre there for the exhibition of his 'penny geggies', which included songs, dancing, a puppet show, and sometimes a lecture by Mumford on the evils of drink, often delivered in a state of intoxication.

Somewhere between Mumford's and the theatre proper lay the music hall. The first was the Royal Coliseum, built in the early 1860s in the Cowcaddens (in fact, the building taken over by Glover and converted into the Theatre Royal in 1869). Then there were the Scotia Music Hall (later the Metropole) in Stockwell Street, the Britannia Music Hall in the Trongate, the Star in Partick, the Gaiety (later the Empire) in Stockwell Street, the only one that laid claim to respectability ('the safest theatre in Glasgow') and others, some of which were little more than glorified public houses. Here every kind of variety turn could be found, from crude melodramas to acrobatics, and here the 'Scotch comics' of Glasgow made their first appearance (Harry Lauder first appeared at the Scotia). Famous English music-hall artists would visit Glasgow in the latter part of the century, appearing not only in the larger music halls but also in the City Hall and St Andrew's Halls (an impressive and acoustically excellent classical building erected in Berkeley Street in 1873 and burned down in 1963).

On 1 November 1884 a disaster occurred at the Star Music Hall similar to that which had occurred at Dunlop Street in 1849. Some persons raised a false alarm of fire, and fourteen people were killed and eighteen badly injured in the resulting stampede. As a consequence of this accident stricter bye-laws were enacted controlling means of exit from places of public entertainment.

At the end of the century Glasgow had five theatres and four music halls, as well as Hengler's Circus in Wellington Street and the Zoo-Circus in Cowcaddens. The premier theatre at this time was the Royal; the Royalty in Sauchiehall Street (later the Lyric) specialized in comic opera and burlesque, and was to move on to musical comedy; the Grand in Cowcaddens went in for melodrama; the Royal Princess's (Main Street, Gorbals) specialized in long-run pantomimes; the Queen's in Watson Street, East End, formerly the People's Palace, was the most rollicking. The music halls were the Scotia, the Gaiety (which at the turn of the century had just been rebuilt as the Empire and was becoming a legitimate theatre), the Britannia, near Glasgow Cross, the toughest of the music halls, and the Tivoli at Anderston. J. J. Bell recalled the music halls of the 1880s:

> The only Halls of importance were the Gaiety and the Scotia . . . , and because of its locality the Scotia seemed the more sinister, and we decided to go there. In those days Stockwell Street was none too savoury. Constables in pairs walked up and down; there were smells of frying fish and drink, scenes of squalor and frowsiness, sounds of foulness and blasphemy . . . The Scotia was a spacious theatre, not garish, and . . . there was nothing about it to suggest unseemliness. The audience was almost entirely working-class.

Hengler's Circus, however, Bell recalled, was a perfectly proper place for grandpapas to take their grandchildren to at Christmas time. He remembered the series of magnificent water spectacles 'invented, designed and produced by Mr Hengler'. He remembered Glasgow's pantomimes of the period, always culminating in the 'gorgeous transformation' to be followed by the Harlequinade, an old-fashioned practice later abandoned. He remembered, too, how the young bloods, having emerged from the music hall feeling that the night was still young, and intending to sup at Godenzi's, 'the favourite night restaurant' in Sauchiehall Street, would call in at a place next door to Godenzi's, calling itself the Garden of Eden, 'a sort of café, with a few plants and a stage, which was guarded by an iron fence, lest the charms of the syrens who sang and danced should prove too much for the passions of the "gilded youths".' And he described the departure from Godenzi's in the small hours:

> They come out of 'old Godenzi's' to a dusky street, watched by the yellow eyes of gas lamps. The last tram-car has long since plodded its weary way to the stables. Two drunk men pursue their erratic

brotherly course homeward. A third, who will not sleep in his own bed tonight, has the support of a pair of constables; a fourth, having subsided against a shop door, will be called for in due course. It rains. The gentlemen from Godenzi's turn up their collars – also the hems of their trousers, which were not turned up by the tailor. Those who still have some gilt to shed take a hansom or 'growler' – double fare after midnight; those who have frugal minds, or lean purses, tramp it.

There were much lower forms of entertainment. In 1871 the *Glasgow Daily Mail* (not to be confused with the *North British Daily Mail*, which in 1901 became the *Glasgow Daily Mail*) published its famous exposure of what it called the 'Dark Side of Glasgow', revealing that in the old central part of the city there were 200 brothels and 150 shebeens in an area of less than one-sixteenth of a square mile. There were different grades of shebeens, from the larger and highly profitable concerns, operating in rooms holding thirty or forty people with a smaller room for favoured customers and overflow space in the kitchen, to smaller shebeens in the wynds, to 'wee shebeens' on the stairheads, which the police found hard to identify because they could so easily disappear, down to the lowest grade, those which operated simultaneously as shebeens, brothels and thieves' kitchens. Activity went on all night in these places. The police found themselves frustrated by the elusiveness of the operators and frequenters of these dens. The irony was that some of them were owned by the most respectable landlords, who were powerless to keep their tenants in order. Glasgow Corporation itself owned one of the worst areas in central Glasgow, the Laigh Kirk Close at 59 Trongate, which contained twenty brothels and three shebeens.

An account of Victorian Glasgow should end on a more elevated note. That is conveniently provided by an event which took place in the very last year of Queen Victoria's reign, Glasgow's second great International Exhibition (known as 'The Groveries'), laid out over 73 acres on the same site as that of the 1888 Exhibition by the architect James Miller and dedicated to a demonstration of progress in art, science and industry during the century that had just ended. Queen Victoria herself died when it was in progress, but contrary to expectation and press announcements the theatres did not close. This was the high point of Glasgow's self-confidence. In November 1899 J. K. M'Dowall prefaced his *People's History of Glasgow* with a proud declaration of faith:

The story of Glasgow should be more correctly realised. I should even presume to have it taught in schools and colleges to its future

HENGLER'S
GRAND CIRQUE,
WELLINGTON STREET, GLASGOW.

PROGRAMME.

MARCH, ...	"Grand Manœuvres,"	*Desormes*
OPERATIC SELECTION, ...	"The Gondoliers,"	*Sullivan*

1—Evolutions on Horseback by Mr. JAMES FRANKS.

    Clown, ... LINDON.

2—Entree by the LEONARDS.

3—Race by the DIMINUTIVE PONIES, ridden by MONKEY JOCKEYS.

4—Dexterous Feats of Juggling on Horseback by SIGNOR LUIGI.

    Clown . ... CATTLE.

5—The BROS. QUAGLIENI, Acrobats.

6—"GOOD OLD TIMES" Quadrilles on Horseback, by Mesdames JESSIE, ALICE, BERTIE, and MAUDE, and Messrs. FRANCISCO, SEAL, CLARKE, and FRANKS.

7—Gymnastic Exercises on the Triple Horizontal Bars, by Messrs. HORTON and LINDER.

8—Mr. CHARLES CLARKE, Tumbling and Somersault Throwing on Horseback.

    Clown ... ... YORICK, THE FOOL.

9—Eccentricities by YORICK, the Fool.

10—The Bros. PINDER, Musical Grotesques.

11—Trotting Act on Horseback by Miss LENA.

    Jester, ... DAVID ABBEY SEAL.

12—Interlude by the LEONARDS.

13—The Trained Steeds, "ROMULUS" and "PIONEER," introduced by Mr. LOUIS FRANCISCO.

14— AN ENTIRELY NEW AND ORIGINAL
GROTESQUE PANTOMIME,
ENTITLED—A
VILLAGE WEDDING
OR TRAMPS ABROAD,
IN TWO SCENES AND NUMEROUS TABLEAUX.
Introducing Hengler's Great
WATER NOVELTY.

Dresses and Costumes by Madame Saroni and Assistants; Properties and Paraphernalia by Mr. Balsall and Assistants; Mechanical Effects by Mr. Fred Cattle; Limelight by Mr. W. Proctor and Assistants; Scenery Painted by Mr. W. Shaw; Engineering Fittings by Mr. G. H. Williams; Music by Mr. George Clemens; The Beautiful Chime of Bells by Harrison & Co., Musical Tube Manufacturers, Coventry.

The Whole of the Spectacle
Invented, Designed & Produced by Mr. ALBERT HENGLER

NOTICE—Mr. HENGLER desires to publicly acknowledge his indebtedness to Mr. ALFRED POWELL, Sen., for his most valuable assistance in the Engineering department of this production.

Characters:—

The Bride, ...	.	..	Miss BERTIE
The Bridegroom,	...	..	Mr FRANKS
The Tramps,	...	..	{ Mr FRED CATTLE { Mr LINDON
The Squire, ..	...	..	Mr SEAL
The Lady, ..	...	..	Miss ALICE
The Master Blacksmith,	...	..	Mr CLARKE
The Mother-in-Law,	...	..	Mr YORICK
The Policemen,	...	...	{ Mr MITCHELL { Mr LINDER
The Landlord,	..	..	Mr WEBSTER
The Landlady,	...	..	Mr WATSON

Wedding Guests, Blacksmiths, Villagers, Soldiers, School Children &c., &c., by Members of the Company, and Auxiliaries numbering nearly 100 persons.

Synopsis of Scenery and Incidents:—
Scene 1.—The VILLAGE GREEN & BLACKSMITH'S FORGE
.. Early Morning—Smiths at Work
The Tramps
THE HARMONIOUS BLACKSMITH.

Children's Romps—Arrival of the Villagers and the Squire—Some Refreshments—Haste to the Wedding—The Police—The Return—The Squire's Wedding Present—The Pickpockets—Departure of the Happy Couple—The Garland Dance—Return of the Bride-groom who has discovered his loss—The Thieves searched—Recovery of the Stolen Goods—Off to Prison—The Escape.

Scene 2.—A FETE ON THE RIVER.

NOTE.—In this Scene an absolute and unequalled Novelty will be presented to the astonished gaze of the public, in the incredibly short space of 55 seconds, the large Arena is flooded with
23,000 GALLONS OF REAL WATER.

Arrival of Villagers and the Wedding Party—A little Regatta, and some fun on the Water—The Fishermen—A good catch—The old Lady in trouble—A gallant Rescue—The Police again—Lively Work—More Fun, and
SCREAMING FINALE.

Eccentricities throughout the Performance by YORICK, the Fool

citizens, who might thus learn to honour the spirit which gave Glasgow the ambition to be a hive of useful industry. If they knew of the life, the blood, and the treasure spent by the self-reliant and self-respecting generations of the past, and learned the lesson that the city's greatness has been due to corporate endeavour inspired by, and seconding, individual effort, they would be incited to emulate and carry on those activities which have made Glasgow the first municipality in the world and the second city of the British empire.

CHAPTER 16

'The high, tragic pageant of the Clyde'

GLASGOW'S growing prosperity throughout the nineteenth century largely derived from its being the centre of an area of heavy industry, particularly shipbuilding and engineering. It is often claimed that it was the undue dependence of Glasgow and Clydeside on shipbuilding and heavy engineering that made them so vulnerable to depression in the 1930s. Yet Glasgow could also boast of its industrial diversity in the years before the depression. In 1915, the Town Clerk said with pride:

> No city has rivalled, far less surpassed, the commercial metropolis of Scotland. This has chiefly arisen from the city being – if the expression may be used – *cosmopolitan* in its commerce and manufactures. Glasgow unites within itself a portion of the cotton spinning and weaving manufactures of Manchester, the printed calicoes of Lancashire, the stuffs of Norwich, the shawls and mousselines of France, the silk-throwing of Macclesfield, the flax-spinning of Ireland, the carpets of Kidderminster, the iron and engineering works of Wolverhampton, Sheffield, and Birmingham, the pottery and glass-making of Staffordshire and Newcastle, the coal trade of the Tyne and Wear, and all the handicrafts connected with or dependent on the full development of these. Glasgow also has its distilleries, breweries, chemical works, tan-works, dye-works, bleachfields, and paper manufactures, besides a vast number of staple and fancy hand-loom fabrics which may be strictly said to belong to that locality. Glasgow also, in its commercial relations, trades with every quarter of the globe; and its merchants deal in the various products of every country. It hence appears that one branch of manufacture or trade may be dull while another may be prosperous; and, accordingly, Glasgow does not feel any of those universal depressions which so frequently occur in places limited to one or two branches of manufacture or commerce.

While the Town Clerk's boast was essentially justified, he ignored the fact that Glasgow was by now the centre of a large conurbation and that the remainder of the Clyde Valley, the rest of Lanarkshire, Renfrewshire, Dunbartonshire and Northern Ayrshire, was more dependent on heavy industry than the city of Glasgow itself and that a severe drop in the level of employment in the heavy industries of the Clyde Valley would affect the consumer goods industries and service trades of the city. This is just what happened in the 1930s.

But a long period of glory preceded the depressed years, most notably in shipbuilding. The rapid growth of the Clyde shipyards after 1841 was the result of the adoption of steam propulsion and the increasing use of iron instead of wood. By the late 1860s wood was no longer used in Clyde shipbuilding except for very small craft. The last wooden Cunard liner, the *Arabia* of 2,400 tons, was built in 1852. The replacement of iron by mild steel was the next great advance. It was the famous firm of William Denny and Brothers of Dumbarton that built the first ocean-going steamer of mild steel, the *Rotamahana*, launched in 1879, for the Union Steamship Company of New Zealand. The following year the same firm launched the first steel ship for the transatlantic service, the *Buenos Ayrean* for the Allan Line. William Denny's pioneering use of mild steel was, as a result of his influence and advocacy, followed by other Clydeside shipbuilders, but Denny long remained the leader. Between 1879 and 1889 the tonnage of steel shipping launched on the Clyde rose from 18,000 to 326,136 and the proportion of steel-built ships rose from 10.3 per cent to 97.2 per cent, a record unmatched anywhere else in the country.

It was the growth of steelworks in the area that made Clydeside such a leader in steel shipbuilding. The founding of the Steel Company of Scotland in 1871 and the building two years later of its first open-hearth plant at Hallside, south of the river beyond the city's south-east boundary, speeded up the process. And not only did the proximity of the works encourage steel shipbuilding: in 1899 there was a famous case of a steel manufacturer from elsewhere going into Clydeside shipbuilding in order to use his steel. In 1899 the Sheffield steel firm of John Brown and Co. acquired the Clydebank Engineering and Shipbuilding Works to find an outlet in the ship-building trade for their heavy forgings.

To steam propulsion and the increasing availability (and cheapness) of mild steel can be added a third factor contributing to the massive growth of Clyde shipbuilding. This was the development of marine engineering, especially the introduction of new boiler designs to cope with the higher steam pressures required. The first 'triple-expansion' engine, built by John Elder and Co. to the design of

A. C. Kirk (who developed a three-stage process for the expansion of the steam to eliminate pressure loss) was fitted in the ship *Propontis* in 1874. Although the boilers as originally designed were not satisfactory, it was not long before improved triple-expansion engines were in service on Clyde-built ships. The first of these to be fitted on a ship for deep-sea service, also designed by Kirk, was installed in the *Aberdeen*, built in 1882 for service to Australia and China. The triple-expansion engine, increasingly used to achieve economy in fuel rather than increased power, became a great feature of Clyde-built ships, and was associated in the popular mind with the city of Glasgow, as the ineffable McGonagall testified:

> O, wonderful city of Glasgow, with your triple expansion engines,
> At the making of which your workmen get may singeins.

What McGonagall would have said had he known about Clydeside's quadruple-expansion engines (which have been called 'the ultimate stage in the search for economy with the reciprocating steam engine') can only be imagined.

The next significant advance in marine engineering on Clydeside was the development of the steam turbine at the beginning of this century. The Parsons steam turbine had been first demonstrated in Royal Navy vessels at the Diamond Jubilee Naval Review at Spithead in 1897, but in 1901 Denny's introduced a Parsons turbine in the passenger vessel *King Edward* built for service on the Clyde, and after this the use of turbines in high-powered Clyde-built passenger ships increased rapidly. It was a Glasgow University Professor, Sir John Biles, who devised new means of increasing efficiency in turbine machinery and extending its use, culminating in the installation of direct-drive turbines on the *Aquitania*, built by John Brown and Co. for Cunard at Clydebank in 1914.

The volume of shipbuilding on the Clyde grew from about 100,000 tons in the early 1860s to 750,000 in 1913, in which year there were about 60,000 men employed in Clyde shipyards and marine engineering shops, while the total number of workers dependent on the industry was about 100,000. In 1919 the number employed in the shipyards alone was over 43,000, but the figure had dropped to 29,310 by April 1930, by which time the industry was feeling the effects of the great depression. One yard after another stopped all production and the sight of empty berths on Clydeside became increasingly common. In 1931 the most dramatic sign of depression came with the suspension of work on the *Queen Mary*, which was eventually completed and launched in 1934. The *Queen Elizabeth* was launched in 1938. The construction of these two ships represented a remarkable achievement, all the more so as they were completed in a conscious endeavour to provide work in a period of continuing depression. In the two years after the launching of the *Queen Mary* the output of the shipyards fell to 60,000 tons, a record low since the beginning of the growth of Clydeside shipbuilding in the mid-nineteenth-century. At least two thirds of the men normally engaged in the industry were unemployed.

Unemployment in Glasgow and on the Clyde, with the spectacle of skilled workers lounging listlessly on street corners, has become a bitter Glasgow memory that will not be easily forgotten. George Blake, in his novel *The Shipbuilders*, published in 1935, captured the mood of the early 1930s. In Chapter Six there is an account of the head of a shipbuilding firm, sailing down the Clyde on the trials of the *Estramadura*, the last ship his firm built before closure was forced on him by an empty order book.

> It was in a sense a procession that he witnessed, the high, tragic pageant of the Clyde. Yard after yard passed by, the berths empty, the grass growing about the sinking keel-blocks. He remembered how, in the brave days, there would be scores of ships ready for the launching along this reach, their sterns hanging over the tide, and how the men at work on them on high stagings would turn from the job and tug off their caps and cheer the new ship setting out to sea. And now only the gaunt, dumb poles and groups of men, workless, watching in silence the mocking passage of the vessel. It was bitter to know that they knew – that almost every man among them was an artist in one of the arts that go to the building of a ship; that every feature of the *Estramadura* would come under an expert and loving scrutiny, that her passing would remind them of the joy of work and tell them how many among them would never work again . . .
>
> It was a tragedy beyond economics. It was not that so many thousands of homes lacked bread and butter. It was that a tradition, a skill, a glory, a passion, was visibly in decay and all the acquired and inherited loveliness of artistry rotting along the banks of the stream.
>
> Into himself he counted and named the yards they passed. The number and variety stirred him to wonder, now that he had ceased to take them for granted. His mental eye moving backwards up the river, he saw the historic place at Govan, Henderson's of Meadowside at the mouth of the Kelvin, and the long stretch of Fairfield on the southern bank opposite. There came Stephens' of Linthouse next, and Clydeholm facing it across the narrow, yellow ditch of the ship-channel. From thence down river the range along the northern

bank was almost continuous for miles – Connel, Inglis, Blythswood, and the rest: so many that he could hardly remember their order. He was distracted for a moment to professionalism by the lean grey forms of destroyers building for a foreign Power in the sheds of a yard that had dramatically deserted Thames for Clyde . . . There came John Brown's, stretching along half a mile of waterfront at Clydebank, the monstrous red hull of Number 534 [the future *Queen Mary*, but at this time incomplete and abandoned] looming in its abandonment like a monument to the glory departed; as if shipbuilding man had tried to do too much and had been defeated by the mightiness of his own conception. Then came, seeming to point the moral, the vast desolation of Beardmore's at Dalmuir, cradle of the mightiest battleships and now a scrapheap, empty and silent forever, the great gantry over the basin proclaiming stagnation and an end.

The shipping needs of the First World War had inflated the ship-building capacity of the country as a whole by about one third, and the reduction in the demand for new ships after the war, once the war losses had been made good, faced the industry with problems that it tried to solve by concentrating its activities in a smaller number of yards to which the best plant of the closed yards was made available. But while this strategy mitigated the disaster in some degree, it did not prevent massive unemployment and growing political bitterness. Matters were made worse immediately after the end of the war by the selling of confiscated German ships at far less than the cost of new ships.

The 'rationalizing' of shipbuilding in an endeavour to combat depression by increasing efficiency and cutting costs was part of a larger pattern in Scottish industry after the First World War that hit Glasgow particularly hard. The merging of firms to eliminate competition and the movement southward of industrial control helped to make Scotland a depressed area. Already by 1922 there were over 80,000 unemployed in Glasgow. The great railway merger of 1923, when the London, Midland and Scottish Railway absorbed the Caledonian and the Glasgow and South-Western while the London and North-Eastern Railway took over the North British and its subsidiaries, brought the control of Scotland's railways to London with the resultant moving of associated industries to England, notably the locomotive building and repair work that had been so important in the west of Scotland. Indeed, Glasgow's locomotive engineering works had been second only to shipbuilding among the city's heavy industries, but their functions, as well as

The 'Wild Clydesiders' in the election year of
1922, as seen by the *Bailie* – a weekly
magazine which ran a series of portraits of
contemporary personalities. From left to right:
James Maxton, George Buchanan,
John Wheatley and Campbell Stephen

those of the engineering works at Kilmarnock, now became greatly
restricted and their labour force diminished correspondingly.

All these developments helped the growth of left-wing political
activism in Glasgow and on Clydeside. After the Reform Act of 1832,

Glasgow had voted almost continuously for the Liberal party. Between 1832 and 1868 Glasgow returned two members and between 1868 and 1885 it returned three. Seven electoral divisions were established in 1885 and growing population and enlarged boundaries led to the establishment of fifteen divisions in 1915. In the General Election of 1922 ten out of Glasgow's fifteen seats were won by the Independent Labour Party. This was the climax of a series of events that went back to the early days of the First World War, a war which had been opposed on principle by James Maxton (born at Pollokshaws in 1885) and his fellow members of the I. L. P. Under Maxton's influence Glasgow became a centre of pacifist agitation during the war. He and the older John Wheatley and others organized the great Clyde strike of 1915 for a wage increase of twopence an hour, which brought Glasgow wages up to the same level of those of other industrial cities. There was another great strike of Clydesiders just after the war, in January 1919, in support of a forty-hour week.* Maxton was imprisoned for a year for a speech he made at an anti-war demonstration on Glasgow Green on May Day 1916. He emerged from prison the following year eager to battle against war profiteers, rack-renting landlords, and for better housing, for a forty-hour week on Clydeside, and above all for peace. Together with John Wheatley and William Stewart, Maxton led thousands of I. L. P. members in a massive May Day march in Glasgow in 1918.

Maxton was returned for Bridgeton in 1922, and his three close friends John Wheatley, George Buchanan and Campbell Stephen were also elected, representing Shettleston, Gorbals and Camlachie respectively. David Kirkwood was elected I. L. P. member for Clydebank.

An enormous demonstration in St Enoch Square saw the successful I. L. P. members off on the night train for London. And so the 'wild Clydesiders' came to Westminster. 'Not since the days of the Chartists', David Kirkwood later wrote, 'had any group of men so fully captured the imagination of the people as our team, and never had any group of men gone to the House of Commons with higher resolve than the Clyde Brigade of 1922.' They regarded themselves as the spearhead of the 142 Labour members returned to Parliament in that general election. Before they left for Westminster they jointly issued a manifesto (referred to in the *Glasgow Herald* by Sir George Adam Smith, Principal of Aberdeen University, as

*On 'Black Friday', 31 January 1919, there was a massive demonstration in George Square in support of the strike. It provoked police and military intervention in which 53 people were injured and a number of workers' leaders (including David Kirkwood, William Gallacher and Emmanuel Shinwell) were arrested.

'breathing the noble spirit of the Covenanters') which they read out at a great victory meeting after singing the 124th Psalm ('If it had not been the Lord who was on our side . . .'). Its first clause ran thus:

> The Labour Members of Parliament for the City of Glasgow and the West of Scotland, inspired by zeal for the welfare of humanity and the prosperity of all peoples and strengthened by the trust reposed in them by their fellow-citizens, have resolved to dedicate themselves to the reconciliation and unity of the nations of the world and the development and happiness of the people of these islands.

But, though Glasgow and Clydeside remained 'red', the realities of political life and of party politics led to the frustration of many a noble dream. The Labour Government of 1924 was, in David Kirkwood's disillusioned words, 'a pitiful affair', in spite of Wheatley's shrewd yet imaginative Housing Act under which over 75,000 houses were built by the local authorities in Scotland and which would have achieved still more had it not been curtailed in 1926. After the defeat of the General Strike in 1926 relations between the I. L. P. and the Labour Party were increasingly hostile. In the Labour Government of 1929 Wheatley was excluded from the Cabinet, but Emmanuel Shinwell and Tom Johnston, who had both been elected I. L. P. members in 1922 but who were now fighting against the independent I. L. P. position of Wheatley and Maxton, were given minor office. The I. L. P. faded away as a significant force, except in Glasgow, where Bridgeton, Shettleston, Gorbals and Camlachie together gave four I. L. P. candidates 73,993 votes as against the 7,722 polled by the official Labour Party candidates in the general election of 1935. By now Glasgow and the country were well into the great depression, whose advent had destroyed the Labour Government of 1929. The impetus of the I. L. P. in Glasgow was not yet spent, however, for it was David Kirkwood whose ceaseless agitation moved the Chancellor of the Exchequer on 13 December 1933 to speak in the House of Commons words which, in Kirkwood's excited phrase, 'sentenced Clydebank to Life'. It was announced that work would re-commence on the '534' in John Brown's shipyard. For a while Kirkwood believed that this was a true reprieve for the unemployed on the Clyde:

> And as I looked at him, [the Chancellor], juggling with the happiness of thousands, I saw behind him the long Dumbarton Road through Clydebank with four thousand men moving along towards Brown's Yard while the horn sang out the morning welcome. I saw some whose pockets bulged with their 'pieces' and some who would march

out at dinner-time with a new ring in their step. These were the men who, years later, would tell their children:

'I worked on the "534".'

Behind them I saw their homes, now so bare, gradually brighten with furniture and carpet and waxcloth, and children setting out for school, well fed and well clad. And I saw the wrinkles of care and anxiety smooth out from the faces of the mothers. And I saw the boys and youths eagerly awaiting the word 'Go!' to rush forward to begin the life that had so far been denied to them.

It was a splendid vision of regeneration. But although there was a real increase in employment as a result of the building of the two Queens there was no coherent or effective policy, either by the National Government or by individual industrialists, to re-invigorate industry in the area (or in Scotland as a whole). Some attempt was made in the late 1930s to attract new industries to depressed areas by the provision of industrial estates, and though Glasgow itself was excluded from the 'Special' or 'Development' Area which central Scotland was designated in 1934, in 1938 a large industrial estate was established at Hillington, just outside Glasgow, to accommodate some seventy firms of which the most important was the Air Ministry's shadow factory for Rolls-Royce aero engines. More work was brought to the Glasgow area by rearmament in response to the threat posed by Hitler and the feverish expansion of war production after the actual outbreak of war. It was not always easy to re-organize full production in the traditional heavy industries, for there had been a steady drift of key workers away from these vulnerable kinds of employment during the years of stagnation. But eventually the requisite skilled labour was obtained, and ship-building and engineering firms were effectively geared to war produc-tion, which included ships, army vehicles, guns and other equipment as well as the imaginatively conceived Mulberry Harbour, a major part of which was built on Clydeside. In 1941 surplus labour in the Glasgow area was directed to the south and only then did unemploy-ment virtually disappear for the duration of the war.

The Second World War did not find Glasgow workers in the same mood as during the First World War, when, under the guidance of I. L. P. leaders, many saw the struggle as an attack on fellow workers in another country in the interests of capitalism. The struggle against Hitler and his aims for Europe could bear no such construction, and even the few pacifists of the period did not argue on this ground. But, as Clifford Hanley (himself a conscientious objector in this war) has testified, Glasgow had more than its statistical quota of 'Conchies' here too. The workers survived without loss of morale the heavy and prolonged night raids on Clydebank and Greenock in the spring of 1941 – raids specifically designed to lower workers' morale seriously by destroying their homes while they were at work. In these raids on 13, 14 and 15 March 1,083 people were killed and 1,602 injured; on 7 and 8 April raids killed 64 and seriously injured 71; and in the raids on 5 and 8 May, 341 were killed and 312 seriously injured. Only seven houses in Clydebank were left undamaged and of the population of 55,000 all but 2,000 had to leave the town and live where they could, sometimes having to travel up to 60 miles daily to work. Glasgow itself got off lightly compared with London and some other cities. The first raid on the city was on 19 July 1940 and on the night of 18 September bombs dropped on George Square luckily missed all the main buildings. The city's most serious loss was the destruction by fire-bombs of 'Greek' Thomson's Queen's Park Church in the last air-raid on the night of 23 March 1943.

With the country's southerly ports more vulnerable to enemy bombing, the Clyde shared with Liverpool the handling of the bulk of merchant shipping coming into wartime Britain. Loading and unloading were generally done when the ships were at anchor – I well remember being ferried out from Greenock to the *Île de France*, then being used as a troop ship, in 1944 – and a Clyde Anchorages Emergency Port was set up to facilitate this. Not only was an enormous amount of war material and merchandise brought into and sent out of the Clyde during the six years of war – 52 million tons altogether – but 2.1 million troops were embarked and 2.4 million disembarked. The two Queens between them brought one and a quarter million soldiers, mostly Americans, across the Atlantic to Gourock.

For a decade after the end of the Second World War the Clyde shipyards were kept busy with replacements. But their techniques and layout remained old-fashioned: as so often in British industry the penalty for having been pioneers in the nineteenth century was a reluctance to adopt radically new methods and techniques in the middle of the twentieth. And the old trade union tradition of 'one union one job' meant a proliferation of small unions and interminable demarcation disputes. These factors were to produce a new crisis after the post-war prosperity came to an end.

One casualty of the Second World War was Glasgow's regular passenger service across the Atlantic. A direct service from Glasgow to New York had begun as early as 1850 with the screw steamer *City of Glasgow*, and six years later the Anchor Line (which had run services between Glasgow and Lisbon since 1838) founded a regular passenger and cargo service on this route. Immediately before the First World War they had a splendid fleet of four vessels, the *Columbia*, the *Caledonia*, the *California* and the *Cameronia*, which maintained a weekly Glasgow–New York service. Many still living will remember the fine Anchor Line fleet that maintained this service between the wars, the *Cameronia* (1920), the *Tuscania* (1922: I myself first sailed to America on this pleasant ship in 1937), the *California* (1923), the *Transylvania* (1925) and the *Caledonia* (1925: a fine and comfortable ship). The Allan Line (eventually absorbed by the Canadian Pacific) ran regular services from Glasgow to Montreal from 1854, and forty years later was running, in addition to weekly services from Glasgow to Canada and from Glasgow to New York, fortnightly services from Glasgow to Boston and from Glasgow to Philadelphia. Early in this century the Donaldson Line converted their Glasgow–Canada cargo service into a passenger service. Thus, as the writer in the *Third Statistical Account of Scotland* put it, 'early in the century there were three large liners leaving the Clyde every Saturday for America – an Anchor with two or three black funnels, an Allan with a red, white and black one, and a Donaldson with a black, white and black stack – capable among them of carrying 4,500 people.' After 1935 the Donaldson Atlantic Line, a new company, ran the *Athenia* and the *Letitia* to Canada. The former was sunk by a German submarine on 3 September 1939, on its way out from Glasgow to Montreal, the first shipping casualty of the Second World War. The Anchor Line *Cameronia* slipped quietly out of Glasgow two days later, on its way to Boston and New York, carrying mostly American tourists home. The crew were still busy camouflaging it with grey paint as it sailed down the Clyde.

All the normal civilian services were cancelled during the war, although the Queens carried special persons on occasion. After the war the services were resumed for cargo only, and no more passenger ships sailed from Glasgow to America. The passenger traffic moved to Liverpool and Southampton, and eventually it was very largely taken over by the aeroplane. The Second World War made some amends to Glasgow by transforming Prestwick into a major international airport, the chief terminal for the numerous wartime ferrying and transport operations across the Atlantic. R.A.F. Transport Command operated a regular service (for both military and civilian personnel) between Dorval (Montreal) and Prestwick, which was the airport for the whole country not just for Glasgow. There were also almost continuous flights between Prestwick and the United States. And at Renfrew airfield, which was also developed during the war into a major airport, the Lockheed Aircraft Corporation of California assembled thousands of American aircraft that had been brought by sea in sections to the Clyde. After the war Renfrew became Glasgow's airport for an increasing amount of domestic traffic (it was eventually supplanted by Abbotsinch), while Prestwick remained a major international airport, particularly valuable because of its freedom from fog.

CHAPTER 17

Before the Lights Went Out

THERE was an intellectual and artistic ferment in early twentieth-century Glasgow which some people have gone so far as to call a second Scottish Enlightenment. We have already referred to the Glasgow School of painters that flourished at the end of the nineteenth century. Of greater significance as an artistic pioneer and an international figure in the 'Modern Movement' was the Glasgow architect Charles Rennie Mackintosh (1868–1928), who is still perhaps better known on the Continent than in his native Scotland. Mackintosh was apprenticed to an architect while a student at the Glasgow School of Art, and then joined the Glasgow firm of architects Honeyman and Keppie. (John Honeyman, who died in 1914, was an expert on Gothic and designed some of the best Victorian Gothic churches in Glasgow and elsewhere in addition to doing important restoration work on old buildings. John Keppie (1863–1945) joined Honeyman in 1889; Mackintosh joined the firm in the same year and his influence on both Honeyman and Keppie was considerable.) In 1890 Mackintosh won the 'Greek' Thomson travelling scholarship and visited France and Italy. On his return he became associated with Herbert McNair and the sisters Frances and Margaret Macdonald, the latter of whom he married. McNair (married to Frances), the two Macdonalds and Mackintosh exhibited together as 'The Four', showing craftwork and graphic designs in the Art Nouveau style, to which Margaret Macdonald remained addicted although it was neither an essential nor a permanent feature of Mackintosh's vision. In 1896 Mackintosh won the competition for the Glasgow School of Art, his greatest claim to fame. The eastern section of the building went up at 167 Renfrew Street in 1897 and the western section was not added until 1907.

The Glasgow School of Art was a pioneering example of a functional architecture which is in many respects an original development of a native Scottish building tradition of the sixteenth and seventeenth centuries, the style known as the Scots Vernacular.

Mackintosh's sense of functionalism was linked to his belief that all aspects of a building, both exterior and interior, were part of a single artistic unity, and he showed this in his houses, especially: Windy-hill, Kilmalcolm, Renfrewshire and the Hill House, Helensburgh. This demand that the architect should control every detail of interior decoration and of the design of all objects within the building has been criticized on the grounds that it left little scope for the taste of the owner, but it derived from Mackintosh's overwhelming sense of the visual and functional unity of a building and to his own interest in interior design. His finest achievement in interior decoration was the Willow Tea Room at 217 Sauchiehall Street, which he designed for Kate Cranston in 1903. Kate Cranston and her brother Stuart – their family had earlier owned the Crown Hotel in George Square on the site where the Merchant's House was built by James Burnet in the 1870s – introduced to Glasgow elegant tea-rooms where both men and women could take meals in wholly respectable surroundings. Stuart Cranston opened his first tea-room in Argyle Street in 1898 and Mackintosh did the interiors for this and also for Kate's first tea-room in Ingram Street which opened in 1900. But it was the Sauchiehall Street tea-room, where Mackintosh and his wife designed everything down to the teaspoons, that created the greatest impression. As an alternative to the public house, the Cranston tea-room was a genteel source of middle-class refreshment that caused astonishment among some members of Glasgow's working class. That astonishment is well caught in one of the stories by 'Hugh Foulis' (Neil Munro) where Erchie the waiter tells how he took Duffy the coalman to Miss Cranston's. Erchie is speaking:

'Ye'll no guess where I had Duffy. Him and me was in thon new tea-room wi' the comic windows. Yin o' his horses dee'd on him, and he was doon the toon liftin' the insurance for't. I met him comin' hame wi' his Sunday claes on, and the three pound ten he got for the horse . . .'

[Erchie persuades Duffy to come with him into the tea-room:]

'When we came fornent it, he glowered, and "Michty!" says he, "wha did this?"

' "Miss Cranston," says I.

' "Was she tryin'?" says Duffy.

' "She took baith hands to't," I tellt him. "And a gey smert wum-man, too, if ye ask me."

'He stood five meenutes aforre I could get him in, wi' his een glued on the fancy doors.

' "Do ye hae to break yer way in?" says he.

' "No, nor out," I tells him; "look slippy in case some o 'yer customers sees ye!"

' "Man!" I says, "ye've henned – that's whit's wrang wi' ye: come in jist for the pant; naebody 'll touch ye, and ye'll come oot if it's sore." . . .

' "It'll cost ye nae mair than the Mull o' Kintyre Vaults [Duffy's favourite pub]," I tellt him, and we began sclimmin' the stairs. Between every rail there was a piece o' gless like the bottom of a soda-water bottle, hangin' on a wire; Duffy touched every yin o' them for luck.

' "Whit dae ye think o' that, noo?" I asked him.

' "It's gey fancy," says Duffy; "will we be lang?" . . .

' "This way for the threepenny cups and the guid bargains," I says to Duffy, and I lands him into whit they ca' the Room de Looks. Maybe ye havena seen the Room de Looks; it's the colour o' a goon Jinnet used to hae afore we mairried: there's whit Jinnet ca's insertion on the table-cloths, and wee beeds stitched a' ower the wa's the same as if somebody had done it themsel's. The chairs is no' like ony ither chairs ever I clapped eyes on, but ye could easy guess they were chairs; and a' roond the place there's a lump of lookin'-gless wi' purple leeks pented onit every noo and then. The gasalier in the middle was the thing that stunned me. It's hung a' roond wi' hunners o' big gless bools, the size o' yer nief – but we don't get pappin' onything at them.

'Duffy could only speak in whispers. "My jove!" says he, "ye'll no' get smokin' here, I'll bate."

' "Smokin'!" says I; "ye micht as well talk o gowfin'."

' "I never in a' my life saw the like o't afore. This cows a'!" says he, quite nervous and frichtened looking . . .'

It was perhaps reactions of this kind on the part of some Glaswegians that decided Mackintosh that Glasgow was too philistine a city for him. He left suddenly in 1913, to settle in London. Later, he lived in the south of France, painting some remarkable water-colours. But his career as an architect was over when he left Glasgow. He left behind him the two country houses, the interiors of the tea-rooms (which have not survived) and a number of other buildings, including Queen's Cross Church, Garscube Road, and the impressive Scotland Street School (225 Scotland Street, Kingston), with its remarkable circular staircases enclosed in cylinders largely of glass. But his masterpiece remains the College of Art.

In spite of his association at an early stage in his career with some other Glasgow artists and his influence on his friend, the architect

James Salmon (who was much more closely in contact with continental Art Nouveau than Mackintosh), Mackintosh was essentially an isolated figure in Glasgow. More clearly associated with the early twentieth-century Glasgow Enlightenment were the group of young men who wrote for the Glasgow University Magazine, *G.U.M.*, in the decade before the start of the Second World War. H. O. Mavor (better known as the dramatist James Bridie, 1888–1951) was first cartoonist, then editor, of the *G.U.M.* at a time when Walter Elliot was a contributor; Elliot was to go on to become a distinguished Conservative politician (though his generous independence of mind always kept him something of an outsider in party politics) but this did not prevent him from forming a close friendship with another fellow-student, James Maxton, a friendship that endured through fierce political differences. Another member of this generation of students was Tom Johnston, who during the Second World War was to distinguish himself as the most imaginative and vigorous of all Secretaries of State for Scotland. Bridie, in his autobiography, described the Glasgow student of that time as 'lively, violent, unprejudiced, friendly, noisy, sympathetic, moderate even in riot, interested, disinterested, intelligent, balanced, unaffected, chaste, adaptable, knowledgeable, humorous, companionable, wrapt like a mantle in commonsense yet radiating poetry, downright, upright, a considerer of the lilies, a philosopher,' and while we need not take this deliberately outrageous description literally, it is clear that there was a special kind of intellectual and artistic excitement about that generation of Glasgow students, which can be seen in the pages of the *G.U.M.*, then perhaps the best university magazine in the country. It is significant of the versatility of the Glasgow student of that generation that both Bridie and his exact contemporary Elliot took medical degrees before going on to become respectively playwright and politician, while Maxton trained and worked as a teacher before going into politics professionally. Another Glasgow University student of this generation was Tom Honeyman, and he also took a medical degree and practised medicine before becoming Director of the Glasgow Art Gallery in 1939 and with Bridie founding the Glasgow Citizens' Theatre in 1942.

It was this generation that produced the extraordinary Glasgow University song 'Ygorra', which was apparently based on a muddled recollection of a Welsh song heard at an Eisteddfod: it became the tradition to sing it vigorously at rectorial elections. It was also this generation that was involved in a remarkable riot at the Coliseum Music Hall in November 1909. An entertainer and musician had been prosecuted for printing the letters M.D. after his name, and on his explaining that the letters meant Merry Devil, not Doctor of Medicine, he had been let off with a small fine. Medical students like Bridie, who took seven years to obtain his medical degree, with many re-sits, took a poor view of this, and they formed a group to go to the theatre for the sole purpose of hissing the magician. He replied with a speech contemptuous of medical students. This so provoked the students that they packed the Coliseum the following Thursday armed with a great variety of missiles intended for the offending magician. The missiles included, according to Bridie (who was a ringleader), 'peasemeal bombs, bags of maize, eggs, potatoes, tomatoes, herring, soot,' and when police intervened to prevent the proposed punishment of the magician a pitched battle between police and students developed, in which these missiles were freely used. Five students later appeared in the police court on charges connected with the incident, but they were so successfully defended by two K.C.s and their juniors that only one was fined (one pound), another was admonished, and the other three were found not guilty.

James Bridie and his friends were also doing more important things apart from rioting in theatres. They rallied to the support of the Glasgow Repertory Theatre founded in 1909 by Alfred Wareing on the model of Miss Horniman's Gaiety Theatre in Manchester. It took over the Royalty Theatre, which had hitherto specialized in musical plays but had been losing its audiences ever since Howard and Wyndham had opened the King's Theatre in 1904. The Glasgow Repertory Theatre did not survive the First World War, but, even before its dissolution, a new movement, the Scottish National Theatre Society, had developed in Glasgow with the intention of starting a theatre company more specifically Scottish in orientation than the Glasgow Repertory ever was. It was not until January 1921 that this had concrete results, when the Scottish National Players were founded with the professed aims of developing Scottish national drama, encouraging in Scotland a taste for good drama, and founding a Scottish national theatre. In spite of the activities of Bridie, Honeyman and others, the Scottish National Players never developed into a full professional theatre, and its productions were marked by an increasingly feeble amateurism. It disappeared on the outbreak of war in 1939. But three years later Bridie and Honeyman founded the Glasgow Citizens' Theatre, which in 1945 moved to the old Princess's Theatre in the Gorbals, after which it never looked back. The part it has subsequently played in training Scottish actors and encouraging Scottish drama has been of immense significance, and has made Glasgow a focal point for drama in Scotland. It is not too much to say that the original inspiration goes back to that generation of pre-First World War students among whom Bridie, Elliot and Honeyman were so active.

There were other developments in the Glasgow theatre during the Second World War. In 1939 Molly Urquhart turned an abandoned church in Rutherglen into a little theatre, in which the distinguished actor Duncan Macrae first made his name. Both Molly Urquhart and Duncan Macrae later joined the Citizens' Theatre and played leading parts there. A new, tiny theatre in Glasgow, called 'The Park', also opened in the early days of the Second World War, as a result of the enterprise of John Stewart, who later built the Pitlochry Festival Theatre. Bridie, opening 'The Park' in uniform, remarked that 'a new venture like this in the middle of a war seems to me to have the right kind of lunatic, daft, Scottish panache about it that deserves the heartiest encouragement.' Another war-time development in Glasgow was the lively left-wing Unity Theatre, which catered especially for working-class audiences and had its greatest, specifically Glasgow success with *The Gorbals Story* by Robert McLeish.

Glasgow's contribution to Scottish culture in the early twentieth century was not confined to architecture and drama. Neil Munro (1864–1930), whose fictional account of a Glasgow working man's response to Kate Cranston's Willow Tea Room has already been quoted, was not Glasgow born (he was born on a farm near Inverary) and his Scottish historical novels, from *The Lost Pibroch* (1896) to *The New Road* (1918), are mainly concerned with Highland life and history. But Munro came to Glasgow to earn his living as a journalist and was editor of the *Glasgow Evening News* from 1918 to 1927; he came to know the city intimately and the stories he wrote for the *Evening News* in the early years of the century under the pen-name of Hugh Foulis, as well as his autobiography *The Brave Days* (1931), are important sources for an understanding of what might be called the social feel of Glasgow at the turn of the century. The settings of the tales of Para Handy, skipper of the Clyde 'puffer' (small coastal steamer), and his crew return again and again to Glasgow pubs and streets in spite of the peripatetic activities of the characters, while those concerned with Erchie the Glasgow waiter and Jimmy Swan the Glasgow commercial traveller revel in intimate social detail of lower-class Glasgow life. The stories about Para Handy often have the somewhat contrived humour of the Scottish music hall and those about Erchie and Jimmy Swan can be crudely sentimental, and yet they reveal Glasgow with affectionate accuracy. The split in Munro's work between his historical novels (moving between the Celtic twilight and Stevensonian romance) and his humorous–sentimental tales of contemporary Glasgow is symptomatic of a split in the

Wee MacGreegor

Scottish imagination of the time, particularly acute in a Highland-born Glaswegian. Glasgow was, of course, full of Highlanders and their descendants, who have contributed a great deal to the city's character. A different kind of split is shown in the autobiography of Edwin Muir (first published as *The Story and the Fable* in 1940 and revised as simply his *Autobiography* in 1954). He was born and raised on a farm in Orkney and faced the horrors of industrial Glasgow at its worst when his family had to move there when he was a young teenager.

Muir's painfully squalid Glasgow is the same as the cosy Glasgow of Erchie and Jimmy Swan, but seen by different eyes. Cosier still was the Glasgow of the native writer J. J. Bell (1871–1934) who, as his autobiographical writings clearly show, came from a comfortable middle-class Glasgow family and grew up in Hillhead, then a pleasant suburb. Bell's *Wee MacGreegor* stories, which began publication in the Glasgow *Evening Times* in 1902, rendered Glasgow character and Glasgow family life with an interesting combination of sociological accuracy, humour, and unabashed sentimentality, a mixture that delighted the readers. Glasgow was now widely recognized as a city that produced characters, and outside Scotland Glasgow character and Scottish character were often taken to be synonymous – so much so that if one spoke with a Scottish accent that was not Glasgow, one was liable to be accused of not having a Scottish accent at all.

This was to a considerable degree the result of the large Glasgow element in the 'Scotch comic' of the period. As Jack House has said, 'most Scotch comics either belong to Glasgow or pretend that they do'. Will Fyffe, who sent the song 'I belong to Glasgow' round the world, in fact came from Dundee. Harry Lauder was born near Edinburgh, but he made his first professional appearance at the Scotia Music Hall in Glasgow and though (after a spell with Irish comic songs) he went on to make his reputation singing Scottish comic songs in London, he was much involved with Glasgow and always received an especially warm welcome when he performed there. Tommy Lorne, who is still affectionately remembered as a great 'Scotch comic', was a genuine Glaswegian and the greatest of all the Glasgow comics. By the early years of this century Glasgow had established itself as a home of music-hall entertainment, centred on the Scotch comic. The tradition continued well after the Second World War, with Glaswegian comics such as Tommy Morgan, Dave Willis, Alec Finlay, Jack Anthony, Duncan Macrae (who was more than a comic), Jimmy Logan, Stanley Baxter and Billy Connolly. Glasgow was also a great centre for pantomime in the early twentieth century, and that tradition, too, survived into the decades after the

Second World War. The Theatre Royal and the Princess's both excelled in pantomime, the Princess's pioneering this form of seasonal entertainment (in which, of course, the Scotch comic was prominent).

In the years immediately preceding the First World War, Glasgow's music halls included the Alhambra, the Coliseum, the Savoy, the Pavilion, the Hippodrome, the Empress, all opened since the beginning of the century, the Palace (which became the Empire), and the Scotia (which became the Metropole, to survive as the oldest music hall in Scotland, noted for its pantomimes). The regular theatres, besides the Theatre Royal and the Princess's, included the King's, the Royalty, the Grand, the Olympia in Bridgeton and the Lyceum in Govan. The King's was opened by Howard and Wyndham in 1904 and, with its genteel audience (of both sexes) in the stalls and dress circle in evening clothes, it marked the final emergence of the Glasgow theatre into full – even conspicuous – respectability.

Cinemas first appeared in Glasgow in the form of converted shops and were already well established by the beginning of the First World War. By 1917 the city boasted a hundred cinemas, said to have been the highest number in proportion to population in the country. The most famous pre-war cinema was opened in 1909, called simply the Picture House (later enlarged as the Gaumont); its Palm Court was a favourite rendezvous. The Coliseum became a cinema and on 7 January 1929 showed Glasgow's first 'talkie', *The Singing Fool*. The cinema remained popular until television took over as the primary source of mass entertainment. In 1929 the Glasgow Film Society, claimed by Jack House to be the oldest film society in the world, was started to show to a specialist audience, foreign (non-American) films. But entertainment in Glasgow, as in any city, is bound up with patterns of living and problems of housing and city development, which are discussed in the next chapter.

The public house was still the main form of entertainment for working-class men, and Glasgow pubs were, as many still are, grim utilitarian affairs where the customer stood at the bar to consume the traditional Glasgow 'hauf an' a hauf pint' (half a gill of whisky plus a half pint of beer: the Edinburgh equivalent was 'a nip an' a pint'). But the great popular entertainment of Glaswegians in the early years of the century was, as it remains today, football as a spectator sport.

It was partly in order to draw men out of pubs that a football association was formed in Glasgow in March 1873. The previous year 154,446 persons had been apprehended in Glasgow for being drunk, incapable and disorderly. It was, significantly, in Dewar's Temperance Hotel in Bridge Street that a group of men met on 13 March of the following year, representing seven football clubs, and decided 'that the clubs here represented form themselves into an association for the promoting of football according to the rules of the Football Association'. It was in 1867 that the first Scottish football club, Queen's Park, had been formed in Glasgow and by the end of the first season of the Scottish Football Association there were sixteen clubs. They then spread to other parts of the west of Scotland and to Edinburgh, and by the end of 1875 there were fifty clubs in Scotland. In 1872 the first international football match, Scotland versus England, was played in Glasgow at the West of Scotland Cricket Club's ground in Hamilton Crescent. From then on there was no looking back. By 1875 there were twenty-six registered clubs in Glasgow, and the following year there were thirty-five.

The Scottish Football League was formed in Glasgow in 1880, and Glasgow became established as the administrative centre of the game. 'And soon', in the words of John Rafferty's article on Glasgow as the 'Football Centre of Scotland' that appeared in a special supplement of *The Scotsman* on 9 May 1975 to mark the 800th anniversary of the founding of the city, 'Glasgow was to be the spectating wonder of the world.' Rafferty continued:

> Queen's Park built their second Hampden Park before the turn of the century. Then Celtic challenged their right to international fixtures with a ground measured to hold 50,000 and with a double-decker stand and a world championship cycling track. Queen's Park reacted by building their third Hampden Park and one which before the First World War held the first 100,000 crowd in the world.
>
> Rangers challenged Hampden in the '20s when they enlarged Ibrox stadium, so in the city there were three football grounds, Hampden Park, Ibrox Stadium and Celtic Park, measured to hold over 100,000 spectators. No other city in the world could boast of such spectating capacity.

The polarization of feeling between supporters of Celtic and of Rangers has long been part of Glasgow folklore. Celtic was originally started as a club to provide soup kitchens for the poor immigrant Irish, and the early feeling against them was quite simply a feeling against Irish immigrants. Later, the religious issue replaced the national one. ('There'll be sair hearts in the Vatican this nicht', a Rangers supporter is alleged to have said happily after a match in which Celtic had been defeated.) Later still the loyalty to one team or the other became a matter of deeply ingrained custom and feeling, with no specific religious or racial element.

The objective of using football to wean men from drink can hardly be said to have been realized, for not only did supporters tend to tank up before and (more seriously) after a match, but many well-known footballers have become proprietors or managers of Glasgow pubs on retirement, thus encouraging the Glasgow phenomenon of the footballers' pub, in which football was (and is) virtually the sole topic of conversation.

Of the other senior football clubs in Glasgow most have traditionally drawn on regional support, and there appears to be a social element involved too. Jack House has noted the allegation 'that most of the supporters of Queen's Park wear bowler hats and speak with a "refained" accent'. House, too, has given a classic description of a unique element in Glasgow football: 'The "Hampden Roar" is the name given to the amazing ululations produced from thousands of throats when the Scottish football fans are urging on the Scottish team in an international match, especially against England. It is an almost frightening sound, and English football players have been quoted as saying that the Hampden Roar is the equivalent of two goals for Scotland. Unfortunately this has not always proved true.'

We have mentioned in an earlier chapter the two Glasgow exhibitions of 1888 and 1901. An account of intellectual life and entertainment in the early twentieth century can appropriately close with some mention of the city's next two exhibitions, those of 1911 and 1938. The 1911 exhibition, designed to raise funds to endow a Chair of Scottish History and Literature at the University, was on a smaller scale than the others. The guarantee fund was £143,000 and the attendance 9,400,000. Although modest in scale, the exhibition – at Kelvingrove, extending from Sauchiehall Street to Gibson Street, and from Kelvin Way to Gray Street – provided an imaginative and varied display. As C. A. Oakley described it:

> The Stewart Memorial Fountain in the park was its focal point, the architect setting around it his major palaces – of industries, history, fine arts, and machinery – the grand concert hall with 300 seats, and the conference halls. In other parts of Kelvingrove were erected an old-world Scottish 'toonie', a Highland Village, a Pavilion on Old Glasgow, a Garden Club, an Aerial Railway, a Mountain Slide, a West African Village, and various side-shows. The chief Palace was that of History – it was modelled on the Palace of Falkland – and contained the most comprehensive collection of Scottish relics ever brought together. Good use was made of the River Kelvin, in which a cavalcade of modern ships floated, but the great thrill was the aerial railway, which did a circular trip from the heights, where the Earl Roberts Statue now stands, to the University grounds – and went 130 feet above the Kelvin.

The weather throughout was splendid, except for the final night, when a fierce storm took off the tops of several of the main buildings.

The exhibition of 1938 was more an act of faith than a spontaneous assertion of civic pride, coming as it did after years of depression and with the Second World War looming. It called itself grandiosely the Empire Exhibition (Scotland) 1938 and it was held on 175 acres at Bellahouston Park. The architect, Thomas Tait, designed a three-hundred-foot-high tower as the exhibition's focal point, and as the tower was built on top of Bellahouston Hill it dominated the exhibition dramatically. Some of the other buildings were unusually well designed; the concert hall had remarkably good acoustics, and the amusement park was officially described as 'the biggest and most original amusement park in Europe'. It had attractive water displays and spectacular floodlighting at night. The exhibition attracted thirteen and a half million people, and on the last day 364,000 attended, a record for the British Isles. But the weather was terrible, with constant wind and rain. This was the west of Scotland's worst summer for almost a hundred years. The people, however, were determined to visit it and to enjoy themselves, even though – or perhaps because – the exhibition seemed to be defying both history and the elements. When war came, within a year of the official closing of the exhibition in a downpour, Tait's Tower, which had been intended to stand as a permanent memorial to the exhibition, had to be hastily dismantled, as it was seen as a possible navigational aid to German airmen.

In spite of the thirteen-and-a-half million visitors, the 1938 exhibition was the only one that had to call on its guarantors to make good a loss. They had to pay 3s. 5d. in the pound, which was not excessive considering the awful weather during the whole exhibition.

CHAPTER 18

Today and Tomorrow

IN 1967 a sub-committee of the Scottish Housing Advisory Committee reported on unfit housing in Scotland. The report, entitled *Scotland's Older Houses*, records some of the conditions found in Glasgow by the investigators. In spite of the activities of the City Improvement Trust and the provision of Corporation housing described in Chapter Twelve, the conditions encountered by the sub-committee in 1967 are uncomfortably reminiscent of those described by Edwin Chadwick in 1842. The sub-committee themselves declared that they were 'forcefully' reminded of the Report of the Royal Commission on the Housing of the Industrial Population of Scotland published in 1917, which had spoken out eloquently against slum conditions. 'Glasgow has a bad reputation for bad housing conditions,' they said, 'and, despite great efforts by the Corporation, we have found that this reputation is unfortunately justified. The statistics alone cannot adequately describe the problem: indeed, they misleadingly suggest that the problem is not as great as it is. We have seen conditions in Glasgow that can be described only as appalling. Families are condemned to live in atrocious conditions which should shock the national conscience – and, we believe, would do so if they were better known. But even the Glaswegian who sees only the often imposing (yet, on closer inspection, often crumbling) front exterior seldom appreciates how revolting and inhumane are the conditions inside the closes, on the common staircases, and in the back courts.' They return to Glasgow in a later section of the report: 'We were particularly appalled at some of the conditions which we saw, particularly in Glasgow: gutters choked with refuse of every description; burst and choked drains; heaps of uncollected garbage and rubbish; pools of stagnant and foul smelling water – the catalogue could be extended almost indefinitely.'

The sub-committee did see some compensating advantages in Glasgow's slum tenements: 'solidity of construction, warmth, relative freedom from damp' and proximity to work, but they pointed out that 'their very solidity of construction . . . carried the seeds of to-day's problems, since the stone structures of these nineteenth-century buildings have remained sound while the woodwork and internal fittings have become dilapidated and grossly inadequate for modern standards of sanitation and living space'. But how did they look and feel to those who lived in them?

> The close known as 150 South Wellington Street was like thousands of other Glasgow slum closes, a short, narrow walled-in passage leading up to three landings and through to a grassless earthen or broken-bricked backcourt, with its small, mean communal wash-house and open, insanitary midden. In such backcourts the women of the tenements, after taking their weekly turn in the washhouse, hang out the family washing and take it in dried with sunshine or strong seawind and half-dirtied with industrial smoke and grime. They are the only playground of many thousands of the city's children, where the youngsters play football and children's games, climb on the midden and washhouse roofs and escape death or injury from the perilous traffic of the streets.
>
> They look like tunnels cut through solid cliffs of masonry, these closes, and in the slums are decorated in the crudest style. Halfway up their walls are painted a stone or chocolate colour which is separated from whitewash by a stencilled border of another shade. There are often great holes in the walls of these closes, left unplastered or, if filled in, left unpainted and presenting unsightly daubs or crudely plastered cement. As the walls are for long periods unrefreshed with new paint, the old paint cracks and peels and the dingy whitewash flakes and falls before factors will spend money on property renovation. Many tenement dwellers live indifferent to all this ugliness and those with some spirit, who are angered by it all, lose heart in their long, unequal struggle against the tight-fistedness of factors, and live on and die in homes too narrow for fuller life, from which it seems there is no escape. These closes, badly lit, with their dangerous broken-stepped stairs, often filthy and malodorous, smelling of catspiss and drunkards' spew, have been for generations of Glas-wegians the favourite, and for thousands, the only courting-place, and many hurried, unhappy marriages have originated there. 'Stonnin' at the close' or 'closemooth' is a social habit of tenement dwellers and at all hours lone individuals lounge, staring vacantly.

This description comes from *The Dance of the Apprentices* (1948) by the Glasgow writer Edward Gaitens remembering his childhood in the Gorbals in the years immediately before the First World War (the scene described here is set in 1913), in a novel that also covers the First World War and the years between the wars. It seems to bear out the criticisms of the Royal Commission of 1917 and the sub-committee of 1967. Yet the reference to the children's games and the courting suggest that, in spite of the appalling physical conditions, there was a certain amount of life and colour and simple human happiness in this environment. Gaitens does not, perhaps, give a distinct impression of that relish for life in this passage, but another Glasgow writer, born in the Gallowgate, in the very heart of old Glasgow, has made it clear that, side by side with all the conditions deplored in official reports and made notorious throughout the world, there was a special kind of zest for living that Glaswegians cannot help harking back to in fascination, long after they have escaped to more salubrious and genteel parts of the city. 'Out of its horrible smoke-bleary streets,' wrote Clifford Hanley of Glasgow in his autobiography *Dancing in the Streets* (1958) [it is perhaps no coincidence that the titles of both Hanley's and Gaitens' books contain a form of the word 'dance'], 'it keeps throwing up jokes and songs and poetry as well as bloody murder. A dark jollity of life bubbles through it as if it were not a city at all but a monster, an enormous octopus or the kraken itself, except that this kraken has never slept.' And when criticizing the suburban Council houses and high-rise modern blocks where the inhabitants of demolished slums were transferred, Hanley adds:

> It's easy to say this from outside Gallowgate or Gorbals, when nobody in his senses would deliberately choose to live in Gallowgate or Gorbals if he didn't have to . . . But something has gone out of life in these great airy suburbs. A string has been broken and left the children rootless and starved of tradition, and tradition means a lot to children. They don't have the handed-down legends of the slum streets, and they don't have the different legends of children in country villages. The people in the enormous new suburbs know this very well in their hearts. There's an unease and an unrest in the biggest of the new districts, and television isn't a complete substitute for the feeling that has gone.

Such a sentiment has often been voiced by Glaswegians, and has now been officially noted by the planners, and anyone who seeks to discover the image of Glasgow held by its more articulate citizens will find it expressed again and again. Of course, there has been a lot of sentimentality uttered about Glasgow, by 'Hugh Foulis' and J. J. Bell and generations of music-hall singers, but the nostalgia for a vitality amid the ugliness represents something genuine. Sometimes the ugliness itself is seen as a symptom of vitality. The appalling gang violence that flourished between the wars especially in the Gorbals, Calton and Bridgeton, was seen by Clifford Hanley as something that 'existed for fun'. Unlike American gangsters, Hanley observed, Glasgow gangs never made any money or acquired any political influence. 'They just wanted a fight. They started poor and they finished poor and they stayed poor in between.' The gangs were indeed a result of poverty and unemployment working on particular social, psychological and historical conditions. There was a Glasgow tradition of rival stone-throwing groups of youngsters going back to the eighteenth century, as we have seen in Chapter Six. The gangs that appeared in the 1920s may well have begun, as J. A. Mack has suggested, 'as an extension into later adolescence of the collective stone-throwing exploits of schoolboys'. There was also the traditional religious rivalry. Though most of the gangs took their names from the streets or districts where they had their headquarters (for instance, the South Side Stickers, the Calton Entry, the Briggate Boys), others took names that reflected the religious divide: the Billy Boys, for example, took their name from William of Orange. The Twelfth of July Orange Walk, with its ceremonial parading of Protestant anti-Catholic feeling ('The Twelfth of July, the Papes'll die') inevitably exacerbated any religious element in gang warfare. But if they 'existed for fun' the gangs, in Mack's words, 'could and did become fully criminal and dangerous', and it was only after vigorous planned action by the police (and the ingenious tactics of Police-Sergeant 'Tommy' Morrison, who soon became a legendary figure in Glasgow) that order was restored to the streets of the Gorbals, Calton, Bridgeton and other affected areas in the 1930s. Other kinds of violence, including razor-slashing, that developed after the Second World War, represented a different phenomenon from the gangs of the 1920s and 1930s. But at least it can be said that Glasgow's Pakistani and Indian population, much increased after the Second World War, has never provoked the kind of racial violence that has sometimes arisen in other cities. Race relations in Glasgow have remained consistently good, as though Glasgow's fund of racial feeling has been spent in the rivalry between Celtic and Rangers.

Nevertheless, modern Glasgow remains a violent city and violence is built into its street lore. Hanley quotes a Glasgow tenement children's rhyme:

> Murder murder polis
> Three sterrs up
> The wummin in the middle door
> Hit me wi' a cup

Ma face is a' bleedin'
My heid's a' cut
Murder murder polis
Three sterrs up.

This speaks vividly for Glasgow's slum children, evoking that amalgam of violence, humour, vitality and matter-of-fact resilience to which those who know them best (or have themselves been part of them) have so often testified. The slums were rich in street games, the boys playing 'bools' or 'jauries' (with ordinary 'wally jauries' or fancy glass marbles called 'glessies'), peeries, billy-nuts, moshie and rounders and the girls specializing in varieties of skipping-rope games and ba' beds or peevers.

But the reality of the slum squalor remained, in spite of the efforts of generations of municipal and national reformers. With the passing of the Housing (Scotland) Act 1930 slum clearance began in Glasgow on a large scale, the Act granting local authorities a subsidy of £2 10s. for forty years for each person rehoused from a clearance or an improvement area or from insanitary houses demolished or closed. The Housing (Scotland) Act 1935 for the first time fixed minimum standards for the definition of overcrowding and provided a further subsidy for each house built to relieve overcrowding, the priority now moving from slum clearance to relief of overcrowding. Slum clearance received priority with the passing of the Housing (Repairs and Rents) (Scotland) Act 1954, which obliged local authorities to submit three-year programmes for slum clearance. In the following ten years 32,000 houses in Glasgow were closed or demolished. But the 1961 census showed 11,000 dwellings in Glasgow as unfit, though the report of 1967 already cited estimated that on a more adequate criterion there would have been as many as 70,000 unfit houses in the city. The 1971 census showed 14,500 houses previously occupied now vacant. In 1961 there were 98.9 persons per acre in the Gorbals compared with 11.9 in Pollokshields and 18.7 in Kelvinside. With some buildings demolished and some empty awaiting demolition (and some new high-rise flats) the density of population in the Gorbals had fallen to 77.55 per hectare in the 1971 census as compared with 28.92 in Pollokshields. (A hectare is 2.471 acres.)

With new houses – first traditional council houses then huge high-rise council flats – unable to keep up with the decay and demolition, the planned movement of the population out of Glasgow into new towns seemed one solution to the problem. Between 1958 and 1965, 8,667 houses for Glasgow families were completed by New Towns Development Corporations and 3,843 were completed for Glasgow families in new towns by the Scottish Special Housing Association. This did not, of course, completely take care of Glasgow's problem, although it alleviated it. What was happening was an actual decline in the city's population. The population of Glasgow shown in the 1951 census was 1,089,767; in 1961 it was 1,055,017; in 1971 it was 897,483. From 1 April to 30 September 1975, 3,228 houses were demolished in Glasgow while in roughly the same period 2,628 new houses were completed by the New Towns Development Corporations of Cumbernauld, East Kilbride, Glenrothes, Irvine and Livingston. And of course not all of these were for people from Glasgow. What was going on?

What was, in fact, going on was the direct result of Glasgow Corporation's slum clearance and comprehensive redevelopment policies. Their effect has been seen most vividly in the central area of the city, where in the late 1960s the number of houses built was halved (to just over 6,000) and the population reduced from 24,000 to 16,000. Bound up with this was a communications policy, clearing paths for new motorways to enter and leave Glasgow. By the time that Glasgow became a district of the new Strathclyde Region, the Town Council had planned seventy-five miles of urban motorway (compared with thirty-nine miles planned by the Greater London Council) which involved grievous damage to the townscape and the separation of the city centre from the northern and western suburbs by what one critic called 'a channel of noise and smell'. It would be an exaggeration to say that the planning has involved the destruction of a city in order to facilitate the means of reaching and leaving it. The destruction of older houses on the city's north-western approaches in the interests of the M8 and the M74 running westward past the now non-existent Cowcaddens before turning south through the demolished Charing Cross region to cross the river west of the Broomielaw did not exactly involve the destruction of Glasgow. But the proposal to make Great Western Road part of this urban expressway system by widening it and building underpasses involved the destruction not only of some noble terraces but also of the living communities of Maryhill, Great Western Road itself, Byres Road, Hyndland and Partick, and this aroused fierce protest which led to the project's being postponed while the authorities had second thoughts. So Great Western Road has been reprieved, although its eastern end is now a tangled ribbon of motorway built over a demolished part of the old city.

There have been compensations. The pedestrianized Buchanan Street, with its tubs of flowers and seats for those who wish to observe the passing show, can on a sunny day present an attractive and in some ways a Continental scene. Although several of the famous and stately nineteenth-century stores have had to go both here and in the pedestrianized sections of Sauchiehall Street, so that much of the impressiveness of Victorian commercial Glasgow has gone, plans for new buildings are bold and ambitious. But so far there have been no compensating attractions in the old heart of Glasgow. Drygate is now lost in the middle of a massive housing estate, which doubtless provides much better accommodation for its inhabitants than the old slum buildings but which obscures the nature and pattern of this historical quarter. There are more dismal areas of desolation nearby. On the other hand, after wandering around what little remained of really old Glasgow in the neighbourhood of Glasgow Cross immediately after the fateful day of 16 May 1975 when the city became a district of Strathclyde Region, I took an agreeable stroll along the prettified river front between Victoria Bridge and the railway bridge: the riverside walk was attractively laid out; the sun was shining; and – it was about half-past-twelve – many office workers were eating an open-air lunch on the seats provided I had the feeling that Glasgow was enjoying itself.

The debate about modern developments in Glasgow has been fierce. The redevelopment of the Gorbals – announced in 1955 but the first new flats were not ready until 1958 – with its removal of inhabitants into enormous blocks of high-rise flats ('multi-storey residential penitentiaries', James Cameron has called them), has been much criticized for the lack of social imagination involved, but Sir Basil Spence won international prizes for his design. The social consequences of redevelopment could sometimes only be discovered after the event, and with the best will – and skill – in the world planners and architects could make mistakes that were hard to foresee. Even so, the redevelopment of the Gorbals is a long and slow process and is not expected to be complete until the mid-1980s. When Gorbals is replaced by Laurieston and Oatlands (the giving of a new significance to these old names illustrated the desire to abolish the old image of the Gorbals) it may be that much that was heartbreaking in the old area will have gone for good. Not everybody is convinced of this. 'The problem is', remarked Geoffrey Shaw, housing convener of Strathclyde Region, in 1975, 'that while people could live with violence and poverty, we've never quite learned to live with concrete.'

Is this sentimentality? In an article written in May 1975 for the eight hundredth anniversary of the city charter John Rafferty criticized the critics. 'Is the Glasgow, which all those wordy characters claim is the city that is being vandalised in its rebuilding, the same

Glasgow which not so long ago other wordy characters or maybe the same ones were describing as a cancer on the face of the Empire?' he asked. He saw 'something inconsistent in the emotional campaign to save something which not so long ago was universally condemned as nasty and ugly'. While understanding the regret that Charing Cross Anderston, Cross, Townhead, Gorbals and Cowcaddens have gone, he pointed to the rediscovery of some beautiful Victorian buildings in the centre of the city exposed as the rubbish around them was removed, to the preservation of the magnificent frontage of St Andrew's Halls in Granville Street with a new library extension, to the saving of the 'lovely shell' of the Royal Bank of Scotland in Buchanan Street, to the skilled restoration work being done on the old Royal Exchange, now Stirling's Library, and to the development of attractively laid-out pedestrianized areas and riverside walks. All this is undeniably praiseworthy. So are the ambitious and imaginative plans for new city patterns and for rehabilitating central Glasgow by linking the provision of new housing, new opportunities for employment (with hopes of attracting Government Departments from the south), new developments in communications (with a proposal for two new railway stations for the electrified services), and new shopping and recreational facilities. All this looks forward to the 1980s, and still leaves Glasgow in the middle and late 1970s in a curious betwixt-and-between position, uncertain when the necessary Government money will be provided for those of the schemes that require it, poised between a half-demolished past and a beckoning but uncertain future.

But at least the flight from Glasgow has been stopped. On 12 May 1976 the Government announced that it would scrap forthwith Britain's latest new town at Stonehouse, eighteen miles from Glasgow, only three years after its designation and after four million pounds had been spent on it. It was to be abandoned in favour of 'urban renewal' in Glasgow. It was in that week that the Strathclyde Regional Council unveiled its strategic five-year plan for the region and expressed itself firmly against the development of Stonehouse. In announcing the decision, the Secretary of State for Scotland endorsed a change by both central and local government in social and economic policies towards urban renewal in west-central Scotland; later he announced that a big urban renewal project for Glasgow was being planned. So just a year after the coming into force of the Local Government (Scotland) Act 1973, which drastically reorganized local government in Scotland and made the City of Glasgow (the former 'county of the city of Glasgow') a district of the enormous Strathclyde Region, extending from the Island of Mull to the Cumnock and

Doon Valley in Ayrshire, a major change in policy for Glasgow was announced.

It would perhaps be most fitting to end this account with the celebration in May 1975 of the eight hundredth anniversary of the city's charter and the implementation on the 16th of that month of the legislation that abolished the City of Glasgow as a separate entity. Yet it is worth pointing out that this change, in many respects so drastic, did not in itself alter the movement of history in the city. Nor did it alter the city's traditions as much as might have been expected. The traditional title of Lord Provost, for example (although the original title was simply Provost), will continue to be used by the Chairman of the Glasgow District Council. 'In each region there shall be local government areas to be known as districts', the Act stated; each region and each district were to have a 'council consisting of a chairman and councillors' and 'the chairman of each council . . . shall be elected by the council from among the councillors'. The District Council of Glasgow shares with the District Councils of Aberdeen, Dundee and Edinburgh the right to have its chairman designated Lord Provost. Under the new system education and environment (including roads) are the responsibility of the Regional Council while housing comes under the District Council, though provision is made for involving the Regional Council here as well.

Other things were changing in the life of the city. Patterns of entertainment changed, with a steady drop in the number of theatres and cinemas in the 1950s and 1960s. The Queen's (which, in Clifford Hanley's words, used to put on 'the roughest, bawdiest, longest-running pantomimes in the world') burned down in 1952, and a similar fate befell the Royalty (renamed the Lyric) in 1953 and the Metropole in 1961. But what shocked Glasgow people most, and set up a great wave of nostalgia, was the closing in 1962 of the Empire, that home of variety and the most famous music hall in Britain outside London. Today opposite its site in Sauchiehall Street is the Electricity Board's headquarters. Suburban cinemas disappeared steadily. So did the music halls in districts such as Bridgeton, Gorbals, Govan and Partick. Tea-rooms, a feature of Glasgow life since the late nineteenth century, disappeared or altered their character; their place was often taken by pretentious restaurants as the habit of dining out replaced the habit of going out for tea or going to the theatre among a section of Glasgow's middle classes. Clubs, a picturesque feature of the city since the early eighteenth century, continued to decline. More and more people stayed at home in the evening and watched television.

But not all is loss and nostalgia. The reconstruction of the Theatre

Royal into a home for Scottish Opera, a first-rate opera house which opened in triumph in October 1975, was the climax to a long and honourable tradition of opera in the city as well as the beginning of a new chapter in Glasgow's history as the opera centre of Scotland. Clifford Hanley referred to 'the incessant urge of Glaswegians to burst into song; Burns songs, pop songs, folk songs, operatic songs, patriotic songs, all kinds of songs'. Hanley saw this as reflecting a popular sentimentality, but this love of song had its more serious and disciplined side. It was in Glasgow that the first British performance of Mozart's *Idomeneo* took place, in 1934, and in 1935 the city saw the British première of Berlioz's *The Trojans*. These were both presented by the Glasgow Grand Opera Society, an ambitious amateur group that would tackle almost anything. At the same time the city welcomed seasons of professional opera from a number of distinguished companies. But the foundation in 1962 of Scottish Opera by Alexander Gibson (its present artistic director), together with Robin Orr, Ian Rodger and others who shared his high ambitions for music in Scotland, gave a wholly new impetus to opera in Glasgow and in Scotland generally. Gibson had been since 1959 musical director of the Scottish National Orchestra (a full-time orchestra which succeeded the part-time Scottish Orchestra in 1950 and was based in St Andrew's Halls until the building burned down in 1962), and was responsible for building it into an orchestra of high international class. Now, in founding Scotland's first professional opera company, on a severely limited budget and to considerable head-shaking by wiseacres, he gave notice of further plans for Scottish music. Between the founding of Scottish Opera and the opening of its new permanent home in Glasgow, it had given some eight hundred performances of a total of fifty operas, ranging from Monteverdi to Britten. The company's performances included one of *Full Circle*, a short Scottish opera by Robin Orr (at one time Professor of Music at Glasgow University) and also, for the first time anywhere, an uncut version of *The Trojans* in English. They put on the first complete performance of Wagner's *Ring* in Glasgow since 1921. This was when the company had temporary headquarters at the former Engineer's Institute in Elmbank Street, and was contending against many difficulties; with a permanent home its future looks altogether more assured.

Peter Hemmings, the general administrator of Scottish Opera, was largely responsible for raising the £3 million required for rebuilding the old Theatre Royal (which had closed in 1956, when it was modified to provide studios and offices for Scottish Television) as an opera house. He got the blessing of the city fathers, and an appeal was launched in three directions – to the public, to industry and to the Government. By the beginning of 1974, about £835,000 had been raised from commerce and industry. The public appeal was launched in April 1974, and the first donation was of £1,000 from a man in Bearsden. The Government hung back, but political rivalries in a year that saw two elections helped the cause. Mr Heath, as Leader of the Opposition, pledged support in September 1974 if his party were elected, and shortly afterwards the Labour Government announced that they would match the promised £1 million from industry with the same amount. With the City of Glasgow offering a bridging loan, all was set for the successful conclusion of the operation.

Meanwhile, Hemmings had gone ahead with plans for the rebuilding. When he heard, early in 1972, that Scottish Television would be vacating the Theatre Royal when their new premises round the corner in Cowcaddens were ready (these new premises now dominate the demolished and cleared Cowcaddens), he at once formed a sub-committee to look into the possibility of acquiring and remodelling the theatre for Scottish Opera. They commissioned Arup Associates (who had converted the Maltings at Snape) to propose a scheme. This scheme, when completed, showed that it was possible to restore the lost glories of an old theatre while converting it into a building with admirable acoustics, furnished with the most advanced technical equipment. It was a great triumph for Glasgow, all the more so as Edinburgh, the capital city, home of a great International Festival, had dithered for decades about building an opera house and at the time of writing still has not got one or any firm plans for one. When, therefore, on 16 October 1975 the new opera house officially opened with the Scottish Opera's presentation of Verdi's *Otello*, Glasgow firmly took its place as the music capital of Scotland. The situation had changed indeed since 'Jupiter' Carlyle complained of the lack of music in Glasgow in 1743.

In the visual arts, Glasgow has been maintaining the tradition begun by the Foulis brothers' Academy in the eighteenth century. The fine Hunterian collection, bequeathed to the University by William Hunter, a student of the Foulis brothers, in 1783 and moved to an unsuitable new Hunterian Museum, designed by Gilbert Scott, when the University moved in 1870, is now housed in a splendid Hunterian Museum, with an adjacent harmonizing library. Glasgow's main art collection, which since 1902 has been housed in the red sandstone Art Gallery and Museum in Kelvingrove Park, has been described by Sir John Rothenstein as 'the finest civic collection in Britain'. It includes the impressive Graham-Gilbert collection, bequeathed in 1877, which has some important Rembrandts among forty-seven Dutch and Flemish paintings: together with the paintings from the original McLennan bequest by Ruisdale, Cuyp, Jordaens and others, these provide Kelvingrove with (again in Rothenstein's words) 'a Dutch–Belgian collection with which there is none comparable in any British municipal gallery'. It also has some important French and Italian paintings and a fine representation of British painters.

Glasgow has also been enriched by the magnificent collection assembled by Sir William Burrell (1861–1958), a Glasgow shipping magnate with wide-ranging and discriminating artistic tastes. While his collection includes some remarkable examples of ancient art – Mesopotamian, Assyrian, Egyptian, Greek, Persian and Roman – its most complete section is that representing nineteenth-century French painting, with twenty-two pictures by Degas and seventeen by Daumier. The problem has been housing this collection adequately, and after long delays it was finally decided to build a Burrell Museum in the ample grounds of Pollok House (three miles south-west of the city centre, off Pollokshaws Road). Pollok House was built in 1747–52 by William Adam (father of the famous Adam brothers) for Sir John Maxwell and it was presented to the National Trust for Scotland and to Glasgow Corporation, with the Stirling–Maxwell collection which it contained, by Mrs Anne Maxwell Macdonald and family in 1966 and opened to the public the following year. The collection was assembled between 1842 and 1859 by Sir William Stirling Maxwell (1818–78), who was an authority on Spanish art, on which he wrote an important book, and who acquired a great many important and representative Spanish paintings, including works by Goya, El Greco and Murillo. Pollok House also contains a fine collection of furniture, silver, porcelain and glass. Mrs Macdonald's gift to the city also included the surrounding 361-acre Pollok Park, where the Burrell Museum is to be built. When that is complete Glasgow, with the Pollok complex, the new Hunterian Museum and the Kelvingrove Art Gallery and Museum, will have a place of rank as an art centre among European cities.

So amid the fierce debates about high-rise flats and motorways, grandiose plans for urban renewal and general controversy about the city's future, Glasgow has been quietly establishing its right to be considered a great city of the arts. Meanwhile, what had been happening on the Clyde, the source of Glasgow's original prosperity? 'The Clyde made Glasgow and Glasgow made the Clyde', the old saying goes. As Glasgow moved during the present century from being a centre of manufacturing to a centre of service and distribution, the Clyde inevitably became less important. As recently as 1955, 48 per

R   227

cent of the working population of the Glasgow conurbation was engaged in manufacturing and 44 per cent in service and distribution. By 1973, the share of manufacturing had fallen to below 33 per cent and that of services and distribution had risen to almost 60 per cent. During those eighteen years the working population declined by about 100,000, for reasons we have already discussed. It may be that, as the centre of the British National Oil Corporation and the home of the Offshore Supplies Office, Glasgow will develop a new industrial impetus and the Clyde will take on a new role. Indeed, a reconsideration of the needs of the Clyde was already evident in 1965 when the Clyde Navigation Trust, which had done so much for the upper reaches of the Clyde, ceased to exist and in 1966 the Clyde Port Authority, the first estuarial authority in Britain, came into being. The emphasis is increasingly on the deeper sheltered water of the lower Clyde, accommodating ever larger ships. At the same time the use of container vessels has cut drastically the amount of cargo shipping coming into Glasgow: between 1966 and 1975 the annual throughput of general cargo in Glasgow's docks fell by about a million tonnes, as more and more cargo was handled in boxes through the Clydeport Container Terminal at Greenock. In Glasgow itself the handling of the Clyde's 'break-bulk' cargo is centred on King George V Dock, while Shieldhall Quay has been specially equipped to handle exports from the Scottish steelworks. Activities associated with offshore oil, notably the construction of platforms, have grown up on the lower Clyde estuary and adjacent sea-lochs.

As for shipbuilding, so long the glory of Glasgow and the Clyde, although in 1975 there were still over 18,000 people directly employed on shipbuilding on the river and over three times that number engaged in the supply industry or as sub-contractors associated with shipbuilding, the decline has been steady and drastic. In addition to the factors discussed earlier, competition from overseas shipbuilders, particularly in Japan, has proved hard to meet. In spite of North Sea oil, and the diversification of companies to manufacture oilrigs or associated equipment, the position of Clyde shipbuilding at the time of writing remains doubtful and confused. Whatever the coming years may bring, it looks as though Glasgow's future as a sea-trading city must depend on the deeper waters of the lower reaches of the Clyde. The heroic dredging and deepening operations of the eighteenth and nineteenth centuries, which enabled Glasgow to emerge as a great world port and without which it might well have remained (as Hugh Cochrane has suggested) a modest cathedral city like Worcester on the Severn, have proved largely irrelevant to Glasgow's needs in the second half of the twentieth century.

Glasgow has come a long way since St Mungo. From the 'dear green place' by the Molendinar Burn to the pretty town admired by Defoe, the bustling commercial city of the tobacco lords, the great industrial city that followed, the proud Victorian show-place, the Glasgow of slums and pubs and comics and legends – throughout all its long history it has never lacked vitality or character. It has been re-made more than once, and it will be re-made again. Whatever its future, it is hard to believe that it will ever lose its characteristic combination of nobility and vulgarity, of friendliness and roughness, of Lowland prudence and Highland recklessness. It is a city that has traditionally engendered among its citizens a special kind of exasperated love, a city that people have become nostalgic about before they have left it.

Let Glasgow Flourish.

Select Bibliography

W. Bannister, *James Bridie and his Theatre*, London, 1955

W. Baynham, *The Glasgow Stage*, Glasgow, 1892

J. J. Bell, *Do you Remember?* Edinburgh, 1934

    I Remember, Edinburgh, 1932

    Wee MacGreegor, Glasgow, 1900

G. Blair, *Biographical Sketches of the Glasgow Necropolis*, Glasgow, 1857

G. Blake, *The Shipbuilders*, London, 1935

J. Bridie, *One Way of Living*, London, 1939

A. Brown, *History of Glasgow*, Glasgow, 1795

E. Burt, *Letters from a Gentleman in the North of Scotland*, London, 1754

R. G. Cant and I. D. Lindsay, *Old Glasgow*, Edinburgh, 1947

A. Carlyle, *Autobiography*, ed. J. H. Burton, London and Edinburgh, 1910

A. K. Chalmers, *A New Life Table for Glasgow*, Glasgow, 1894

J. Cleland, *Annals of Glasgow*, Glasgow, 1816

    Enumeration of the Inhabitants of Glasgow, Glasgow, 1832

    The Rise and Progress of the City of Glasgow, Glasgow, 1820

R. Cowan, *Vital Statistics of Glasgow*, Glasgow and Edinburgh, 1838

M. E. Craig, *The Scottish Periodical Press 1750–1789*, Edinburgh, 1931

J. Cunnison and J. B. S. Gilfillan (eds.), *The Third Statistical Account of Scotland: Glasgow*, Glasgow, 1958

D. Defoe, *A Tour thro' the Whole Island of Great Britain*, ed. G. D. H. Cole, London, 1927

J. Denholm, *History of the City of Glasgow*, Glasgow, 1804

T. M. Devine, *The Tobacco Lords*, Edinburgh, 1975

A. O. Ewing of Ballikinrain, *View of the Merchants House of Glasgow*, 1866

G. Eyre-Todd and R. Renwick, *History of Glasgow*, 3 vols., Glasgow, 1921–34

I. Finlay, *Art in Scotland*, London, 1948

R. Forsyth, *The Beauties of Scotland*, 5 vols., Edinburgh, 1805

J. G. Fyfe (ed.), *Scottish Diaries and Memoirs, 1550–1746*, Stirling, n.d.

E. Gaitens, *Dance of the Apprentices*, Glasgow, 1948

A. Gomme and D. Walker, *Architecture of Glasgow*, London, 1968

J. Gibson, *History of Glasgow*, Glasgow, 1777

I. F. Grant, *The Economic History of Scotland*, London, 1934

    The Social and Economic History of Scotland before 1603, Edinburgh, 1930

H. H. Hamilton, *An Economic History of Scotland in the Eighteenth Century*, Oxford, 1963

The Industrial Revolution in Scotland, Oxford, 1932

C. Hanley, *Dancing in the Streets*, London, 1958

W. H. Hill, *History of Hutcheson's Hospital and School*, Glasgow, 1881

J. House, *The Heart of Glasgow*, London, 1972

T. Howarth, *Charles Rennie Mackintosh and the Modern Movement*, London, 1953

D. Johnson, *Music and Society in Lowland Scotland in the Eighteenth Century*, London, 1972

J. R. Kellett, *The Impact of Railways on Victorian Cities*, London, 1969

D. Kirkwood, *My Life of Revolt*, London, 1935

M. Lindsay, *Portrait of Glasgow*, London, 1972

F. N. McCoy, *Robert Baillie and the Second Scots Reformation*, 1974

J. K. McDowall, *The People's History of Glasgow*, with new introduction by J. B. S. Gilfillan, Wakefield, 1970

R. D. M'Ewan and W. MacLean, *Old Glasgow Weavers*, Glasgow, 1933

J. MacKinnon, *The Social and Industrial History of Scotland*, I, to 1707, 1920; II, from the Union to the Present Time, London, 1921

P. Mackenzie, *Reminiscences of Glasgow*, 2 vols., Glasgow, 1865–6

W. M. Mackenzie, *The Scottish Burghs*, Edinburgh, 1948

K. Macleod, *Charles Rennie Mackintosh*, London, 1968

J. McNair, *James Maxton, the Beloved Rebel*, London, 1955

J. M'Ure, *The History of Glasgow*, Glasgow, 1736

C. McWilliam, *Scottish Townscape*, London, 1975

D. M. Malloch, *The Book of Glasgow Anecdote*, London and Edinburgh, 1912

Sir J. D. Marwick, *Early Glasgow*, Glasgow, 1911

The River Clyde and the Clyde Burghs, Glasgow, 1909

R. Miller and J. Tivy (eds.), *The Glasgow Region*, Glasgow, 1958

J. O. Mitchell, *Old Glasgow Essays*, Glasgow, 1905

M. Moss and J. Hume, *Glasgow as It Was*, Glasgow, 1975

N. Munro, *The Brave Days*, Edinburgh, 1931

('Hugh Foulis'), *Para Handy and other Tales*, Edinburgh and London, 1931

Memorabilia of the City of Glasgow selected from the Minute Book of the Burgh, MDLXXVIII – MDCCL, Glasgow, 1868

C. A. Oakley, *The Second City*, Glasgow 1975

J. Pagan, *Sketches of the History of Glasgow*, Glasgow, 1847

T. Pagan, *The Convention of the Royal Burghs of Scotland*, Glasgow, 1926

M. Plant, *The Domestic Life of Scotland in the Eighteenth Century*, Edinburgh, 1952

R. Pococke, *Tours in Scotland 1747, 1750, 1760*, Edinburgh, 1887

J. M. Reid, *Glasgow*, Glasgow, 1956

R. Renwick and Sir J. Lindsay, *History of Glasgow*, Glasgow, 1921

'Senex' (R. Reid), *Glasgow Past and Present*, Glasgow, 1884

Sir J. Sinclair, *The Statistical Account of Scotland*, Vol. V, 1793; Vol. XII, Edinburgh, 1794

SELECT BIBLIOGRAPHY

T. C. Smout, *A History of the Scottish People 1560–1830*, London, 1969
J. Strang, *Glasgow and Its Clubs*, London and Glasgow, 1856
J. Swan, *Select Views of Glasgow and Environs*, 1829
J. Tweed, *Biographical Sketches of the Hon. the Lord Provosts of Glasgow*, Glasgow, 1883
   Guide to Glasgow and the Clyde, Glasgow, 1872
A. Wilson, *The Chartist Movement in Scotland*, Manchester, 1970
L. C. Wright, *Scottish Chartism*, Edinburgh, 1953

Census figures and other H.M.S.O. publications.

Index

Abbotsinch Airport, 203
Aberdeen, 194
Achaius, John, Bishop, 1
Adam, James, 111
Adam, Robert, 32
Adam, William, 227
Adelaide, Queen, 123
Agricola, 3
Airdrie, 151
Albert, Prince, 171
Alexander III, King of Scots, 12
Alexander, J. H., 184, 185
Allan Line, 202
Alms House, 15
American War of Independence, 50, 52, 71, 76, 97, 100
Anchor Line, 201, 202
Anderson, George, 32
Anderson, J. H., 185
Anderson, John, 88
Anderson, Provost James, 172
Anderson, Rev. William, 60
Anderson's Institution, 88–9
Anderson, William, 20
Anderston, 63, 95, 112, 148, 152, 170, 189, 222
Angles, 4
Annales Cambriae, 1
Annand, William, 23
Anne, Queen, 44
Anthony, Jack, 211
Antonine Wall, 3, 4
Antoninus Pius, Emperor, 3
Architects
  Anderson, Robert Rowland, 167
  Baird, John, 160, 163
  Barclay, David, 167
  Barclay, Hugh, 165, 167
  Bell, George, 163
  Black, Robert, 164
  Brash, John, 158
  Bryce, John, 160
  Burnet, John, 165, 167
  Burnet, John James, 166, 178, 205
  Clarke, William, 162, 163
  Emmett, J. T., 165
  Hamilton, David, 167
  Hamilton, James, 167

Honeyman, John, 163, 165, 204
Keppie, John, 204
Kirkland, Alexander, 160, 163
Leiper, William, 165, 166
Mackintosh, Charles Rennie, 178–9, 204–7
Miller, James, 190
Paxton, Joseph, 159, 160, 163, 167
Pearson, J. L., 166
Rhind, David, 164
Rochead, J. R., 159, 160
Salmon, James, 163, 207
Scott, Sir George Gilbert, 165
Sellars, James, 164, 165, 166, 167
Smith, George, 159, 160
Stevenson, J. J., 166
Tait, Thomas, 215
Taylor, George Ledwell, 167
Thomson, Alexander ('Greek Thomson'), 159, 161–2, 164, 165, 167, 201
Wright, Frank Lloyd, 163
Wilson, Charles, 159, 160, 164
Young, William, 166
Argyll, Archibald Campbell, Marquis and eighth Earl of, 24
Argyll, Campbell Archibald, fourth Duke of, 59
Argyll, John Campbell, second Duke of, 54
Arkwright, Richard, 74, 95
Arthur, John, 52
Art Galleries, Libraries & Museums
  Art Gallery and Museum (Kelvingrove Park), 226, 227
  Burrell Museum, 227
  Hunterian Museum, 226, 227
  Institute of Fine Art, 178
  Kelvingrove Museum, 177
  McLellan Galleries, 178
  Mitchell Library, 177
  Municipal Art Gallery, 178
  Stirling's Library, 51, 223
Athenia, 202

Baillie, Robert, 23, 26, 29, 35, 37
Banton Ironstone Mines, 102
Barrhead, 95
Baxter, Stanley, 211

Baynham, Walter, 182, 183
Beaker folk, 2
Beaton, David, Cardinal Archbishop of St. Andrews, 22
Beaton, James, Archbishop, 22
Beck, Bishop of Durham, 8
Bede, 6
Bell, J. J., 180–1, 189–90, 211, 218
Bell, John, 178
Bellamy, Mrs. George Anne, 89
Bell, Henry, 98
Bell, John, 32
Bell, Patrick, 25
Berthollet, Claude Louis, 96
Bile, King of Strathclyde, 7
Biles, Sir John, 194
Birnet, Duncan, 32
Blacader, Robert, Bishop, 10, 14
Black Bull Inn, 65
Blair, Goerge, 139, 140
Black, Joseph, 83
Black, George, 195
Bleaching, 96–7
Blind Harry, 8
Birkbeck, Dr. George, 88
Bogle, Robert, 53
Bogles, 51, 52
Bondington, William de, Bishop, 10
Boswell, James, 81
Bothwell Brig, battle of, 39
Bowling, 70, 72, 142
Boyd, Zachary, 29
Brereton, Sir William, 36
Brewster, Rev. Patrick, 131, 132
Bridei, King of Picts, 7
Bridgeton, 148, 199, 212, 219, 224
Britannia, 100
Bridie, James, *see* Mavor, H. O.
British Broadcasting Corporation, 178
British National Oil Corporation, 228
Britons of Strathclyde, 4, 6–7, 12
Brown, John, and Co., 193, 194, 199
Browne, John, 38
Bruce, Robert, King of Scots, 8
Buchanan, Alexander, 51
Buchanan, Andrew, 51, 52, 53, 102
Buchanan, George (tobacco lord), 51, 57
Buchanan, George (Labour M.P.), 198
Buchanan, Steven & Co., 98
Buenos Ayrean, 193
Buildings (see also under 'Art Galleries, Libraries and Museums', 'Schools and Colleges')
    Assembly Rooms, 185
    Barony Church, 166
    Barony North Church, 165
    Belhaven Church, 166
    Belmont and Hillhead Parish Church, 166
    Buck's Head, 167
    Caledonia Road Church, 161, 165
    Camphill Church of Scotland, 165
    Central Station Hotel, 167
    City and County Buildings, 163, 173

City Chambers, 166, 173
City of Glasgow Bank (Queen Street), 164, 166
Clydesdale Bank (St. Vincent Place), 165
County Buildings, 173
Custom House (Clyde Street), 167
Dowanhill Church of Scotland, 165
Eagle Buildings, 163
Egyptian Halls, 167
Elgin Place Congregational Church, 165
Finnieston (later Kelvingrove) Parish Church, 165
Free Church College, 160
Glasgow Cathedral, 1, 10, 14, 18, 24, 29, 59, 109
Glasgow Herald Buildings, 179
Glasgow School of Art, 178, 179, 204, 206
Grecian Building, 167
Govanhill Public School, 167
Hill House, Helensburgh, 205
Hutcheson's Girls' School, 167
Holmwood House, 162
Hutchesons' Hospital, 32, 60, 85, 103, 145, 156, 166, 167
Hutcheson's School (Crown Street), 167
Justiciary Court House, 121
Kelvinside Academy, 167, 175, 176
Kibble Palace, 173
Lansdowne Church, 165
Merchants' House, 15, 45, 126, 139, 140, 205
North Park House, 178
Park Church, 160
Queen's Cross Church, 206
Queen's Park United Presbyterian Church, 165, 201
Royal Bank of Scotland (Buchanan St.), 164
Royal Exchange, 51, 68, 110, 223
Royal Glasgow Institute of Fine Arts, 178
St. Enoch's Hotel, 143
St. Mary's Episcopal Cathedral, 165
St. Andrew's Halls, 225
St. George's-in-the-Fields, 165
St. Matthew Blythswood, 165
St. Vincent Street Church, 164, 165
Scotland Street School, 206
Shawfield Mansion, 55, 57, 59, 112
Stevenson Memorial Church, 166
Stock Exchange, 167
Surgeon's Hall, 54
'The Knowe', 162
Trinity College, 160
Tolbooth, 10, 19, 27, 48, 79, 173
Town House, 48
Trades Hall, 15
Trades House, 15, 60, 126
Virginia Mansion, 51, 57
'Windyhill', Kilmalcolm, 205

Burgh reform, 125–6, 169
Burnet, Alexander, Archbishop, 38
Burns, George, 100
Burns, James, 27
Burns, Robert, 38
Burrell, Sir William, 227
Burt, Captain Edward, 48
Bushel, Captain, 55
Buses, 148

Cadell family, 101
Cadell, William, 101
Caledonia, 202
Caledonii, 3, 4
California, 202
Calton weavers' riots, 102, 103
Calton, 152, 169, 219
Cambuslang, 136
Cameron, Bishop, 10
Cameronia, 202
Cameron, James, 222
Camlachie, 99, 189, 199
Campbell, Archibald, of Blythswood, 120–1, 122
Campbell, Colin, 32
Campbell, Daniel & Shawfield, 54
Campbell, Frederick, Lord, 70
Campbell, Patrick, 29
Campbell, Richard, 106
Candle factories, 42
Caracalla, Emperor, 4
Cargill, Donald, 40
Carlyle, Alexander ('Jupiter'), 61, 64–5, 81, 226
Caroline, Queen, 107
Carrick, Robert, 115
Carron Company, 52, 84, 101
Cathcart, 148, 162
Celtic (Football Club), 213
Celtic Society, 172
Chadwick, Edwin, 128, 216
Chalmers, Dr. A. K., 155
Chalmers, Dr. Thomas, 175
Chambers of Commerce and Manufactures, 76, 93
Chapman, Robert, 93
Charles I, 22, 23, 25, 26, 28, 29, 43
Charles II, 29, 31, 38, 39
Chartism, 130–5
Chartist Circular, 130, 131
Cholera, 154
Cinemas, 212
City Improvement Trust, 155, 156, 157, 162
City of Glasgow, 201
City of Glasgow Bank, 164
City of Glasgow Improvement Act, 155, 156
Clark, John, 32
Cleland, James, 116
Cloth factories, 42
Clubs, 63–5
Cluthas, 146, 152
Clydebank, 147, 198, 201

Clyde burghs, 120–3, 125
Clyde Iron Works, 101
Clydeport Container Terminal, 228
Clyde, River, 1, 2, 3, 10, 12, 13, 15, 36, 41, 52, 53, 59, 68, 70, 71–2, 96, 97, 100, 103, 115, 128, 137, 142, 143, 144–6, 151, 154, 155, 168, 192–203, 227–8
Clyde Tunnel, 153–4
Clydeside, 134, 136, 138, 193–203
Clydeville, 155
Coal mining, 52, 100–1, 102, 136
Coatbridge, 147, 151
Cobbett, William, 182
Cockburn, Henry, Lord, 66, 105, 122, 126
Coffee House, first, 42
Colquhoun, James, 33
Colquhoun, Sir James, of Luss, 142
Colquhoun, Patrick, 76, 93
Columba, 146
Columbia, 202
Comet, 98–9, 100
Commonwealth, 36, 38
Company of Scotland Trading in Africa and the Indies, 41–2
Connolly, Billy, 211
Convention of Royal Burghs, 15, 21, 52, 70, 73
Cooke, George Frederick, 182
Copland, Professor Patrick, 96
Corbett, Cameron, 151
Cotton, 52, 53, 73–5, 95–8, 102, 130, 136
Coulter, Lowrie, 72
Covenanters, 24–9, 39
Cowlairs, 142
Craigie, J. H., 121
Cramond Iron Works, 101
Cranston, Kate, 205, 209
Cranston, Stuart, 205
Crompton, Samuel, 95
Cromwell, Oliver, 26, 28, 29, 30, 31, 36, 37
Crosshill, 148, 150, 153
Crum and Co., 96
Cullen, William, 53
Cumbernauld, 221
Cunard Company, 100
Cunard, Samuel, 100
Cunninghame, William, and Co., 50, 51, 52, 53
Custom House, 98, 115, 167

Dale, David, 72, 74, 95
Dalglish, Robert, 121
Dalmarnock, 154
Dalmuir, 154
Dalnotter Iron Works, 101
Dalrymple, James, 17
Dalrymple, James, 150, 151
Dalsholm, 96
Dalswinton Loch, 98
Damnonii, 2, 3
Dance of the Apprentices, The, 217–18
Dancing in the Streets, 218
Darien Scheme, 41–2
Darnley, Henry Stewart, Earl of, 18

David I, King of Scots, 1, 12
Deacon Convenor, 15
Dean of Guild, 15
Defoe, Daniel, 46, 48, 229
Denholm, James, 67
Denny, William, 193, 194
De Origine, Moribus, et Rebus Scotorum,
    17–18
Dickens, Charles, 185
Dilettanti Society, 178
Dewar's Temperance Hotel, 212
Dio Cassius, 4
Disraeli, Benjamin, 173
Disruption, 131, 175
Dixon, Jacob, 123
Dixon, Joseph, 122, 125
'Dixon's Blazes', 101–2
Dixon, William, 123
Donalds, 51
Donaldson Atlantic Line, 202
Donaldson Line, 202
Douglas, Sir Robert, of Blakerston, 60
Dreghorn, Allan, 68
Dreghorn, Robert, 72
Drumclog, skirmish of, 39
Duchess of Rothesay, 146
Ducrow, Andrew, 185
Dumbarton, 4, 12, 13, 57, 120, 122, 123,
    159
Dumbuck, 13, 71
Dunbar, battle of, 29
Dunbar, Gavin, Archbishop, 22
Duncan, Alexander, 93
Dunlop, Dr. John, 129, 130
Dunlop, Provost, 170–1
Dunlops, 51
Dunmore, Robert and Co., 53

East Kilbride, 221
Edington, Thomas, 101
Education (Scotland) Act, 1872, 175, 176
Edward I, King of England, 8
Elder, John, and Co., 193
Elliot, Walter, 207, 209
Elphinstone, William, 15
Electric light, 152
Engineer's Institute, 225
Eugenie, Empress, 172
Evening Times, 211
Exhibitions
    Empire Exhibition (Scotland) 1938,
        215
    Exhibition of 1911, 214
    International Exhibition of 1888 ('The
        Groveries'), 190, 214
    International Exhibition of Science
        and Art, 177, 180, 214
Ewen or Eugenius, 5
Ewing, James of Strathleven, 125
Eyre, Charles, Archbishop, 138

Fairfowl, Andrew, Archbishop, 38
Fairy Queen, 100
Fall, Dr. James, 77

Fergus Mór, 4
Finlay, Alec, 211
Finlay, Ian, 178
Finlay, Kirkman, 121, 122, 123
Fleming, would-be Provost, 170–1
Finlaystone, 115
Finnieston, 112, 151
Football, 212–14
Forsyth, Robert, 90, 97, 98, 109–12
Forth–Clyde Canal, 70–1, 98, 141
Foulis, Hugh, *see* Munro, Neil
Foulis, Robert and Andrew, 90–1, 177,
    226
First World War, 150, 212, 217–18
Frame, Robert, 148
Frank, Richard, 36
Free Press, 131
French Revolution, 103, 125
Fyffe, Will, 211

Gallacher, William, 198
Garbett, Samuel, 101
Garden, Alexander, 121
Garden, William Hamilton, 158
Gairdner, Dr. W. T., 154
Gaitens, Edward, 217–18
Gardens, Parks, etc.
    Alexandra Park, 156, 167
    College Gardens, 60
    Glasgow Green, 58, 59, 69, 83, 103,
        110, 114, 121, 130, 131, 132, 133, 134,
        138, 145, 167–8, 173, 185, 198
    Pollok Park, 227
    Kelvingrove Park, 160, 178, 226
    Physic Garden, 60
    Queen's Park, 148, 163, 165, 167
    Rouken Glen, 151
    Royal Botanic Gardens, 159, 167, 173
    Skinners' Green, 173
    West End Park, 160, 167, 168, 177
Garnet, Dr. Thomas, 88
General Strike, 199
George I, 54
Gibson, Alexander, 225
Gillespie, Patrick, 26, 29, 30, 37–8
Gillies, John, 101
Gilmorehill, 155, 165
Gilmorehill Land Company, 156
Gladstone, W. E., 173
Glasgow Advertiser, 93
Glasgow Argus, 131
Glasgow Arms Bank, 51
Glasgow Bridge, 72, 145
Glasgow Building Company, 156
Glasgow–Carlisle diligence, first, 141
Glasgow Chronicle, 131, 140
Glasgow Corporation and Police Act
    (1895), 170
Glasgow Corporation Improvement and
    General Powers Act, 156
Glasgow Courant, 91, 92, 93
Glasgow Daily Mail, 190
Glasgow District Council, 224
Glasgow Evening News, 209

Glasgow Examiner, 132
Glasgow Fair, 9, 183
Glasgow Film Society, 212
Glasgow Gas Light Company, 152
Glasgow Grand Opera Society, 225
Glasgow–Greenock coach, first, 141
Glasgow Group of painters, 178, 204
Glasgow Herald, 94, 198
Glasgow Journal, 91
Glasgow Magazine and Review, 94
Glasgow Mercury, 93
Glasgow Museum or Weekly Instructor, 1733, 94
Glasgow Necropolis, 139–40
Glasgow Police Act (1809), 109
Glasgow Political Union, 124
Glasgow punch, 63
Glasgow Reform Association, 134
Glasgow School Board, 175
Glasgow Subway Railway Company, 151
Glasgow Tramway and Omnibus Company Ltd., 148
Glasgow Universal Magazine of Knowledge and Pleasure, 94
Glasgow Universal Suffrage Association, 131
Glasgow University Magazine (*G.U.M.*), 207
Glasgow Weekly Chronicle, 93
Glasgow Weekly History, 91
Glassford, John, 50, 52, 70, 102
Glass Works, 42
Glencairn, William Cunningham, ninth Earl of, 31
Glenrothes, 221
Glorious Revolution, 43
Glover, Edmund, 183, 185, 186, 188
Godenzi's restaurant, 189–90
Golbourne, John, 71
Gomme, A., and Walker, D., 158, 160, 163
Gorbals, 20, 42, 60, 68, 103, 143, 152, 153, 155, 156, 161, 170, 189, 198, 199, 208, 218, 219, 220, 222, 224
Gourock, 146
Govan, 84, 136, 150, 151, 153, 161, 212, 224
Govan Iron Works, 102
Graham, H. H., 68
Graham, James, of Claverhouse, 39
Grahamston, 89
Grant, I. F., 13, 21
Graham, John, 39
Greenock, 71, 76, 97, 98, 99, 130, 146, 201
Grey, Charles, second Earl Grey, 122
Grieve, John, 101
Guide to Glasgow and the Clyde (Tweed), 135, 144, 146, 167, 168

Hadrian's Wall, 4
Hamilton, Alexander Hamilton Douglas, tenth Duke of, 69, 124
Hamilton, Andrew, 120
Hamilton, Archibald, Lord, 107–8, 125
Hamilton, David, 51

Hamilton, James, third Marquis and first Duke of Hamilton, 24, 26, 27
Hamilton, William, 68
Hamilton, William, Earl of Lanark and second Duke of Hamilton, 28
Hampden Park, 213
'Hampden Roar', 214
Hanley, Clifford, 200–1, 218, 219, 224, 225
Hardie, Andrew, 106
Hargreaves, James, 95
Havannah slums, 158
Helensburgh, 98, 142
Hemmings, Peter, 225, 226
Hendry, John, 43
Herbertson, Richard, 20
Highland Clearances, 75, 138
History of Glasgow (Denholm), 67
Hogganfield Loch, 1
Home, Dr. Francis, 96
Honeyman, Tom, 207, 208, 209
House, Jack, 211, 212, 214
Housing, 155–7, 216–22
Housing (Repairs and Rents) (Scotland) Act, 1954, 220
Housing (Scotland) Act, 1930, 220
Housing (Scotland) Act, 1935, 220
Howe, Frederic Clemson, 151
Hume, David, 78, 83
Hume, William, 42
Hunts, William, 226

Irvine, 221
Isle of Arran, 146
Ivanhoe, 99

Jackson, John, 90
Jamaica Street Bridge, 68, 145, 148, 172
James I, King of Scots, 12
James II, King of Scots, 11, 13
James III, King of Scots, 11
James IV, King of Scots, 11, 14, 16
James VI of Scotland and I of England, 19, 23
James VII of Scotland and II of England, 40, 77
Jeffrey, Francis, 104, 122, 125, 183
Jenner, Edward, 117
Jews, 139–41
Jocelin (monk of Furness), 1, 5, 6
Jocelin, Bishop, 1, 10
Johnston, Tom, 207
Johnston, Thomas, 95
Johnstone, Harry, 182
Jutes, 4

Kean, Edmund, 182, 184
Kellet, John, 147, 155
Kelvin Bridge, 175
Kelvingrove, 159, 165, 214, 216, 227
Kelvin, River, 70, 96, 151, 159, 166, 177, 178
Kelvinside, 167, 220
Kelvin, William Thomson, Lord, 152

Kennedy, T. F., of Dunure, 122
Kentigern, Saint, 1, 4–5, 6, 10, 229
Kibble, John, 173
King George V Dock, 228
Kingston, 161, 206
Kingston Dock, 144
Kirk, A. C., 194
Kirkintulloch Bridge, 54
Kirkwood, David, 198, 199
Knox, John, 22

Lanarkshire Universal Suffrage Association, 130
Langside, 147, 148
Langside, battle of, 18
Largs, battle of, 8
Lauder, Harry, 211
Laud, William, Archbishop of Canterbury, 23
Lauderdale, John Maitland, second Earl and first Duke of, 39
'Laud's Liturgy', 23, 24
Laurie, David and James, 155
Lauriston, 72, 222
Leechman, William, 81
Lennox, Dukes of [family name Stewart], 17
Lennox, Matthew Stewart, fourth Earl of, 18
Leslie, General Alexander, 25
Leslie, General David, 27, 29
Leslie, John, Bishop of Ross, 17
Letitia, 202
Letter of Guildry, 15
Levi, Joseph, 139
Levy, P., 140
Liberator, 130
Lind, Jenny, 185
Lindsay, Archbishop Patrick, 23
Linen, 47, 52, 53, 73–5
Livingston, 221
Livingstone, David, 171
Lloyd George, David, 157
Local Government (Scotland) Act, 1973, 174, 223
Lochhead, James, 65
Logan, David, 99
Logan, Jimmy, 211
Lollius, Urbicus, 3
Lorne, Tommy, 211
Loth, 5
Louis de France, music master, 44
Lyceum Rooms, 124

MacAlpin, Kenneth, King of Scots, 7
Macaulay, Thomas Babington, Lord, 171
Macdonald, Mrs. Anne Maxwell, 227
Macdonald, Frances and Margaret, 204
McDowall, J., 144, 175, 177, 190–1
McGill, James, 84
McGonagall, William, 194
MacGregor, Duncan, 148
McGregor, James, 96
Macgregor, W. Y., 178

McIver, David, 100
Mackay, Charles, 183
MacKenzie, John, 101
Mackenzie, Henry, 66
Mackenzie, Peter, 107, 115, 120, 122, 124, 132
McLellan, Archibald, 178
M'Leod, Rev. John, 67
McNair, Herbert, 204
Macrae, Duncan, 209, 211
MacRae, James, 51
Macready, William, 182
M'Ure, John, 58, 59
McWilliam, Colin, 113
Maeatae, 4
Mail coaches, 69, 141, 143
Malcolm II, King of Scots, 7
Malcolm, Robert, 131
Marine engineering, 136, 193–4
Mar, John Erskine, eleventh Earl of, 54
Marshall, Richard, 69
Martin of Tours, 6
Maryhill, 150, 151, 153, 221
Mary, Queen (wife of William of Orange), 40, 77
Mary of Guise, 15
Mary, Queen of Scots, 18, 22
Mavor, H. O., ('James Bridie'), 207, 208, 209
Maxton, James, 198, 199, 207
Maxwell, Sir John, 227
Maxwell, William Stirling, 227
Medical Officer of Health, 135, 154
Medwyn, John Hay Forbes, Lord, 133
Mendoza, Daniel, 69–70
Mennons, John, 79
Menzies, Andrew, 148
Merchant guilds, 14–15
Millar, Archibald, 86
Millar, John, 82
Millar, Charles, 55
Miller, D. P., 185
Miller, Robert, 147
Milngavie, 129
Mitchell, Stephen, 177
Model lodging houses, 156
Moir, James, 132, 135
Molendinar Burn, 1, 5, 10, 11, 110, 140, 156, 229
Monkland Canal, 52, 71, 100, 101, 141
Monteith, James, 73
Montgomerie, Hugh, seventh Earl of Eglinton, 24
Montgomerie, Hugh, of Busbie, 44
Montrose, James Graham, first Marquis and fifth Earl of, 25, 26, 27, 28, 33
Morgan, Tommy, 211
Morrison, 'Tommy', 219
Mugdock, 129
Muir, Edwin, 211
Muirkirk, 101
Muirkirk Iron Works, 101
Mungo, Saint, see Kentigern, Saint
Munro, Neil, 205–6, 209, 218

Murdochs, 51
Mure, John, 19
Music hall, 180, 188–9
Muslin, 47

Napier, David, 99, 100
Napier, Robert, 100
Napoleon III, 172
Nasmyth, James, 100
National Covenant, 23
National Radical Association, 130
Navigation Acts, 41
Nechtansmere, battle of, 6
Necropolis Glasguensis, 139
Neilson, J. B., 100, 101
Newark Bay (later Port Glasgow), 41
New Assembly Hall, 67
Newcomen, John, 83
New Lanark, 74, 95
Newspapers, 91–4
Newton, 136, 147
New Towns Development Corporation, 220, 221
Nicholas V, Pope, 13
Ninian, Saint, 6
Nisbet, Sir Philip, 27
Norsemen, 8
Northern Looking Glass, 118
Nova Erectio, 77, 78

Oakley, C. A., 214
Oatlands, 222
O'Connell, Daniel, 138
O'Connor, Feargus, 132, 134
Oengus, King of Picts, 7
Ogilvie of Innerquarity, 27
Old Mortality, 39
Orr, Robin, 225
Oswald, James, of Shieldhall, 125
Oswalds, 51
Overnewton, 177
Owen, Robert, 95
Owen the Bald, King of Strathclyde, 7

Pacification of Berwick, 25
Pagan, J., 159, 160
Paisley, 76, 151
Para Handy, 209–10
Partick, 138, 188, 221
Partick Gas Works, 174
Paterson, Alan, 146
Paul, Lewis, 95
P-Celtic, 2, 3, 7
'Penny geggies', 188
People's History of Glasgow (McDowall), 144–5
Picts, 3, 4, 7
Plan of the City of Glasgow (J. Arthur), 52
Pitlochry Festival Theatre, 209
Plantation, 155
Plantation Quay, 144
Pococke, Richard, Bishop of Meath, 59
Polok, James, 31
Pollokshaws, 103, 147, 148, 153, 198

Pollokshields, 143, 148, 150, 153, 162, 163, 180, 220
Population, 41, 128, 136, 137, 153, 155, 174, 220–1
Port Dundas, 98
Porterfield, George, 24, 28, 38
Port Glasgow, 50, 97
Prestwick Airport, 202–3
Pride, George, 14
Prince of Wales (later Edward VII), 173, 177
Princess of Wales (later Queen Alexandra), 173, 177
Princeton University, 84
Pritchard, Dr. Edward W., 173
Provand, John, 106
Ptolemy (Greek geographer), 2

Q-Celtic, 6, 7
Queen Elizabeth, 194, 200, 201
Queen Mary, 194, 195, 200–1
Queen's Dock, 144
Queen's Hotel, 173
Queen's Park (Football Club), 213, 214

Radcliffe, William, 95
Rafferty, John, 222
Railways, 141–3, 147–8, 153
 Caledonian Railway, 142, 143, 147, 155, 156, 196
 Cathcart District Railway, 148
 Edinburgh and Glasgow Railway Company, 142, 143
 Glasgow and South-Western Railway Company, 143, 155, 156, 196
 Glasgow, Paisley, Kilmarnock and Ayr Railway Company, 143
 Glasgow, Dumbarton and Helensburgh Railway, 142
 Glasgow, Dumfries and Carlisle Railway Company, 143
 Glasgow–Garnkirk Railway, 142
 London and North-Eastern Railway, 196
 London Midland and Scottish Railway, 196
 North British Railway Company, 142, 143, 172, 196
 Paisley and Renfrew Railway, 142
 Pollok and Govan Railway Company, 142
 Rutherglen Railway Company, 142
Railway Stations
 Bridge Street Station, 142, 143
 Buchanan Street Station, 143
 Central Station, 89, 134, 143, 148
 College Goods Station, 155
 Dundas Street Station, 172
 Queen Street Station, 143
 St. Enoch Station, 143, 152, 186,
 St. Rollox Station, 142
Ramsay, David, 19
Ram's Horn Church, 111, 116
Rangers (Football Club), 213

Ray, John, 38
Reformation, 17, 18, 22, 59
Reid, Thomas, 83
Reform Bill, 121–2, 124, 125, 132, 141
Reform Bill (Scotland), 120, 122, 124, 125, 126, 132, 169, 197
Reid, Alexander, 178
Reid, Robert ('Senex'), 115, 116
Renfrew, 12, 13, 107, 120, 121, 136
Renfrew Airport, 202–3
Rennie, John, 71
Report on the Sanitary Condition of the Labouring Population of Great Britain, 128
Rhydderch, King of Strathclyde, 5
Richmond, Alexander, 103
Riddrie, 151
Ritchie, John, 70
Robert III, King of Scots, 11
Robertson, John, 99
Robertson, William, 101
Robison, John, 83
Rob Roy, 45
Robroyston, 8
Rodger, Ian, 225
Roebuck, Dr. John, 84, 96, 101
Rollo, Sir William, 27
Romans in Scotland, 3, 6
Rope works, 42
Ross, George, 130
Rothenstein, Sir John, 228
Rowan, Robert, 33
Royal College of Science and Technology, 89
Royal Infirmary, 176
Rupert, Prince, 26
Russell, Dr. J. R., 154
Russell, Jerome, 22
Rutherglen, 8, 12, 13, 107, 120, 121, 122–5, 209
Rutherglen Bridge, 145, 168

St. Andrew's Suspension Bridge, 145
St. Ninian's Hospital, 20
Sanders, James, 32
Sanders, Robert, 32
Saracen's Head, 65, 66
Saxons, 4
Scheele, Carl, 96
Schools and Colleges, 85–7, 175–6
    Allan Glen's Institution, 176
    Glasgow Academy, 175, 176
    Glasgow and West of Scotland Technical College, 89, 176
    Glasgow School of Art, 178, 179
    Grammar School, 14, 51, 68, 175
    High School, *see* Grammar School
    Hutcheson's Grammar School for Boys, 167, 176
    Hutcheson's Grammar School for Girls, 166, 177
    Kelvinside Academy, 167, 175, 176
    Normal School for the Training of Teachers, 175
    Park School for Girls, 176
    Queen Margaret College, 178
    Scotland Street School, 206
    West of Scotland Academy, 178
'Scotch Comics', 211–12
Scotland's Older Houses, 216
Scots, 4
Scots Times, 131, 132
Scott, Sir Walter, 39, 45, 64, 96, 183
Scottish Enlightenment, 78–83
Scottish Football Association, 213
Scottish Football League, 213
Scottish National Opera, 90, 188, 225–6
Scottish National Players, 208
Scottish National Theatre Society, 208
Scottish Patriot, 130, 131
Scottish Special Housing Association, 220
Scottish Television, 225
Second World War, 200–3, 207, 209, 211, 212, 219
Serf, Saint, 5
Severus, Emperor, 4
Seymour, Frank, 184
Sharp, James, Archbishop of St. Andrews, 39
Shawfield Riots, 55–6
Shaw, Geoffrey, 222
Shawlands, 148, 151
Shettleston, 198, 199
Shieldhall, 154
Shieldhall Quay, 228
Shinwell, Emmanuel, 198, 199
Ship Bank, 51, 64, 115, 164
Shipbuilding, 102, 136, 193–201
Shortridge, John, 59
Siddons, Mrs. Sarah, 90
Silvercraigs House, 29
Simpson, Mercer, 186
Sleeman, John, 150
Smeaton, John, 70, 71
Smith, Adam, 80–1
Smith, George, 133
Smith, John, dancing master, 43
Smith, Madeleine, 159
Smith, Sir George Adam, 198–9
Smout, T. C., 116
Soap factory, 42
Solemn League and Covenant, 26, 28
Speirs, Alexander, 50, 51, 52
Spence, Sir Basil, 222
Spinners, 106–7
Springburn, 150
Stage coach, Glasgow to Edinburgh, 42
Stark, William, 121
Statistical Account of Scotland, 74, 85, 117
Steel, 102, 136, 193
Stephen, Campbell, 198
Stewart, Margaret, 19
Stewart, John, 209
Stewart, John, of Minto, 16
Stewart, William, 198
Stirling, Gordon & Co., 98
Stirling, Walter, 98
Stirling, William, 96

Stobcross Dock, 144
Stobcross Ferry, 151, 153
Stobcross Proprietors, 156
Stockwell Bridge, 145
Stonehouse, 223
Stow, David, 175
Strang, John, 117, 119, 131, 139
Strathclyde Region, 221, 222, 223-4
Strathclyde Regional Council, 223
Streets, Squares, etc.
  Abbotsford Place, 155
  Albany Place, 159
  Albert Bridge, 103, 145, 171
  Albert Drive, 162
  Alston Street, 134
  Annette Street, 167
  Argyle Street, 59, 63, 65, 110, 111, 112,
    115, 128, 159, 160, 162, 163, 167, 172,
    205
  Back Cow Loan, 57
  Balvicar Drive, 165
  Barrowfield Toll, 148
  Bellshaugh Road, 167
  Berkeley Street, 188
  Bath Street, 135, 158, 162, 165
  Belmont Street, 166
  Bell Street, 111
  Bridgegate (Briggait), 15, 33, 103, 111
  Bridgend, 60
  Blythswood Hill, 158
  Blythswood Square, 158, 163
  Bothwell Street, 163
  Bridge Wharf, 146
  Broomielaw, 41, 98, 99, 111, 146
  Buchanan Street, 53, 111, 112, 115,
    164, 172, 221
  Buckingham Terrace, 159
  Cambridge Street, 148
  Campbell Street, 110
  Camperdown Place, 112
  Candleriggs, 42, 58, 111, 116
  Carlton Place, 68
  Castle Street, 166
  Cathcart Road, 161
  Cathedral Square, 15, 165, 166
  Cessnock Bank, 155
  Charing Cross, 158, 159, 177, 221, 222
  Charlotte Street, 110
  Claremont Terrace, 160
  Clyde Street, 172
  Cochran Street, 112
  College Vennel, 39
  Common Loan, 58
  Cowcaddens, 57, 159, 188, 189, 221,
    222, 226
  Cow Loan, 51, 57
  Crown Street, 20, 102, 145, 167
  Currie's Close, 63
  Derby Street, 165
  Dowanhill, 166
  Drygate, 4, 10, 11, 18, 35, 59, 79, 109,
    156
  Duke Street, 102, 112
  Dumbarton Road, 154, 159

Dunlop Street, 111, 134, 153
East Russell Street, 156
Eglinton Street, 161
Eglinton Toll, 148
Elgin Street, 167
Elmbank Street, 175, 225
Franklin Terrace, 162
Frederick Street, 112
Gallowgate, 10, 39, 64, 65, 79, 96, 110,
  167, 218
Garden Square, 158
Garscube Road, 206
George Square, 112, 135, 158, 166,
  172, 173, 201
George Street, 109, 112, 135, 205
Gibson Street, 214
Glasgow Cross, 10, 67, 110, 189
Glassford Street, 55, 59, 111, 112, 115
Gorbals Cross, 151
Gorbals Street, 161
Gordon Street, 51, 112, 167
Govanhill, 150, 153, 161, 167
Govan Road, 161
Granby Terrace, 162
Gray Street, 214
Great Clyde Street, 106
Great Western Road, 159, 160, 162,
  165, 166, 180, 221
Great Western Terrace, 159
Green Bank, 155
Grosvenor Terrace, 159
Hanover Street, 112
Heatheryhall, 155
High Street, 10, 11, 14, 20, 33, 35, 53,
  57, 59, 60, 63, 68, 79, 110, 111, 112,
  135, 155, 172
Hillhead, 150, 151, 153
Hillhead Street, 162
Hill Street, 135
Hope Street, 167
Hyndland Road, 165
Hutchesontown Bridge, 103, 145
Hutcheson Street, 32
Ingram Street, 32, 51, 57, 67, 111, 112
  158, 163, 173, 177, 185
Jail Square, 168
Jamaica Street, 53, 72, 111, 112, 145,
  163, 172
John Street, 112
Kelvin Way, 214
Kent Road, 162
Kent Street, 110
King Street, 58, 111
Kirklee Terrace, 159
Laigh Kirk Close, 190
Limmerfield Lane, 18
Lynedock Street, 160
Main Street, 20
Mansionhouse Road, 162-3
Mavis Bank, 155
Maxwell Street, 111
Mercat Cross, 10, 35
Miller Street, 53, 111, 112, 141, 163, 177
Mitchell Street, 150, 179

Streets, Squares, etc.—*continued*
Montrose Street, 112
Netherlee Road, 162
New City Road, 148
Newton Place, 159
Nithsdale Road, 163
Norfolk Street, 161
North Street, 177
Old Kirk Street, 15
Park Circus, 160
Park Circus Place, 160
Partickhill, 162
Pollok Street, 161
Queen's Crescent, 160
Queen's Park Terrace, 161
Queen Street, 51, 53, 90, 111, 112
Renfield Street, 148
Renfrew Street, 179, 204
Rotten Row, 10, 33, 35, 59, 109, 112
Royal Crescent, 159
Royal Exchange Square, 51
St. Andrew Square, 110
St. Enoch's Gait, 58
St. Enoch Square, 51, 53, 58, 111, 143, 152, 198
St. George's Cross, 148, 151, 160
St. George's Road, 165
St. Vincent Crescent, 160
St. Vincent Place, 165
St. Vincent Street, 135, 158, 163
Saltmarket, 10, 11, 20, 29, 33, 79, 103, 110, 145, 156, 188
Sauchiehall Street, 135, 148, 158–9, 167, 178, 189, 205, 214, 221, 224
Saltoun Street, 166
Scotland Street, 206
Shieldhall Road, 153
South Portland Street, 145
South Wellington Street, 217
Stable Green Port, 18
Steel Street, 29
Stockwell Street, 25, 64, 68, 84, 111, 188
Suffolk Street, 110
Trongate, 11, 32, 51, 53, 58, 59, 68, 111, 112, 158, 172
Union Place, 112
Union Street, 167
University Avenue, 162
Vennel slums, 155, 222
Virginia Street, 51, 53, 111
Walworth Terrace, 162
Waterloo Street, 152
Watson Street, 189
Wellington Street, 189
West George Street, 135, 158, 172
West Nile Street, 185
West Regent Street, 135, 158,
West Scotland Street, 151
West Port, 59
West Port Well, 59
Wilson Street, 111, 112, 163, 173
Woodlands Hill, 113 160
Woodside, 165

Woodside Place, 159
Woodside Crescent, 159, 160
Woodside Terrace, 159–60
York Street, 184
Subway, 151–2
Sugar refineries, 42, 47
Sunday Schools, 56
Symington, William, 98
Symons, J. C., 129

Tacitus, 3
Telford, Thomas, 142, 145
Tennent, Charles, 96
Teudebur, King of Strathclyde, 7
Textile industry, 50, 73–5, 102, 116, 136
Theatre, Music Halls, etc., 89–90, 180–9, 207–9, 211–12
Adelphi Theatre, 185
Alhambra Music Hall, 212
Britannia Music Hall, 188, 189
Caledonian Theatre, 184, 188
Citizens' Theatre, 207, 208
City Theatre, 185
Dunlop Street Theatre, 90, 134, 181, 182, 183–4, 185, 186, 188
Empire Theatre, 188, 189, 212, 224
Empress Theatre, 212
Gaiety Theatre, 188, 189
Glasgow Repertory Theatre, 208
Grand Theatre, 189, 212
Hengler's Circus, 189
Hippodrome, 212
King's Theatre, 208, 212
Lyceum Theatre, 212
Lyric Theatre, 189, 224
Metropole Theatre, 188, 212, 224
Olympia Theatre, 212
Palace Theatre, 212
Park Theatre, 209
Pavilion Music Hall, 212
People's Palace, 189
Princess's Theatre, 208, 212
Prince's Theatre, 185, 186–7
Queen's Theatre, 189, 224
Queen Street Theatre, 181, 182–3, 184
Royal Coliseum, 188
Royal Princess's Theatre, 189
Royalty Theatre, 189, 212, 224
Savoy Music Hall, 212
Scotia Music Hall, 188, 189, 211, 212
Star Music Hall, 188–9
Theatre Royal, 90, 134, 188, 189, 212, 224–5, 226
Tivoli Theatre, 189
Zoo-Circus, 189
Thennoch or Thenew, 4–5
The Shipbuilders, 195–6
Third Statistical Account of Scotland, 202
Thistle Bank, 51
Thomson, David, 51
Thom, William, 84–5, 87
Thornliebank, 97
Tobacco, 47, 48, 49–59, 102
Tobacco Lords, 50–3

Tollcross, 101
Tontine Hotel, 67–8
Touris, John, 19
Tour thro' the Whole Island of Great Britain, 46
Town Council, 15, 17, 18–19, 20, 23, 24, 25, 26, 27, 28, 30–1, 32–3, 34, 35, 40, 41, 42, 43, 52, 55–6, 57, 58, 59, 60, 65, 67, 71, 85, 93, 119, 120, 121, 124, 126, 148, 150, 170, 174, 177, 221
Townhead, 223
Tradestown, 72
Tramcars, 148–52, 153
Transylvania, 202
Tucker, Thomas, 36, 41
Turnbull, William, Bishop, 13, 14
Turnpike Acts, 70
Tuscania, 202
Tweed, J., 135, 144, 146, 167, 168, 171

Uddingston, 151
Union, 42, 43–4, 46, 120
Union Bank of Scotland, 115
University of Glasgow, 13–14, 30, 37–8, 51, 59, 77–83, 84, 87, 110, 112, 151, 152, 165, 171, 172, 176–7, 194, 214, 225
University of Strathclyde, 89
Urquhart, Molly, 209

Vaccination, 117
Victoria, Queen, 129, 166, 171, 172
Votadini, 5
Vale of Leven, 97
Victoria Bridge, 11, 145, 146, 153
Vulcan, 100

Wade, General George, 55
Wallace, Sir William, 8
Wareing, Alfred, 208
Watson, James, 20
Watson, John, 20
Watt, James, 71, 83–4, 96
Weavers, 102–6, 116
'Wee MacGreegor', 210, 211
West Country Intelligence, 91
Wheatley, John, 198, 199
Whitefield, Rev. George, 89
Whiteford, Colonel Walter, 42
Whiteinch Ferry, 146, 153
White, John Forbes, 178
White, W. B., 177
Wilkinson, John, 101
William III, King, 40, 51, 77, 111
William IV, King, 122, 123
William the Lion, King of Scots, 1
Willis, Dave, 211
Willow Tea Room, 205–9
Wilson, James, 106
Wilson, Thomas, 100
Wishart, Bishop, 8
Witherspoon, John, 84
Wood, Rev. Valentine, 142
Wordsworth, Dorothy, 113–15
Wordsworth, William, 113–14
Wyatt, John, 95
Wylie, Hugh, 52
Wylie and Lochhead, 163

Yoker Burn, 70
Yorkhill Quay, 144
Young, John, 150